The simulation of surveillance: hypercontrol in telematic societies is a novel exploration of the imaginary of perceptual control technologies at the beginning of the twenty-first century. From virtual reality to computer profiling, artificial intelligence to genetic mapping, William Bogard constructs a "social science fiction" of how the revolution in simulation technology fundamentally reconfigures and intensifies the role of surveillance in war, work, sexuality, and private life. Increasingly, simulation is becoming a preferred means of supplementing the eyes and ears of the authorities in information societies, enabling forms of control which operate more efficiently in advance of problems, but which also hyperrealize our experiences of time, space, agency, and society itself. Push a button, enter a code, and go anywhere, be anyone or anything. *The simulation of surveillance* offers sustained critique of the imaginary in which control breaks free of its prior limits – an imaginary of unmediated perception, the effects of which we see everywhere in fantastic systems for the relentless conversion of objects, events, and people into information.

The simulation of surveillance

Cambridge Cultural Social Studies

Cambridge Cultural Social Studies is a forum for the most original and thoughtful work in cultural social studies. This includes theoretical works focusing on conceptual strategies, empirical studies covering specific topics such as gender, sexuality, politics, economics, social movements, and crime, and studies that address broad themes such as the culture of modernity. While the perspectives of the individual studies will vary, they will all share the same innovative reach and scholarly quality.

The simulation of surveillance

Hypercontrol in telematic societies

William Bogard
Whitman College

CAMBRIDGE
UNIVERSITY PRESS

Published by the Press Syndicate of the University of Cambridge
The Pitt Building, Trumpington Street, Cambridge CB2 1RP
40 West 20th Street, New York, NY 10011-4211, USA
10 Stamford Road, Oakleigh, Melbourne 3166, Australia

First published 1996

Printed in Great Britain at the University Press, Cambridge

A catalogue record for this book is available from the British Library

Library of Congress cataloguing in publication data
Bogard, William, 1950–
    The simulation of surveillance: hypercontrol in telematic
societies / William Bogard.
       p.   cm. – (Cambridge cultural social studies)
    Includes bibliographical references and index.
    ISBN 0 521 55081 5 (hc) ISBN 0 521 55561 2 (pb)
    1. Computer simulation. 2. Virtual reality (Computer science).
    3. Computers and civilization. I. Title. II. Series.
    QA76.9.C65B64 1996
303.3′3 – dc20 95-14611 CIP

ISBN 0 521 55081 5 hardback
ISBN 0 521 55561 2 paperback

KS

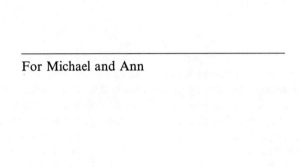

For Michael and Ann

... this state of not being observed would begin to torment him after a while, much more than the knowledge of being observed bothered him earlier, because not being watched would make him feel not worth noticing, not being worth noticing would make him feel disrespected, being disrespected would make him feel insignificant, being insignificant would make him feel meaningless, and, he imagined, the end result might be a hopeless depression, and he would have to conclude that other people suffered as much from not being observed as he did, that they, too, felt meaningless unless they were being observed . . .

Friedrich Dürrenmatt, *The Assignment*

Contents

Introduction

In the last century and a half, western societies have undergone what could be called a revolution in technological systems of control. The origins of that revolution, according to James Beniger (1986: 6), can be traced to a number of problems – in effect "crises" of control – generated by the tremendous expansion of industrial production since the middle of the nineteenth century. In general, these problems had to do with devising more efficient means of extracting and processing raw materials, transporting goods, and searching for new consumer markets. In the West, the dominant response to such recurring crises of industrialization has been increasing bureaucratic control of information. For Max Weber (1958), writing in the early part of the twentieth century, the success, and apparent permanence, of this solution were consequences of its technical superiority. Bureaucratic organization was, all things considered, the most effective means devised to coordinate the rapid development of productive forces in emerging mass societies.

Bureaucracies, for Weber, worked by rationally directing flows of authority and communication. Administrative offices were separated and ranked according to precise criteria, allowing decisions to be made in a routine and predictable manner. The precision operation of the bureaucratic "machine," Weber knew well, however, came with a high price: it concentrated the material means of administrative power in the hands of those at the top of the bureaucratic hierarchy. Even more, it subjected individuals at all levels of the administrative structure to the imperatives of the machine itself. Inefficiencies in the control of production in effect were exchanged for submission to what today we would call the technologies of bureaucratic surveillance – information gathering and storage systems (accounting, recording, and filing mechanisms) and the various devices for encoding and decoding that information (impersonal, standardized rules governing its access, use, and dissemination). As crises of production mounted in industrializing societies, the control of information, through the continuous perfection of the instruments of supervision, monitoring, and disclosure, became the rational, and by implication, best response to growth in the size and complexity of administrative tasks in industrial societies.

Since World War II, computerization has vastly magnified the surveillance dimensions of the control revolution. Dormant as an idea since the 1830s, when Charles Babbage originally formulated the basic principles of an "analytical engine" (having experimented with inventing a primitive calculating machine ten years earlier), the first significant development of computer technology came in response to military needs arising out of the speed and destructiveness of modern warfare in the twentieth century. The earliest successful applications derived from the necessity of more quickly and accurately calculating artillery ranges and trajectories, as well as the need of devising better, more secure ways of coding and transmitting military messages in an age of wireless communications. The advantages in speed, convenience, and secrecy of informated calculation and encryption were obvious, and beyond these first uses it didn't take long to recognize the possibilities of computerized control in other fields. Again, however, there were costs. In the early 1970s, the sociologist James Rule (1973) could already discern the potentially devastating impacts of bureaucratically organized computer surveillance technologies on personal liberty and privacy. At the beginning of the 1980s, David Burnham (1983) warned of the imminent rise of what he termed the "computer state," government and private corporations gathering, storing, and sharing massive amounts of information on individuals, an Orwellian vision of a not-so-distant future of interconnected databases jammed with details about virtually every aspect of human affairs. Today, that future perhaps seems closer than ever. Computer technology is now commonplace across the entire spectrum of social institutions, from the office and the factory, to schools, hospitals, and the home, and by all indications the trend of diffusing and intensifying informational control by digital means, a half-century old, shows absolutely no sign of abating.

Contemporary discussions of informated forms of control have tended for the most part to remain within the historical framework of problems defined by the computerization–surveillance–bureaucracy nexus. Digital technologies, we are told, mark the emergence of "surveillance societies," or they evolve entirely new and usually more menacing forms of surveillance, characterized by greater speed and less public visibility of data-gathering processes, greater intrusion into the personal lives of individuals, and less power of individuals to resist institutional demands for ever larger quantities of information about them. Missing from those discussions, or at least not immediately related to the issues they raise, has been the consideration of another, perhaps more significant, development in information technologies over the past several decades. That, in a word, is simulation, which provisionally can be defined as a *means of verisimilitude* (Der Derian 1990), ways of replacing "actual" with "virtual" processes, or the electronic signs/images of objects and events for their "real" counterparts. In this book, the emerging technologies of virtual reality will provide perhaps some of the clearest examples of contemporary applications of simulation, where one simply straps on the latest head and body gear and plugs in a program to be transported in cyberspace to whatever location and time (fictional or otherwise) one desires. In general, however, I will use simulation as a broad cover term for what actually is quite a diverse multiplicity of procedures and techniques. Beyond virtual reality, they have come to include the modeling of complex physical, biological, and social processes, gaming, profiling, cybernetics, miniaturization, tele-presencing, cloning, and stealth technology, to name just a few.

Some of the first applications of computerized simulation technologies were once again in the military. Early in the development of computers, military planners recognized their strategic importance as aids in preparing for combat operations and began researching ways to perfect the communications interface between humans and information systems in order to exert greater control over the growing uncertainties of modern conflict. During World War II, behavioral models of human learning and task management – reinforcement, operant conditioning – began to be applied to the problem of training soldiers to carry out their missions more effectively on the battlefield. After the war, the emerging fields of systems research and cybernetics joined forces with cognitive and educational psychology to develop instructional mechanisms to train for future wars (training films, mock combat exercises, flight simulation, battlefield decision and management systems) (Noble 1989: 17). In the 1970s and 1980s, tremendous resources were poured into secret agencies like the Defense Advanced Research Projects Agency (DARPA) to conduct basic research and develop the potential of fantastic simulation technologies like artificial intelligence, war-gaming software, robotic and stealth weaponry, and pharmaceutically enhanced fighting forces. All this was just the beginning. Over the last two decades, computerized simulation has increasingly been utilized as a research tool to model processes that, for a host of different reasons, cannot be studied directly (because of expense, safety, complexity, distance, or the simple fact that they have not yet occurred). Today, the interest in and development of these tools have expanded exponentially. They have become routinely employed in medicine (where computerized "experts" are used to assist physicians in making complex medical diagnoses), in mathematics and the natural sciences (in such areas as chaos and catastrophe research), and in the social sciences (social gaming, forecasting, rational planning, public policy, international relations). Engineers use simulations to project design flaws and tolerances, ecologists to model environments (ecosystems), educators as pedagogical tools, and meteorologists to predict the weather. In one of its most recent developments, the new field of nano-science studies ways to miniaturize machines that can be used in areas as diverse as the creation of synthetic molecules to cancer therapy to the production of electronic circuits. Corporations increasingly base investment decisions on market simulations, while the production of simulation technology has itself become a big business, in areas such as the manufacture of video games (the most popular of which often still retain their original military references) and computer software. The list goes on.

In this book, I will explore some of the relations between surveillance and simulation technologies, and their significance for issues of control in postindustrial or, as I prefer to call them, "telematic" societies at the end of the twentieth century. Those relations, I discovered early on, are exceedingly complex, and I should warn the reader that what follows in this book only addresses in a preliminary way technical connections that today are in an almost mind-bending state of flux and development. Despite that complexity, the argument I develop here reduces to a fairly simple observation: technologies of simulation are forms of *hypersurveillant control*, where the prefix "hyper" implies not simply an intensification of surveillance, but the effort to push surveillance technologies to their absolute limit. That limit is an imaginary line beyond which control operates, so to speak, in "advance" of itself and where surveillance – a technology of exposure and recording – evolves into a technology of *pre-*exposure and *pre-*recording, a technical operation in which all control functions are reduced to modulations of preset codes. This book, in that sense, deals with ideas that from another perspective would properly be said to belong to science fiction. And that is exactly my intention. Simulation technology, from the perspective I adopt here, is part of what I will call the *imaginary* of surveillant control – a fantastic dream of seeing everything capable of being seen, recording every fact capable of being recorded, and accomplishing these things, whenever and wherever possible, prior to the event itself. One of the tasks of this book is to think through how that imaginary circulates as an *effective* mechanism in the technical evolution of control in postindustrial societies. There is nothing novel in this idea. For better or worse, in the popular culture of science and technology today, and for some time now (particularly in the United States), the call to arms has been "if we can imagine it, we can build it." In that sense, the best label for the technologies of simulation I will be reviewing here is precisely imaginary machines. For this trip into the imaginary of control, I will rely heavily on the work of poststructuralist or postmodernist discourse as it developed in the philosophical-historical studies of Michel Foucault in the 1970s and the philosophical-literary writings of Jean Baudrillard in the 1980s – Foucault for his important reflections on discipline and its relation to political strategies of observation and visibility (surveillance), Baudrillard for his seminal work on orders of simulation and simulacra. In examining the evolving links between surveillance and simulation technologies, I am thus indirectly exploring both some of the conceptual continuities and, more often, the inherent tensions between these authors. I make no claim, however, of in any way having resolved those tensions in this book, or even, for that matter, of really having begun at all to address them in anything approaching a systematic or consistent way. Rather, I only note in passing how provocative and useful they have been to me in attempting to develop a framework for thinking about a few of the many paradoxes and contradictions of the contemporary "control revolution," and how those in turn derive from the ever more apparent – and increasingly ominous – convergence of surveillance and simulation technologies in telematic societies.

I want to thank the following people for all their thoughtful comments, criticisms, and help in preparing different sections of the manuscript: Philip Turetzky, Steven Seidman, Mark Poster, Stephen Pfohl, Naomi Abrahams, Timothy Kaufman-Osborn, Jan Mejer, Douglas Kellner, Tim Rouse, Catherine Max, Suzanne Unger, Kim Jordan, Shannon Callister, and all the students in the course in Technology and Society I teach at Whitman College, many of whom have grown up with these technologies and have developed an almost intuitive feel for dealing with the difficult conceptual issues I often struggle with in the following chapters. Finally, I also want to thank Whitman College itself for providing me with the time and support I needed to finish the project.

1

A social science fiction

Michel Foucault once said that he didn't know where his books would end when he began them and that his writing was a way to change his thinking about a problem, to bring himself to think differently about it. For that reason, he said, none of his books really developed a theory, at least in any conventional sense. They were more like fictions, or "experiments" in self-transformation, "experience-books" whose very writing would change the terms of thought (Foucault 1991: 27–33). This book is a kind of experience-book, both in its evolution and in terms of examining the fictional elements of its subject. It began with an idea to write a political history of surveillance, of its development and practice as a means of discipline in modern societies, taking Foucault's work on the prison, *Discipline and Punish* (1979), as its starting point. It ended up being a "social science fiction" of its *simulation*, a trip through hyper-surveillance societies, part factual and part imaginary, an account of an uncomfortably close future where a technics of supervision is wedded to an emerging technics of virtualization. I emphasize the conjunction of *social science* and *science fiction*.[1] Throughout this book, fictions of science and technology are woven into accounts of social relations that today are increasingly structured around oppressive methods of cybernetic or telematic control, what Donna Haraway (1985) has called an "informatics of domination."[2] What began as a study of the informatics of domination from the perspective of contemporary surveillance technologies became, over the course of writing, a fantasy of absolute, perfect control in virtual systems where, at the push of a button, anything – image, object, event – can be simulated, and thus made instantly visible, knowable, and manipulable. What started as an attempt to understand surveillance as a disciplinary strategy in information societies, how its methods had adapted to the contemporary revolution in communications and computer technology, wound up depicting a fictive geography of cyborgs, clones, body doubles, and screens – a "biotelematic scene" on the order of *Blade Runner* meets *Dead Ringers*. In that fantastic and melancholy scene, which our own societies today seem so intensely anxious to approximate, nothing escapes the totalizing apparatus of surveillance, because everything, including the surveillor – *especially* the surveillor – is a simulation.

A social science fiction is like a future history. It is not "true," nor is it exactly a prediction. Instead, it chronicles how a fantastic machine might recount *its* past, a past that haunts *our own* technological present and, like some displaced recollection, precedes it. It is a history written in another dimension and another direction, not from a human point of view, but from that of a futuristic technology that traces its genealogy back through the ages to the technical systems of our own time. In his book, *War in the Age of Intelligent Machines*, Eduard de Landa (1991: 2–3) records the evolution of military machines from the standpoint of an intelligent robot that is itself the amazing projection of the self-organizing capacities of those machines:

> If we disregard for a moment the fact that robotic intelligence will probably not follow the anthropomorphic line of development prepared for it by science fiction, we may without much difficulty imagine a future generation of killer robots dedicated to understanding their historical origins. We may even imagine specialized "robot-historians" committed to tracing the various technological lineages that gave rise to their species. And we could further imagine that such a robot historian would write a different kind of history than would its human counterpart. While a human historian might try to understand the way people assembled clockworks, motors, and other physical contraptions, a robot historian would likely place a stronger emphasis on the way these machines affected human evolution.

For de Landa, the robot-historian is the sci-fi counterpart of the robotic soldiers that exist today in crude forms to assist human soldiers in battlefield operations, logistics, and surveillance – the command–control–communications webs, war-game hardware, and artificial intelligence systems that organize the modern, electronic space of war. The robot-historian does not provide us, at least not in the conventional sense, with a "social" history of war and military technology – its focus is not the inventors, the great strategists, or the material struggle of social classes; instead, it chronicles its own history, in which human beings act as mere facilitators of its development, organic extensions of itself, like so many ants who carry out its plan. The robot-historian, we might say, has a virtual existence, as a machinic or cyborgian figure whose presence informs the evolution of military society from its very beginning, in the first techno-human "assemblages" for exerting control over the turbulent forces of war – the hand and the stick, horse and rider, arm and shield. It is an abstract machine, a "singularity" or "strange attractor" where all the chaotic, swirling intensities of war – strategies, tactics, movements, blockages – converge in a coherent and universal military apparatus. The robot-historian, for de Landa, is the future of war only in a very specific sense, viz., as a future already indicated in the earliest design and uses of military weaponry, in the ancient strategic coordination of machinic forces and bodies. It is a figure in which the fictional superimposes itself on and is effective within its own past and, by extension, within the real and present order of things.

A social science fiction, then, aims to describe the social or institutional "effects" of an imaginary technology, not in a causal sense, but in the way a simulacrum is woven into the current technical practices of a society, as the virtual form of their development. In terms of the technologies of surveillance, our focus here, this amounts to a description of how their future development is "signaled" within a crude but already existing structure of organic and machinic connections. These connections, in turn, indicate points of contact or rupture with prior forms of surveillance, as virtual systems of all sorts today – digital communications, tele-presencing, profiling, gaming, genetic modeling – begin to reconfigure many of the control functions of older disciplinary mechanisms (e.g., as cybernetic control replaces direct supervision, virtual environments substitute for real distributions of space and time, bio-electronic sensors for practices of enclosure or confinement).

It is my intention here to supplement, not simply critique, conventional analyses of surveillance. Surveillance is a social technology of power – supervising, monitoring, and recording, its most common methods, are simply ways to control persons and their behavior – and we can certainly describe its uses, causes, and effects in relatively straightforward, sociological terms. This, in fact, has been the dominant approach to the study of surveillance in recent years, i.e., to understand its central role in the maintenance and reproduction of social order. Such analyses are certainly useful. But surveillance is also a fantasy of power, one whose meaning in postindustrial societies, we shall see, extends far beyond the simple idea of supervising or regulating individuals and social relations, to the creation of virtual forms of control within virtual societies, where supervision in fact may no longer be precisely a "social" operation at all, but an imaginary projection of codes, models, and cybernetic assemblages which, in the end, generate only the delusion of sociality. To understand what the technology of surveillance is and the effects it aims for today, increasingly we have to appreciate the fantasy that drives it, and that, in a word, is simulation. Simulation, in its most generic sense, is the "point" where the imaginary and the real coincide, specifically, where the gap between virtual control and actual control disappears. Any language that describes it must be paradoxically both fictive and objective. It is, in the language of this book, a form of *hyper*control – one of its technical aims is to push the disciplinary functions of surveillance to their imaginary limit. To understand the *simulation* of surveillance is to understand the fictive and unbounded possibilities of discipline within a telematic society. ("Tele": from the Greek for "distant." Telematic societies are societies that aim to solve the problem of perceptual control at a distance through technologies for cutting the time of transmission of information to zero.)

A great deal that has been written in the last few years about surveillance has emphasized how information technology has altered the ways in which social control is exercised in postindustrial societies. We hear, for example, about the rise of "surveillance societies," the "new surveillance," and the extension of the surveillance capabilities of the state made possible by modern electronics and communications technology (Lyon 1994; G. Marx 1988; Dandeker 1990; Burnham 1983; Cohen 1985; Rule 1973). The merit of all of this work – and it has a great deal of merit – is that it recognizes the sweeping changes that have occurred in the nature and organization of surveillance practices in recent years, that they have become, in large measure, more detailed but less verifiable, more diffuse and transinstitutional, invading almost all aspects of everyday life, transforming our roles as citizens, consumers, and workers, our sense of privacy and the ways we view issues of risk concerning health, sexuality, and the body. The problem is that none of this work relates these changes in the nature and scope of control in an explicit way to simulation. It is simulation, however, that is the key to explaining the direction that surveillance societies are taking today, a movement that is more about the perfection and totalization of existing surveillance technologies than some kind of radical break in their historical development. This is not a book, then, written from the frame of something new about surveillance, which in relation to observational or recording technologies has always been about control and discipline, but from the perspective of its ancient complicity with technologies for the construction of virtual worlds, of how its forms of control are refined and intensified in a system geared to the frenzied, instantaneous production of images.

Simulation and the virtualization of society

Baudrillard (1983b: 5) defines simulation generally in contrast to dissimulation, as a form of feigning or deception, but then immediately adds the following qualifications:

To dissimulate is to feign not to have what one has. To simulate is to feign what one hasn't. One implies a presence, the other an absence. But the matter is more complicated, since to simulate is not simply to feign: "Someone who feigns an illness can simply go to bed and make believe he is ill. Someone [sic] who simulates an illness produces in himself some of the symptoms." Thus, feigning or dissimulating leaves the reality principle intact: the difference is always clear, it is only masked; whereas simulation threatens the difference between "true" and "false," between "real" and "imaginary."

In *The Logic of Sense*, Gilles Deleuze (1990: 263), in an analysis of simulacra and their meaning in ancient philosophy, also notes that simulation is connected to the idea of masking, but in a special sense that contrasts it to the mere production of appearances or illusions:

Simulation designates the power of producing an *effect*. But this is not intended only in a causal sense, since causality would remain completely hypothetical or indeterminate without the intervention of other meanings. It is intended rather in the sense of a "sign" issued from a process of signalization; it is in the sense of a "costume," or rather a mask, expressing a process of disguising, where [however], behind each mask, there is yet another . . .

Simulation, then, undermines the conventional order of representation, the relation of a signifier to what it signifies, the image to its object. Behind the image, there is only another image. Yet this self-enclosed and self-referring system of images somehow produces effects through a "process of signalization." Baudrillard characterizes this process in terms of the "reproduction of the real" by means of codes or models, in the same way that computerized images are a function of their program. Simulation, that is, aims for the production of a "reality effect," while at the same time concealing the absence of the real, or better, the *redundancy* of the real as a possible signified or referential ground for its image. The use of the term "real" here involves considerable slippage, because its very definition becomes just one more effect of a process of coding, i.e., the real now operates as a reference or signified only *within* the general order of simulation. For Baudrillard, "the very definition of the real has become: *that of which it is possible to give an equivalent reproduction . . .* The real is not only what can be reproduced, *but that which is always already reproduced.* The hyperreal . . . which is entirely in simulation" (Baudrillard 1983b: 146). The "hyperreal" (i.e., the "code," the technologies of signalization) for Baudrillard is what *precedes* the real (the imaginary apparatus that signals or "effects" the real).[3] Simulation, in turn, for Baudrillard becomes the "reigning scheme" of the postindustrial or information age, roughly defined by the concept "telematic society," a scheme whose paradigmatic mode of domination and control is the code (1983b: 83).

For Baudrillard, the contemporary order of simulation is a stage in the evolution (or perhaps better, de-evolution) of the logic and function of images – simulacra – that has deep historical roots (1983b: 11ff.). In the first stage of this evolution, the image is the reflection of a basic reality: it is a "good" image, a "true" representation of its object, and belongs, according to Baudrillard, to the theological order of the sacrament (e.g., the host as true representation of the body of Christ). In the second stage, it masks and perverts a basic reality: it is an "evil" image. This is the stage of ideological representation, the false appearance, the target, in one of its manifestations, of Marx's critique of the illusions or fetishes of the order of capitalist production. In the third stage, corresponding roughly with the development and refinement of modern information technology, the image masks the absence of a basic reality. For Baudrillard, this stage marks the transition from an order of production to one of simulation proper. The first two stages imply a "theology of truth and secrecy," while the third inaugurates an era in which it becomes increasingly difficult to separate the realms of the true and false, appearance and reality, secrecy and transparency. This, for Baudrillard, is our own era, where the circulation and dissemination of sign-images dominate, but rather than being "false" images, now have the function of *concealing* the fact that reality itself is absent behind its representation. It is, in fact, the preliminary stage in the final dissolution of the representational order. Baudrillard does not stop here, however, but carries the logic of this process to its limit. In the fourth stage, Baudrillard's fantastic projection of the evolution of simulation into the future, the image no longer bears any relation to reality whatsoever: it is its own simulacrum. Here, in a world where the historical and experiential gap between the real and its representation has been once and for all bridged, we can imagine a virtual order wherein it is finally impossible to distinguish truth from fiction, real and unreal, the production of goods from the production of signs, persons from their holographic images or bionic reconstructions, or societies from their reincarnations over electronic nets. Of course, this is fiction, but not only fiction. In positing a fourth stage of simulation, Baudrillard serves notice of a dynamic that in cruder forms is already well advanced in the technical systems of the present.

These reflections form the context for Baudrillard's controversial thesis on the "end of the social," the idea that in entering an age of simulated forms, the social, society itself, disappears as a coherent representation. Baudrillard considers three "hypotheses" about the end of the social (1983a: 70ff.):

(1) *The social has basically never existed.* There has never been any "social relation." Nothing has ever functioned socially ... there has never been anything but *simulation* of the social and the social relation. In which case there is no point dreaming about a "real sociality . . . ," this just hypostatises a simulacrum.

(2) *The social has really existed, it exists even more and more . . .* it alone exists. But contrary to the antiquated idea which makes the social into an objective progress of mankind, everything which escapes it being only residue, it is possible to envisage that the social itself is only residue, and that, if it has triumphed in the real, it is precisely as such. In this even we are really even deeper in the social . . . in the fantastic congestion of dead labor, of dead and institutionalized relations within terrorist bureaucracies, of dead languages and grammars . . .

(3) *The social has well and truly existed, but it does not exist anymore.* It has existed as coherent space, as reality principle (the social relation, the social as structure, as dynamic abstraction, as scene of history) ... , all this has only had an end in view, a meaning as power, as work, as capital, from the perspective space of a rational distribution . . . which is also that of production – in short, in the narrow gap of second-order simulacra, and absorbed into third-order simulacra, it is dying.

For our purposes, it is the second and third hypotheses that are the most relevant to our aim of constructing a social science fiction of the relations between surveillance and simulation technology. In both, Baudrillard considers possible implications of the simulation or virtualization of society itself, first as the production of society as informated forms or "residue" – an order in which the images of the social preside over or stand witness to the scene of its death, where the proliferation of the *signs* of the social masks the radical absence or, in more concrete terms, the "wasteland" of contemporary society, a zone of dead (commodified, objectified) labor, excess production, bureaucratic terrorism, and the barrenness of language (language crystallized as object and commodity, i.e., as information and code). For someone who has taken great pains to distance himself from classical sociological concerns, Baudrillard's hypothesis here resonates deeply with radical neo-Marxist and neo-Weberian overtones, a vision of society reduced by its own rationalized and bureaucratized forms of production to the status of detritus.

What distinguishes his vision from these theories, however, is Baudrillard's own sense of the pivotal role of simulation, rather than production or bureaucratization/rationalization per se, as the driving dynamic behind these developments.

Baudrillard's third hypothesis is not so much at odds with his second; rather it frames it in a different way. Here, the simulation of the social order manifests itself not only in the hyperproduction of its signs and images and masks the residualization of society; it signals the end of the social order itself, and with its end the "grand narratives" of the social itself, i.e., the social sciences in general, and sociology in particular. If my reading of Baudrillard is correct, he no longer takes this hypothesis as seriously as his second. In recent works, Baudrillard has distanced himself from contemporary "philosophies of the end" (the end of history, time, and even, I think, of the end of the social), raising rather the question of how those realms are transformed in their subordination to simulation and "hyperization" by the "code." Responding to the whole question of ends that in the last decade has produced a kind of philosophical impasse, Baudrillard has said that he "is no longer sure that it is any longer a question of an end. The word is probably meaningless in any case, because we're no longer sure about the meaning of linearity" (Baudrillard and Lotringer 1987: 67). In his latest work, he refers to the illusory nature of the whole discourse of ends, as itself an effect of simulation (Baudrillard 1994). Perhaps, then, not the "end" of society, nor the "end" of history, time, etc., but as his second hypothesis intimates, *more and more* society and social relations, they alone exist, only not "real" in the sense that framed thought on society since the beginning of the modern era, but "hyperreal" or virtual in a sense appropriate to the information-saturated and media-panicked qualities of a hypermodern world.

From the perspective of this book, the question concerning the "effects" of virtual systems in telematic societies is a question about the role of simulation technology in the constitution, or better, the hyperrealization, of social relations, an inquiry into certain fundamental, technical processes that dismantle or render superfluous the "reality principles" that frame the interpretation and explanation of those relations. We shall see later that these have to do primarily with limits of space, time, and agency in matters of social reproduction. Virtual technologies, to put the matter in a schematic way, generate images directly from coded instructions – images that transcend, or at least are designed to give the appearance of transcending, constraints of distance and difference (simulated events or virtual images always aim to be instantaneous and unmediated). To overcome limits of distance and difference through simulation, however, translates as an effort to resolve problems of order and control whose negotiation is at the heart of the constitution of "societies," as traditionally conceived in social theory. In the imaginary of these systems, no social relation – exchange, production, consumption, collaboration, conflict – is more distant than the space between a keyboard and a screen, or different from the code that governs it. Press a key and make a connection. Virtual systems also work to dissolve boundaries that frame the social actor or agent grounded in a material body, substituting for them what Haraway (1985) has called a "cyborg" figure, the human agent reduced to a machinic–organic interface or, in the case of telematics, the hyperreal "persons" that inhabit data banks as simulated, electronic "communities" or genetic algorithms. All this raises in stark terms the limits of a discourse of "society" for understanding a virtual, literally fictional, order whose contemporary manifestation is signaled today in the growing dominance of informated (and bio-informated) forms.

I shall use the terms simulation, virtualization, and hyperrealization in roughly equivalent ways in this book. Although Baudrillard's reflections on simulation inform a great deal of this text, Deleuze's sense of the "virtual," I think, is perhaps in some ways closer to what I am trying to convey and deserves some brief comments. In *Cinema 2: The Time Image*, Deleuze (1989: 70) contrasts the pair actual:virtual with the pair real:possible. He makes the claim that the virtual is what is *immediately actual*, that an "indiscernible although distinct difference" marks the gap between them:

The actual image and its virtual image thus constitute the smallest internal circuit, ultimately a peak or point, but a physical point which has distinct elements . . . Distinct, but indiscernible, such are the virtual and the actual which are in continual exchange.

In Deleuze's scheme, which he derives in part from Bergson's reflections on temporality and the image (1991), the virtual is not opposed to the *real*; the latter's relevant contrast is rather with the *possible*. Virtual (simulated) images are not "possible" images at all, in the sense of events that could exist "in reality," but do not yet do so. Rather, the virtual is what is *already* actual (e.g., in the same way the image on your television screen is already an actual image, not merely a possible one, i.e., one that somehow could become real). This, again, is why the virtual is not part of the order of visual representation. For Deleuze, the relevant distinction involves an "indiscernible" or imperceptible (although not unintelli-

gible) gap between a "passing present" (the actual) and a "past as preserved" (the virtual). The virtual here takes the general form of the past,
as that which is always already over and fixed, and which organizes the
passage of time as a kind of "repetition in advance," an effect of its code.
In science fiction terms, the passing present, the actual, appears as simulation, and the past as preserved (recorded, encoded, filed), the virtual,
appears as immediately and fully actual. In the following pages, I shall
try to keep some of these distinctions in view and elaborate them further,
although popular discourse generally ignores them. "Virtual reality," for
instance, from a Deleuzian point of view, is something of an oxymoron
– "virtual actuality," or perhaps even just "virtual system" would be better – although I will continue to use the first term because of its current
popularity. The same is true of the Baudrillardian notion that simulation,
or hyperreality, constitutes a challenge to "the reality principle." In one
sense, the notion of the real is not an appropriate context with which to
begin an analysis of virtual or simulated systems. In the many places I
discuss Baudrillard's work here, it is important to keep in mind that the
"hyperreal" is not simply a "possible" real, but an image that in a fundamental sense is always already actualized. As long as we hold this in
mind, we can always refer occasional confusions and ambiguities back to
this distinction.

Simulation, to put matters in more concrete terms, gets hyped today
in the market for things like global online services (simulated communi-
ties/markets, information "highways"), genetic mapping and engineering
(simulated bodies and body parts), expert systems (simulated knowledge), and virtual reality (simulated space and time, fantasy onscreen).
These are technologies, I want to argue, in which surveillance approaches something like an ecstatic form – where a single person wired into a
computer can access millions of files anytime, anywhere, where wars are
fought onscreen in satellite-fed electronic command and control centers
before deciding to fight them "for real," where parents (someday soon)
will choose the genetic "histories" of their children, who in turn will
reflect less the biological differences of their mothers and fathers than the
homogeneity of programmed norms of health and beauty. Such fanciful
scenes invoke a futuristic landscape of surveillance without limits – everything visible in advance, everything transparent, sterilized and risk-free,
nothing secret, absolute foreknowledge of events. But surveillance without limits is exactly what simulation is all about. Simulation, that is, is a
way of satisfying a wish to see everything, and to see it in advance, therefore both as something present (or anticipated) and already over (past).
What sells simulation technology today is the seductive claim that any

image is observable, that any event is programmable, and thus, in a sense, foreseeable (once you discover the algorithm of a video game, you can master it, the game's "future" becomes clear;[4] once you decipher the secret of the genetic code, the body's "destiny" is transparent and securable). Dreams of omniscience, omnipresence, mastery, and security – in short, of control – are, of course, nothing new in the history of technology. Simulation technology is just another way of dealing with limits imposed by time and space, energy, the human body, limits of perception, limits of memory, limits of communication, all problems for which it offers up fantastic, technically imaginative solutions – cybernetic interfaces, computerized prosthetics, genetic identification and verification, universal coding schemes – the list is almost endless. I want to describe that technical imaginary as a dominant force in the current evolution of surveillance societies. That requires a description not so much of what surveillance is and does as of the imaginary that informs the logic of its development.

Surveillance

Most persons today know, or at least sense, how "informated" life is becoming,[5] how much power resides in the control of information, in access to files and codes. The modern bureaucratic state gathers massive amounts of data on citizens, their incomes, their health, their preferences and tastes and dispositions; businesses likewise generate literally mountains of information about workers and consumers, about their debts and balances, credit histories and lifestyles. Information *is* a business – we produce medical records, school records, tax records, welfare records, crime records, by the billions. Computers have made coding, viewing, storing, and recalling information on persons, events, and everything in general, faster and more efficient, and as each day thousands more computers are added to the existing web of networks, sharing and comparing information becomes easier. Almost everything we do, in fact almost everything that happens these days, creates trails of records. Collectively, those records themselves are like a kind of shadow order – the electronic memory-traces of mass society, or perhaps, as Baudrillard (1983a) imagines, the very form of the masses today, the medium into which they have "disappeared."

How does this imaginary circulate in everyday life? Recording information electronically is a means of ordering and systematizing. Anthony Giddens (1984: 183–184) says that coding information for administering subject populations is a key mechanism in the transition from social integration to system imperatives – efficiency, integration, coordination, planning – that defines the modern age.[6] He defines surveillance, appropriately enough, as the strategic control of the *conditions* of disclosure, which essentially means space and time (and, for Giddens, *agency* – you need a human surveillor, at least to run the machines). Not surprisingly, surveillance, as a kind of "making visible" in space, or in the case of time, making a series or succession of durations, produces conformity (Giddens 1984: 127). Giddens adds, however, that conformity is only one consequence of a dynamic that must be framed in the wider context of what he terms a "dialectic of control," an analysis that also focuses on the relative power of human agents to *resist* system imperatives, to elude the apparatuses of disclosure or redeploy them for their own ends, to assert their capacity to "act differently." Little does Giddens suspect, however, where this resistance to disclosure may inadvertently be leading us: to the elusion of the visible and duration itself – simulation technology and telematics, screens to see everything without looking, go everywhere, and arrive before you leave (what else is virtual reality?). Surveillance, contra Giddens, doesn't follow a dialectic of control, but a logic of virtualization and hyperrealization; it is not a process of negation, but one of pure positivity, unimpeded production, and unarrested circulation. Resistance doesn't overcome it, but shifts it into high gear, another register. In focusing on the dialectic of control and its political economy of resistance and opposition, Giddens slides over the whole idea of the imaginary of control and the problem *it* wants to solve – how to close the gap between the passing present and the past as preserved, i.e., between the actual and the virtual, to *simulate the very conditions of disclosure*, space and time, human agency and human perception – all of which would lead him to a consideration of an entirely different set of problems, viz., those of simulation – the production of virtual agents, virtual landscapes and timescapes, and finally, virtual forms of control itself. This is an imaginary that is already very much a real part of our everyday lives.[7]

Academic interest in surveillance isn't new. It has roots, to name just a few, in Marx, who views supervisory practices as tools of capital in managing labor-time and labor-power, in Frederick Taylor's famous time–motion studies of the labor process – scientific management – and in Max Weber's analyses of the use of files and the role of secrecy in consolidating the power of bureaucracy over individuals. Weber's work in particular has influenced the modern institutional theory of surveillance (in recent historical studies of undercover work and military and corporate intelligence, in analyses of the informated office and the domination of administrative forms of organization generally) (see G. Marx 1995; G. Marx 1990; Dandeker 1990; Cohen 1985). Surveillance, from a Weberian slant, becomes the modern metaphor for the bars on the "iron cage" of western civilization, the smooth, silent-running bureaucratic machine, the instrumental, efficient way in supervision.

Beyond Marx and Weber, recent interest in surveillance has its origins in two works by Foucault – *The Birth of the Clinic* (1975), his archaeology of the medical "gaze" as a figure of modern diagnostic practice, and *Discipline and Punish* (1979), on the genealogy of the prison. In *Discipline and Punish*, in particular, Foucault refers explicitly to surveillance as a disciplinary strategy for distributing the forces of bodies in space and time, through continuous practices of hierarchical observation and examination. Some of the interest Foucault has generated centers on his description of panoptics as a generalizable logistics of control in modern societies, the "architectural" model of Bentham's utilitarian dream of a perfect prison, where power is functionalized around the detailed orchestration of space and time, light and visibility. In the prison as panopticon, visibility becomes a trap, both individualizing offenders and inducing them to police their own behavior, transforming them into "subjects," docile bodies. We shall return to this later in the book. For now, it is enough to note that Foucault closes this work with a reflection on the opening of the juvenile reformatory at Mettray in France in 1840, an institution where all the prior disconnected strands of disciplinary practice, in barracks life and military dressage, in the time-tables of the schools and schedules of the academy, in the confines of the factory, the asylum, and the confessional, in the teaching regimen of the clinic, all come together in a coherent carceral method. Beyond incarceration and the prison, one and the same method now will come to serve a variety of institutional functions at the opening of the modern age – from instruction and training, testing and preparing, credentialing and selection, to care, rehabilitation, security and deterrence, production and consumption – a fantastic, seamless web of control linking together the widest and deepest layers of the social body.

How useful is panoptics as an idea for understanding so-called surveillance societies today? Some of Foucault's critics think his work fosters a simplistic or paranoic impression of those societies as prisons writ large (Lyon 1994: 62ff.). Others, in contrast, have radicalized his idea. Mark Poster (1990), for instance, sees modern societies organized around information and communications technology as "Superpanopticons" (a concept, I think, that has much to recommend it). Foucault himself made it clear that the example of the prison in *Discipline and Punish* was not intended so much as a metaphor or explanation for the organization of present societies as a concrete illustration of the operation of panoptic principles in something approaching their most concentrated or pure form. For Foucault, the prison is where the organization of life, of spaces and times and distances, most closely approximates the fiction of absolute control – the surreal, haunting territory where a dying child at Mettray can despair that he must depart the institution so soon, where submission becomes a form of devotion, and even something pleasurable. With regard to contemporary surveillance technologies – computer matching, video scanning, coding, and other electronic or digital forms of monitoring, biological testing, and diagnosis – it is possible to argue that panoptics remains something like a general model (Foucault uses the term "diagram") for a strategy of exposure, i.e., for opening up diverse objects and events, behaviors and transactions, to routine, close inspection, and insuring their compliance – even the pleasure of that compliance – with normative standards. We might even say that modern information technology functions according to panoptic principles in other important senses, when, for example, persons are confined to terminals and electronic work-stations, when their time and space is structured "architecturally" around screens and keyboards, assuring their bodies are continuously plugged in and online. For all this, though, we would do better to reframe the question in terms of simulation. The child at Mettray is as much caught up in a fantasy of control as a material apparatus. To that extent, the idea of surveillance – or panoptics – alone cannot comprehend the direction being taken by contemporary forms of social control.

Simulation, we could say, is the *panoptic imaginary*. Much of what the following chapters try to do is make sense of that complex idea in various contexts – in military logistics and the conduct of modern war, in work, sexuality, and private life. It is a complexity that often verges on paradox and is difficult to capture in a single formula. The strategies and technologies we shall explore here are still very much in the process of development; their connections are fluid and not fully transparent. Our ideas here can only be provisional. We are dealing first of all with a kind of hyperpanoptics – instead of architectures of control, walls and floors and viewing locations, we need to talk about cyberarchitectures, digital structures, and environments; instead of orderings of space and time, virtual space-times and the coding conventions for displaying them onscreen; instead of visibilities and temporal series, about virtual light, programmed images, and cyberloops.[8] We can say that both simulation and surveillance are "strategies of the real," although in different ways –

while simulation masks the absence of the real, surveillance unmasks its presence. As a result, both are also strategies of appearance. Someone who simulates appears real, but a surveillor prefers to mask his appearance. These relations, as it turns out, are both complementary and contradictory. They generate the most subtle tensions and perplexities. Since earliest times, the exercise of surveillance has been dependent on masking (in his analysis of panoptics, Foucault already emphasizes how asymmetrical relations of power materialize not only in the ways observational mechanisms disclose events, but in the ways they themselves are camouflaged). At the same time, masks are precisely what surveillance intends to strip from its object. Surveillance, we shall see, is all about breaking through surfaces of appearance, closing gaps between appearance and reality, practices which themselves demand stealth, deception, and attention to controlling appearances.

Things are even more complicated than this, however. If simulation is a technology for the reproduction of the real, for that very reason it signals the emergence of an order where the real is everywhere in crisis and threatening to disappear (and that, we have seen, for Baudrillard includes the essential "reality" of the social order itself, which everywhere is vanishing and becoming hyperreal). The real in simulation is what is already contained (and projected) in its model, its code, program, or scenario (these terms are not necessarily equivalent, nor do they exhaust the bewilderingly complex array of contemporary simulation technologies). A simulation aims to be more than just a copy. With enough preparation and staging, it could substitute perfectly for the real thing. This isn't just a fantasy. Among many other things, simulations are routinely used today by the military for training purposes. Flight simulators have been around a long time; today's soldiers train on virtual reality machines while their commanders prepare for battle with computerized war games. In fact, we shall see in chapter 4, a good case can be made that simulation, in important ways, is originally related to concerns of military preparedness. Today, police use profiles, or composite images, as aids in making arrests and to instruct officers in targeting suspected offenders; schools use them to identify problem students or to teach required materials in controlled settings; hospitals employ them to assist doctors in diagnosis and treatment (expert systems). In all these examples, some form of coded information (sign-image) anticipates an actual event in order to control its outcome.

The complex logistical functions of simulation and surveillance very often overlap. Both are means of exposure, training, preparation, and deterrence. In the future, perhaps, we will all carry genetic identity markers (or implants!) of some sort, something like biological barcodes that when scanned (surveilled) supply not just our life histories, but our future biographies, to the relevant authorities, who will then tell us what educations we are entitled to, what jobs we are suited for and should prepare for, what special talents we possess and how best to develop them, what illnesses we can expect to encounter and what lifestyles would deter them, how long we are likely to live, how we will probably die. Those codes, filed away in data banks for instant access and comparison, would be like our doubles or shadow selves, designer identities (see Turkle 1984). To the authorities at least, they would become in some ways more real than our real selves, because they would stand in for and verify the reality of those selves in ways that are, or have the potential to be, absolutely certain (the genetic code, as a standard from which all deviations originate and against which they are assessed, doesn't lie). Simulation, in fact, would in such cases carry surveillance, the unmasking of reality, to its logical limit and conclusion – perfect information on individuals, perfect exposure, and perfect discipline (the code becomes a prior and automatic form of normalization).

But then again, simulation functions in ways that are totally contradictory to surveillance – not as a method of exposure or unconcealing, but the fabrication of completely original scenes, pure fictions that bear absolutely no relation to "reality" at all, not even as a signified absence, yet for all that are fully "actual" (someone once remarked that virtual reality was the end of photography as a means of evidence because it would be impossible to distinguish between true and fictional images). If surveillance is about the real, simulation, in the end, is about the hyperreal, the more-than-real. Surveillance uncovers, but simulation, we could say, *is* the cover. Surveillance always looks *through or behind* something; simulation is a projection *onto* something (a screen). However one "scans" a video game or virtual scene, the kind of observation that is involved is never just simple surveillance, never just a form of monitoring or perceptual control, but always (only) a simulation *of* surveillance, a fiction of surveillance, and the relationship that develops is not just discipline, but the simulation of discipline (control, order). Surveillance peers behind the screen, simulation stops *at* the screen.

Much of this book, then, is about identifying these paradoxical connections between simulation and surveillance, how those connections evolve (and are evolving) in telematic societies to produce order out of human multiplicities. As we shall see, that will mean patching together the work of authors who often have deep philosophical differences – Baudrillard and Foucault – with the "objective fictions" of other writers, like Paul Virilio, Donna Haraway, and Michel de Certeau, who among others have posed these problems in different terms and for different reasons. I think these works can be incorporated within a larger framework that examines the question of social control in present-day societies from the point of view of the simulation of surveillance.

I cannot, unfortunately, give a simple definition of this idea, at least one that doesn't almost immediately contradict or deconstruct itself. On a very general level, it refers to a sophisticated means of introducing discipline into the very heart of an operation, so that it becomes fully automatic and "front-ended" (total cybernetic control). Or it can be just the opposite – no longer exactly "discipline" at all, as a method of ordering, but a kind of pure operationalism, a pre-ordering, if you will, or ordering in advance. In the end, we shall be forced to admit that both descriptions are right and both are wrong, yet both are inescapable. Simulated surveillance, we shall see, throughout this book refers to a paradox of control. It is a fantasy of absolute control and the absence of control at the same time, total control and the end (perfection, cancellation) of control. Much of what I have to say about it is through examples and descriptions that bring out this paradoxical character, but which do not, and in a literal sense cannot, resolve it. It simply reflects the generally paradoxical nature of control in telematic orders. Again, I say paradoxical rather than dialectical, because the effort to totalize control does not lead to its surpassing or overcoming in a Hegelian sense, but to its hyperization, its reconfiguration as a simulacrum within an informated order. What we shall call a "disappearance" of control in modern, telematic societies is not a negation as much as it is, to use Felix Guatarri's term, a "reterritorialization," a re-"spatialization" and re-"temporalization" of control as a virtual phenomenon (Deleuze and Guatarri 1987).

Of course, simulation, like surveillance, has a history. It is a strategy of war and politics whose idea is very old, and whose origins are lost in antiquity. Disguise and camouflage, ruse, the staging of images – like careful watching, stalking, preying – these are ways of exercising (and subverting) power that probably are engrained as much in species as in cultures.[9] In the late twentieth century, we are rapidly becoming more familiar with technologies for creating "surrogate" individuals and populations – cloning, profiling, and artificial intelligence, to name just a few. These technologies have modern antecedents in eugenics, in statistical biology, and in demographic studies, in early nineteenth-century efforts in robotics and the mechanization of labor, all of which run parallel to surveillance technologies evolving in prisons, schools, and other bureaucratically organized institutions at that same time.

Like surveillance, this could have been a book about the historical evolution of simulation in the modern age, as a complementary tool of surveillance in the consolidation of national power, bureaucratic
domination, the development of capital, etc. It would have been, at that
level, a history of the present, in Foucault's sense, a genealogy of simulation practices that would supplement Foucault's discussion of panoptic surveillance. Such a historical investigation undoubtedly would be
very valuable. But the topic of simulation itself persuaded me to look at
these things differently. Not a history of simulation, but following Alfred
Jarry (1960: 131), a "pataphysics" of simulation, a "science" of virtualization as an imaginary solution,[10] in this case, a solution to problems
encountered by the technology of surveillance itself – viz., how to control the spatial and temporal distribution of objects and bodies, how to
organize multiplicities of human and machinic forces simply and effectively. This change to a pataphysical – or imaginary – perspective was
dictated by the operative form of simulation itself, which virtualizes all
historical and social frames of reference. One doesn't understand a virtual technology by understanding its history so much as one understands
it through the ways it models or codes histories (i.e., stages events,
chronologies, temporal passages, periods, etc.). Virtual systems – simulations – before anything else, are *indifferent* to history, at least human history. They are like de Landa's robot – human history doesn't matter.
Think of the image of the clone as a virtual body. One can look at the
history of cloning technology to gain a better sense of how it developed
to its present stage, how it furthers bureaucratic/medical/state/corporate
interests, and so forth, or alternatively, one can see the clone as a biotechnical figure that embodies a certain "history in advance," that creates a
"history" ex nihilo, an individual that "will have been," whose destiny is
embodied in the articulation and design of its genetic code. Simulation
technology, for all we hear about the exciting possibilities of its future
development, is in fact more about a kind of nostalgia or melancholy for
the future; it produces a sense that the future is not ahead but in some
fundamental way already over, in the same way the life of a clone is pre-
determined, already over from the start, or the way a video game or artificial intelligence machine contains *all* its possibilities in its program
(despite the best efforts of designers to program in novelty, learning,
interactivity, and ultimately, imagination). A history of technology, or
technologies of power, that would be similar to Foucault's genealogy of
discipline, would miss something essential here. Simulation, one more
time before we begin, is about the hyperreal and the fictional. The hyperreal doesn't have a history, it has a "future past," an imaginary history

that is over before it begins.

Baudrillard (1993b: 1) says that when the world is on a delusional course, we have to use a delusional language to describe it, a language of the imaginary and the fantastic. That language, inevitably, is one of breaking limits, of absolutes, totalities, and virtualities. Increasingly, it seems, we are forced to resort to hallucinogenic, delusional images just to stay "objective" about the present. Nothing less captures the movement of the forces of simulation, and their relations to the technologies of surveillance, at the end of the twentieth century. The delusion of simulation is that it can reproduce the real without remainder, that it can collapse the difference between reality and appearance, the actual and the virtual, make those differences indiscernible. When we relate that delusion to the development of contemporary surveillance technology, a picture emerges of an "observation-machine" that fashions its own images for its own consumption, for which an "outside" no longer exists, where nothing is left to control because everything is under control from the very beginning. This book is not a theory of surveillance. Nor is it an attempt, despite appearances, to reduce everything to technology, a form of technological determinism. It is more like an effort, in Heidegger's (1977) sense, to locate an essence of technology – in my case, an image that signals a process of technical development from a paradoxically close future. It is not, or at least not only, an empirical description of telematic societies, as they exist today. It is an account of a delusion of those societies, which today appear ever more willing to sacrifice themselves to simulation in order to push surveillance to its absolute limit.

2

Surveillance, its simulation, and hypercontrol in virtual systems

Panic for nothing

A true story. Driving out of the Medicine Bow range of the Rocky Mountains toward Laramie, Wyoming, you pass through the little town of Centennial. It's not much more than a truckstop – a gas station/cafe, a small motel, some outbuildings. You wind around a blind curve before dropping onto the valley floor. It's been downhill for twenty miles, almost no traffic, and you're oblivious to how fast you're driving. Just at the edge of town, you spot a patrol car parked on the side of the road by the cafe. Speed trap. You panic and hit the brakes, thinking you might have time to slow down, but it doesn't matter. You've certainly been spotted, probably scanned with a radar gun. You start to pull over. But as you get closer, you notice that no one is sitting inside the car, that in fact it's not really a patrol car at all, just an old junker painted black and white, topped with some fake flashers, and set by the road to make people like you slow down in a hurry. It's probably been sitting there for years. Maybe the owners of the cafe just wanted you to stop and have lunch, spend some money; maybe the highway patrol put it there for local pedestrians, because it doesn't have the money to spend on a real car and driver. Someone, in any case, is playing a bad joke on you. It works. And if you pass through town again, just knowing the patrol car isn't real, that there's no cop inside, doesn't totally overcome the uncertainty of that last curve. You think: there's no trap, don't worry, it's a fake. Or is it? Maybe this time it *is* real. You slow down just to be safe. After a couple of times of this, of course, the apprehension wears off. After all, even the best ruse becomes transparent if it's repeated too often. When that happens, the patrol car becomes just another curiosity along the road (... but still, you slow down).

This is an everyday example, although not a perfect one, of what I mean by the simulation of surveillance. As a strategy of control, it's a simple and also ancient idea, but one that from the beginning develops enormous complexity: feign an observer or a field of observation, and divert, enhance, or arrest a flow – in this case, the motion of your car, but in practice, it could be any process, activity, or rhythm. Virilio (1986: 15) shows how contemporary power – the "observation machine" of postindustrial societies – is *dromological*; it operates on speed, on the *time* of movement. Dromology, literally, is the "logic of the race" – in the present context, the race to *see first*. Who sees first, ultimately, who *fore*sees or sees in advance, wins. Virilio begins his analysis of dromo-logic with a consideration of how political power is organized to control the movement of crowds in the street and immediately links this to the problem of police observation, not, as is conventionally the case, to the dynamics of class struggle: "The State's political power, therefore, is only secondarily 'power organized by one class to oppress another.' More materially, *it is the polis, the police, in other words highway surveillance*, insofar as, since the dawn of the bourgeois revolution, the old communal poliorcetics ... has confused social order with the control of traffic" (ibid.). In the abstract, then, power is the policing of speed, of material flows, by the machinery of observation.

If we link the dromological concept of surveillance to simulation, we arrive at a strategy of war as old as war itself (bourgeois society did not discover it).[1] Make the enemy waste time sorting out appearances. Generate uncertainty and unplanned changes in movement, temporary paralyses, breaks in flows. Deflect the enemy's attention, make him hesitate or misread the conditions of his observation, by using decoys and surrogates, disguising *an absence with a presence*, then surprise him from another direction. In its highest forms, this kind of deception can lead the enemy to hide in the very places that are the most exposed. Power here is not simply the "polis"; ideally, it has no specific locus at all but is always "somewhere else." It is never *the* center but rather *what* centers (see Shorris 1985), not the focus but *what* focuses, a force working along the periphery of its object's vision, at the limits of its perceptual field, behind its back. Or again, it's the force that makes *every place a center* – i.e., a target – *every time a midpoint* between observation and capture. Power here operates as the simulation of surveillance, a projection or a screen. In our own example of "highway surveillance," we might even say that power does not exist at all (at least, not in *this* space or *this* time). That's *not*, however, what whoever stationed the fake patrol car by the side of the road wants speeders to know, namely, that their panic is for nothing, that the trap isn't real.

The simulation of surveillance is a control strategy that informs most of the latest diagnostic and actuarial technologies we associate with the information age – computer profiling and matching, expert decision-systems and cybernetic intelligence, electronic polling, genetic mapping and recombinant procedures, coding practices of all sorts, virtual reality. These technologies *simulate* surveillance in the sense that they *precede and redouble a means of observation*. Computer profiling, for instance, is understood best not just as a technology of surveillance, but as a kind of *surveillance in advance of surveillance*, a technology of "observation before the fact." A profile, as the name suggests, is a kind of prior ordering, in this case a model or figure that organizes multiple sources of information to scan for matching or exceptional cases. Resembling an informated form of stereotyping, profiling technology has become increasingly popular in targeting individuals for specialized messages, instructions, inspection, or treatment. Advertisers use it to determine the timing and placement of ads to reach the widest segment of selected audiences. Educators use it to adjust course content to specific populations of students, police to target potential offenders. Profiling, in turn, is only one of a host of increasingly available computer-assisted actuarial and diagnostic procedures that are being used, among other things, to identify individuals for various tasks or entitlements, to define potential risks or hazards, and to forestall or enhance certain behaviors or traits. Unlike stereotypes, however, profiles are not merely "false images" that are used to justify differences in power. Diagnostic profiles exist rather at the intersection of actual and virtual worlds, and come to have more "reality," more "truth and significance," than the cases to which they are compared. Rather than the profiles resembling the cases, increasingly the cases start to resemble the profiles. In Florida, for example, the highway patrol uses criminal profiles to spot potential drug carriers traveling along a stretch of Interstate 95, long known as a route for drugs moving up the coast from Miami to New York. Based on prior search and arrest records, and criminological simulations, profiles function as preliminaries to surveillance, means of training and selection, allowing the police to scan the passing traffic more efficiently and quickly. If your skin color, sex, age, type of car, state license plate, number of passengers, direction of movement, etc., matches the computer profile each officer carries while on duty, you're a target, whether you've actually done anything wrong or not. Here, the image of the typical offender initiates a series of actions designed to eliminate a risk – in effect, a statistical artifact – rather than respond to an actual offense. The image is not false; it is more like a self-fulfilling prophecy – it creates the offense. If a driver is pulled over and found to be carrying drugs, it doesn't "confirm" the profile, which is always true before the event. The driver – his identity, history, biography – isn't really important. What's important is how the profile is drawn and that it operates in accordance with the parameters around which it was designed. The profile neither fails nor succeeds (here, in capturing an offender); rather, however it's drawn, it *guarantees or serves up* an offender for surveillance. Such higher-order surveillance technologies speed the sorting and analysis of information in an effort to develop full front-end control. They are, in essence, a form of verification prior to identification (if you don't fit the profile, no one really cares who you are; for all practical purposes, you don't exist).[2]

Because they function so efficiently as apparatuses of selection and training, these kinds of technologies undoubtedly extend the already vast surveillance capabilities of the modern bureaucratic state. They are like, if you will, the new "gatekeepers" of the bio-electronic order of the future: if you have the right password (or profile, genetic configuration, image), you can continue on – with your work, with your relations with others, with your life. If not, you're a target. But they are also simply quite unlike earlier forms of surveillance. For one thing, they do not just passively record facts (on the model, for instance, of photography), they *simulate facticity* (on the model of virtual imaging systems); rather than document the truth of events, they exploit and reinforce the uncertainty, the wavering line, between truth and fiction. Finally, they favor deterrence over the punishment aspect of disciplinary strategies, proactive or preventative over reactive measures (Bogard 1991).[3] Our patrol car example conforms to a basic pattern in the development of surveillance technologies: get rid of the "external" surveillor once and for all. Who needs the police? Get the traveler to police himself, and save the time and effort of policing him. In the high-tech imaginary of today's surveillance societies, *you're* in the patrol car, you see yourself coming, so to speak, compare yourself to the profile. You participate in and are responsible for your own observation.[4]

But it's even more complicated than that. In this fantasy, you *are* the patrol car, which is to say, the *apparent* means of observation. "You," the "agent" in all this, as it turns out, exist only as a function of the total simulation – eliminate the car, wipe out the scene, and you eliminate the speeder. "You" aren't the center here, because there is no center. "You" don't control yourself but are only a mobile node in a highly dispersed control environment. In this scenario, the whole polarity of Subject and Object, observer and observed, collapses[5] – "you" aren't even driving down the mountain at all; written into the program, you've already driven down this mountain and been busted, over and over again. And no one is watching because you've already been seen. Violation, arrest, sentencing, everything is over, mapped out, before it's begun – at least that's the fantasy. Power has no "place" whatsoever in these systems, not even along the periphery. Rather, it is always diffuse, atmospheric, and delusional.

When the simulation of surveillance forms the basis of social control strategy, everything suddenly becomes reversible, including the sense and location of control itself – who the authorities are, who breaks the law, who gets caught, all this becomes a tangle, as we shall see. There's no sense to getting "caught" here (unless we mean caught before the act), and no law and no police either, in the sense we normally have come to associate with traditional surveillance practices. Instead, the entire field of observation and all its elements are projected into a scene where everything is capable of circling back in on itself, where the offender is "netted" or captured in advance, the violation is already committed, the sentence already handed down, the time already served. Simulated surveillance is like a Möbius strip, with neither an inside nor an outside surface, or a Mandelbröt function that opens onto endless, nested levels of control, recording, speed traps.

Certainly, it is an unwieldy and strange sounding concept – the simulation of surveillance – but it is what telematic societies are really all about; when they are simulated, the strategic forms and applications of surveillance are almost unlimited. As more human functions – decision-making, calculation, communication, sociation, thinking, seeing, feeling, imagining (especially imagining!) – go "online" today, as more essentially "human" powers are sacrificed or given over to virtual systems – allowing screens to substitute for experience, profiles to make our judgments – the greater the refinement, and the invisibility, of the surveillance apparatus.

As I use it here, the simulation of surveillance refers to a "map" or "diagram" of forces, in Michel Foucault's sense, a display of relations of power and knowledge which are general in, if not exclusive to, a given age, and to an extent serve to define its coherence (when Foucault speaks of "disciplinary societies," this is what he has in mind) (Foucault 1979: 205). Or again, it is like Deleuze's (1988: 37ff.) notion of an "abstract machine," a "singularity" that sets forces in motion and generates concrete functions across a multiplicity of practices. It refers, again, to a social order or generalizable way of ordering, although one that paradoxically calls into question both the idea of the social and the possibility of order. In this order, the "social" tends to disappear (i.e., go online, onscreen); and in this society, order and chaos are often difficult to distinguish (what appears online to be highly ordered in fact masks the radical absence of order) (Baudrillard 1983a; Bogard 1990). I use a number of different terms to convey a sense of the age of simulated surveillance in this book – telematic societies, simulated orders, virtual societies, the postindustrial or postmodern age, the information age, cyborg world. All of these descriptions are interchangeable, and none of them works perfectly. At some point, they all tend to fall back into language that is fundamentally inadequate to their object, specifically, into dualist and categorical frames like human:machine, true:false, fictional:real, male:female, domination:subordination, power:ideology – all distinctions that, as we shall see, virtual systems themselves function so efficiently to deconstruct.

The diagram of simulated surveillance appears to us in concrete form as a fantastic bionic–machinic *assemblage* – networks or webs of computer technology, screens, data entry and exit points, sensors, jammers, prosthetic, genomic, and ergonomic devices, software, hardware, wetware, linking bodies to flows of information. It is an assemblage that not only functions to normalize relations among individuals, and of individuals to themselves, but, if you will, to *supernormalize* those relations in simulation. While normalization, in the sense developed by Foucault, refers to the multiplicity of individualizing and totalizing practices in surveillance or disciplinary societies, supernormalization is the reduction of all differences and similarities to modulations of basic codes. The biomachinic assemblage works to erase permanently the already tenuous distinction between the individual and the totality in modern "mass societies," and substitute instead a kind of pure, cybernetic operationality or connectivity that scales evenly across all levels of experience. The apparent complexity of this assemblage masks a rather simple aim to develop a closed system, where all processes can be translated and managed as flows from and back into information – no longer conformity to a historically variable and continuously contested system of norms, but rather, if you will, production from and return to a singular, universal "norm of norms."

The fact that surveillance as a means of social control can be simulated is nothing new. Cybernetic assemblages are only one example of many technologies dating back to antiquity that wed simulation to practices of observation or inspection. Simulation and surveillance have gone hand in hand, we have already suggested, in war and espionage since their origins. Today, they are routine control functions in most institutional settings, to such an extent that they now almost define the operations and the limits of those institutions. In the following chapters, I examine how the simulation of surveillance infuses work, private life, war, and sexuality, but as privileged fields of the exercise of power which cut across traditional institutional boundaries. Increasingly, these technologies force us to adopt a science fiction vocabulary to account for them. In the "brave new world" of surveillance and its simulation, work, privacy, war, and gender become hyperreal, and workers, soldiers, women, and men become cyborgs, plugged in, electrified, coded bodies. On the information highway, the domestic sphere becomes a global marketplace, a public forum, an electric theater of sex, pleasure, and power, even as the globe, markets, public spaces, sexuality, and power shrink and finally disappear onscreen. The new technologies of this world are those that virtualize perception and experience, and their means of control is cybernetic. Or rather, all their control is hypercontrol, in which the code governs the interactivity of the organism and the machine. Throughout this book, I want to emphasize how difficult it is, in relation to these technologies, to continue to think in conventional terms like social control, institution, discipline, the normalized individual, indeed, surveillance itself; and how hard it is today to define the boundaries of work that is "informated," or when and where electronic wars begin and end, or how sex intersects with, and is to a large degree neutralized by, computerization and biotechnologies.

What does it mean for surveillance to be simulated? It does *not* mean, above all, that surveillance no longer exists, or that it does not produce material effects. Nor does it mean, as in the example with which we began, simply that surveillance practices are deceptive or masked (although this is often the case in its earlier forms, especially when we consider police or military surveillance). In this context, we need to guard against the common idea of simulation as a kind of "illusion." The simulation of surveillance does not exactly mean the "illusion" of surveillance. Modern surveillance is not so much "illusory" as it is elevated to a kind of higher reality or, more exactly, pushed to its spatial and temporal limits by simulation. Simulation always aims for the "more real than real"; as a technical operation, we shall see, it works to *eliminate*, not foster, illusion. The better a simulation, the less awareness there is of the artifice that identifies it *as* a simulation. If we could imagine a perfect simulation of surveillance, of observational control, something that we'll do many times in this book, the question of its "staging" wouldn't even arise, because everything would appear "too real" to leave any room for doubt, for even the slightest suspicion that what was observed was "in reality" a simulation. The simulation of surveillance, then, is not

about creating an illusion of surveillance, but about rendering indiscernible, if you will, the fact of its illusion, viz., that control by observational technologies always involves, to some degree or other, the
diminution of the *appearance* of deception.

Even more, to call these technologies of illusion is to give them far too
much credit. Human beings can perhaps create illusions, can deal in artifice and deception. But any *vital* power of illusion, any of the deeper, creative subtleties of artifice, ultimately are beyond these devices – they are,
in the end, just machines, designed and programmed to do what they do
and nothing more (see Baudrillard 1993b: 54–55). At best, they can make
the line between human and machinic forms of artifice vacillate. Where
the imaginary of simulation is the focus, it is always a question of the
implosion of poles, the play between illusion and reality, human and
machine, the shifting meaning and location of power, Subject and Object,
the undecidability of who is watching and who is watched. To analyze
simulation is to involve oneself immediately in paradoxes, bleeding concepts, and floating senses. We shouldn't view this as a problem, however, but as an essential and productive uncertainty that defines the
operation of simulation itself. We can deal with that uncertainty to some
extent by following Baudrillard's convention in thinking about these
technologies in terms of the creation of hyperreal spaces (and times)
rather than simple illusions, which always prompts us to search for something real in distinction to them.

Simulation technologies are not strictly or exclusively observational or
"inspectional" in nature. Computers are one example, perhaps the main
example today, of a technology whose control functions are fully integrated into its mode of operation rather than imposed externally as a
form of inspection. Computers do not "watch" individuals, although they
are used routinely to record their performance (behavior, thoughts, traits,
transactions). Unlike panoptic systems, their "architectures" of control,
their orders of spatial and temporal relations, are virtual (i.e., orders of
information). In the case of computers, control is more adequately conceived in terms of the network itself, specifically, the set of
human–machine interfaces considered as a whole, rather than an effect
of an external, contingent relation between a "recording" machine and
its operator, between an observer and what it observes.

Simulated surveillance, in its imaginary form, aims for a state of perfect deterrence, in fact a state where deterrence is no longer necessary. Its
strategy is always control *in advance*, hyperized, front-end, programmed
control – regulation as a matter of feedback, models, circuitry design,
interface, and integration. It is an operation that passes *through* bodies

and connects them to the storage and retrieval functions of digital systems, and to the instructions coded in genetic sequences. Control as perfect deterrence is, in one sense, not really control at all, but rather a permanent condition of deferral and elusion, a final solution to all the "problems" arising out of the desire to eliminate surprise and risk – all contingencies are planned for in advance, all problems are dodged, all effects are modulations or permutations of their code. Probably the readiest and most intelligible examples of hypercontrol in telematic societies are video games and virtual reality technologies, where control is a function of the *circuit* established between the operator and the machine, and not the property of either pole considered separately (all surprises in a video game are programmed surprises). With the development and proliferation of computers, imaging technologies, coding and decoding equipment, and the like, this form of control becomes radically transinstitutional, i.e., a universal schematics working indifferently across institutions (economic, cultural, political), translating them as so many flows and breaks of information. All this represents a further refinement – and in some ways the refinement *ne plus ultra* – of the process Max Weber (1958: 155) at the beginning of the century referred to as disenchantment, or what Benjamin (1969: 217ff.) described as the loss of aura in a mechanical age. Computerization, of course, has been the major force in this process recently, but we should remember that it is only the current technological manifestation of a rationalization and standardization of disciplinary methods that "took off" in the modern age but whose real roots are lost in the distant past.

There are four important ways to understand the simulation of surveillance, understandings that will circulate around and through the examples, philosophical analyses, and sociological-fictional-technological reflections in this book. First, as a cyborg assemblage, i.e., in terms of surfaces of contact or interfaces between organic and non-organic orders, between life forms and webs of information, or between organs/body parts and entry/projection systems (e.g., keyboards, screens). Cyborgs are the latest development of human–machine connections which, again, date to ancient times, from the most simple agricultural and war technologies, through Renaissance automata and modern industrial robotics. What makes cyborgs different is their singular linkage of bio-ergonomic, prosthetic, and information technologies and the sophistication of operation introduced by methods of cybernetic control (see Haraway 1985; Schwab 1987; Bergstrom 1986). There will be a fuller discussion of cyborg technology in later chapters, particularly the chapter on cyborg work.

For the rest of this chapter, I want to begin discussing simulated surveillance in terms of its general structure and effects, viz., its relation to
the transparency of surfaces, as the production of sterile zones, as breaks
and flows of informated images, but also, and most importantly, in terms
of its technological *imaginary*. Simulated surveillance is an imaginary of
absolute control, in a word, an *ecstasy* of control. Everything exposed,
everything visible, graspable, naked, no secrets. And we must always
remember it is precisely an imaginary we are talking about here.
Although the term has many psychological connotations, I use it primarily to refer to an essential temporal orientation of simulation.
Simulation is about the imagination of the "future-past," about projecting a future as something already over, ultimately, about mastery over
time (speed and distance) (Bogard 1994). What I describe here is a kind
of future "memory" of the technology of surveillance itself, what it "will
have been" from the standpoint of its simulation (from the point of view
in which the apparatus of surveillance looks back on the "history" of its
perfection as a mode of perceptual control!).

Transparency and disappearance of the surface

In the most general sense, the surveillance apparatus is a machinery for
making a surface *transparent*. What "interests" the apparatus is always
what is on the *other side* of this surface, what "remains to be seen." Body
probes (medical and diagnostic technology), background checks (crime,
levels of credit and debt, political and sexual preference), performance
monitoring (in education and at work) – we are all familiar with these
increasingly routine intrusions that break across the everyday surface of
modern life. For the surveillance apparatus, the surface is *the world as it
appears*, and appearances are construed as a cover that conceals the
world as it "really" is. That cover must be stripped away. Surveillance,
in the first instance, is a technology of truth and depth. It is the *enemy
of appearances*, except where it can enlist appearances to serve its own
ends (i.e., to mask its own operations; I'll return to this below). Cameras,
microphones, transducers, scanners, recording media, and test equipment
of all kinds – along with all the skills to operate them – all these are
designed to exchange horizontal, contingent flows along surfaces for the
permanence of vertical, fixed forms, to expose things for what they really are, identify and essentialize them in a network of relations of visibility, power, and knowledge.[6]

Simulation, on the other hand, has a different, although not opposite,
relation to surfaces. It does not attempt to see *through* a surface so much

as it structures perception *across* a surface. The difference is analogous to that between photographic and virtual images, between representational and self-referential systems. In the former, the real still subsists "behind" the image, which serves as its document. In the latter, the real is reconstituted as the image itself (the identity of the real and its image). The simulation apparatus aims, then, for a kind of transparency of the surface, but on another level and in another sense. Unlike surveillance, it doesn't demand the transparency of the surface *as appearance*, but rather the transparency of the surface *as real*, i.e., the dissolution of the surface as *medium of appearance*. Simulation performs its own operation on reality – not to reveal it as an essence or signified behind the surface, but to dispose of it *as* a visible (perceptible) surface, to dismantle the "real" surface in order to better "realize" the appearances. The paradigm of contemporary simulation has to be the TV screen, which as an imaginary technology would substitute hyperreal for documentary or representational images. The perfect TV, if you can imagine it, is one where you don't "see" the screen (i.e., the real surface of appearance) at all, only the image, fully (in fact, more than fully!) realized. Simulation always works to deconstruct its medium, the surface, to produce a pure, unsupported, unmediated event. (In the next chapter, I will discuss the fantastic imaginary of the Holodeck in the TV series *Star Trek: The Next Generation*, the ultimate simulator, where the surface of the image "disappears" and one enters a world – any world – whose medium of projection is perfectly, absolutely invisible). In fact, at its highest level, simulation is not about the problem of reality versus appearances anymore, but about the coincidence of actual and virtual worlds. The simulation machine creates images of the world not as it really is, or even as it apparently is, but as it (really) will have been. Simulation, the process of signalization, precedes the real, while retaining all its "actuality." In its imaginary form, it has no truck with real worlds, or even apparent worlds, only hyperreal ones. With surveillance technology, the operator's gaze passes through a surface; in simulation, the gaze itself is deployed along a vanishing surface, where it becomes a *surrogate* gaze (watching video is always a vicarious experience, seeing the images that someone, or something, else sees or has already seen) (Olalquiaga 1992: 1–18). With simulation, we move from the problem of the transparency of the medium, the surface, to a kind of pure transparency – what's visible is *all* that's visible – from a stage of mediated seeing to the immediacy, to the ecstasy, of perception.

These relations can become exceedingly complex. Many times, surveillance and simulation work counter to each other, as in the case where someone simulates an activity or stages an appearance to escape observation (the employee pretends to be working, the counter-spy feigns loyalty to his country to elude detection). Here simulation functions to subvert the surveillance apparatus (the boss, the government). Just as often, however, they complement or support one another, usually within the same activity. The surveillance apparatus can employ simulation to conceal its presence (or, for that matter, its absence – our police car example was a crude illustration, but the counter-spy above is also precisely a surveillor who simulates not being a surveillor). For my purposes, the truly interesting cases are where surveillance *converts to* simulation. To take a familiar example, the two-way mirror that hides the surveillance camera still relies on a strategy of concealing the machinery of observation. You enter the room and see only your reflection. Far more advanced would be those technologies in which the machinery of observation is fully integrated into the machinery of its concealment (or better, the machinery that eliminates concealment as a strategy altogether – the mirror that *is* the camera, the camera-mirror, that simultaneously registers as well as reflects, that no longer needs to be "two-way" at all, but instantly records the sign-images displayed on its surface, collapsing the distinction between the observer and the technology of observation). Although this might sound like science fiction, computers are already like this in one sense, at least in the logic of their development: their recording operations are always "on the surface," onscreen, nothing concealed. That is simply how they work; there is nothing distinct "behind" them watching (there are only other computers, or computer-operators, and the multiple networks to which they are connected).

Or consider, once again, the virtual reality apparatus. The prototype headset–treadmill–operator connections that are being tested today foreshadow complex simulation-surveillance machines. Virtual reality opens onto a "view" of the world under the "control" of its operator. But what do "view" and "control" mean here; whose "view" are we dealing with? The view of the operator? Or the view of the programmer? Or both? The operator is an observer, a surveillor (and also controller) of the scene that passes before his or her eyes. But in another sense, what is observed is always the view of another, that "passes for" the view of the operator because it is superimposed on that view. Two views as one. The experience of simulation – the televisual or virtual telematic experience – is *psychasthenic*, i.e., like inhabiting another sensorium, but one that has an uncertain locus, being both present and absent (Olalquiaga 1992). If surveillance is the transparency of the surface, the simulation of surveillance is the *transparency of perception* itself, and its availability to anyone who plugs in. Similar problems of standpoint, perspective, experience plague the contemporary analysis of control, as most of this book will attest to.[7]

In fact, even though the technology is still unsophisticated, we can already discern how it aims for its *own* disappearance, in the same way that virtual reality aims no longer to be either illusion or reality, in the sense that in its final, perfect development this distinction would be meaningless. The highest form of the technology would be the one that constructs the perfect appearance of its absence, and thus one that also deconstructs both appearance and absence. Here, the technology is itself appearance, not just a "surface" of appearance. It is precisely the surface *as* appearance that must be extinguished (in virtual systems, what we *don't* want to see is the surface, the medium). Thus, in the most perverse and paradoxical ways, the assemblage of simulation supports one of the primary goals of surveillance, the abolition of appearances, through the elimination of the medium that supports them.

The absence that is at stake in virtual systems is not only that of the machine, but of the operator too (the person in this space, at this time, plugged into this machine). The technology that disappears is the whole human–machine connection, which gives way to the disembodied traveler, the astral projectionist, the "interface, data cowboy" in cyberspace (see Gibson 1984). The goal is the complete, total elimination of the gap between the real and illusion, the grandest, highest of illusions, really, which literally eliminates illusion and transports one to a radically other (but radically same!) place and time. Here or there? Me, or someone, something, else? In the imaginary of cyberspace, it's a matter of complete indifference.

The promise of virtual reality – its imaginary – is in fact the pure surveillance machine, one where not only the surface of the world is made completely transparent (VR images as pure essences, nothing more behind them, more real than real), but the surface of the technology and indeed the situated body of the observer, who now becomes a cyborg that also, in turn, disappears – no apparent connections to the medium, *crystalline* perception, without material supports, yet with all the "feel" of a real, material world.[8] This is surveillance taken, in imagination, to its highest level, to the very point of surpassing itself. In virtual systems, we are promised essentialized views of unlimited worlds, perfect control, all contingencies, variables, and paths accounted for, a perfect, delusional control – hypercontrol – that succeeds in part because of the sheer number of contingencies that can be programmed as modulations of a single code. A self-contained, ultra-observable, and graspable world.

We feel the compelling need to sort out these fantastic relations and oppositions more exactly, yet as soon as we try, they immediately begin to reverse themselves and fall back into a kind of obscure limbo. There is an important sense in which the issue with regard to simulation is not even transparency at all, but rather a kind of hypertransparency or *obscenity*. (No matter how you characterize objects or events in simulation, you almost always wind up placing the term "hyper" or some equally innocuous equivalent in front of that characterization. "Obscenity," an alternative proposed by Baudrillard (1990b), has the advantage of overcoming this somewhat tired convention, and I shall return to this idea in the final chapter on sex in telematic societies.) The screen in a virtual reality apparatus is not "transparent," you don't see *through* it. But in another sense you do, as far as we can think of that screen as a *window* (it is telling that modern computer programs use the language of windows), that opens onto a world that is not real, but not quite appearance, either, but just (disappearing) surface, the coincidence of virtual and actual. If the image is perfect, however, there is no window, and nothing opaque – everything is "transparent" from the beginning, because everything, in total, is given in advance. Literally, there is nothing more to see – in virtual systems, over cybernetic pathways, what you see, as they say, is what you get. In the movement from surveillance to its simulation, we have moved from penetrating a surface, or seeing behind a screen, to the illusion of seeing behind, to the elaborate artifice of penetration. We shall see that what is involved in this transition is a kind of simulated passage to the Absolute, the fantastic mirage of transcending the limits of time and space and distance, of ultimate speed, of witnessing essences rise and pass away on the invisible screen of the world (this world, any world).

Sterility and the cancellation of evil

The machinery of surveillance, from our perspective, evolves from a military to a police technology, and from there to a general mechanics of control. Surveillance, as a strategy of supervision and a technology of enforcement, first in war and the control of criminality, is now used widely in schools, medical facilities, corporations, and in fact in all bureaucratic settings. Surveillance is not essentially linked to bureaucratization, however, as some authors have suggested (Dandeker 1990). This view of things at least is now too limiting, especially as universal connection to information technology and the pleasures of virtual perception threaten to redefine technical-rational knowledge and secrecy, the traditional foundations of bureaucratic power.[9] Computers have developed from the specialized tools of experts into "toys" for anyone, information networks from restricted access to access saturation (although this isn't to deny that most people on the globe have and will continue to have no access to infotech and will bear the costs of the decisions made by those having hyperaccess). Politically, the Internet is less rule-governed than anarchic, less centered than multicentered or diffused, less hierarchical than sequential and rhizomatic. Linked information systems are not bureaucratic but rather hyperbureaucratic, superadministrative, where every PC is a miniature matrix of authority, a mini-bureau with its own password and files, its own locked spaces. Secrecy likewise is decentered, second-order, and in most cases superfluous (in the glut of information in telematic societies, secrets are only unseen documents of what is already known). When expert knowledge translates into the simple ability to operate a keyboard and authority/power/secrecy into log-on codes and connectivity, bureaucracy goes into orbit – from the particularity and concreteness of a means of organization to the generality and abstraction of an *order*.[10]

Surveillance is always a dream of order, and that links it to a project of sterilization – ordered space is *clean* space. The production of sterile zones – times, places, bodies, cultures – is part of the general imaginary logic of surveillance and, like transparency, what links it to simulation generally and to *its* simulation in particular. The surveillance of the human body, and of life in general, in modern societies raises some of the most interesting questions in this context. In *The History of Sexuality, Vol. 1*, Foucault (1980: 135ff.) writes about how the sovereign's arbitrary right of death in the classical age has been displaced, in modern societies, by the formal power over life, or bio-power.[11] Bio-power has two forms: the disciplines of the body (which Foucault had analyzed in *Discipline and Punish* [1979]) and the administrative control of populations. These two forms subsume a multiplicity of practices which developed in response to problems of order generated by economic, political, and social developments in western European societies in the eighteenth and nineteenth centuries, e.g., the consolidation of industrial capital and global trade, urbanization, health and sanitation problems, militarization, and mass consumer culture. These practices centered in and around the problems of sex, sexuality, and the body. At issue was the ability to foster life in the service of modernizing societies, and sex was the hinge where power could operate both on the production of individual pleasures and the reproductive forces of populations. The analysis of bio-power, for Foucault, is part of a history of the present – we see its effects in the authority of present-day medicine, psychiatry, and the human sciences, their close relations to juridical and legal practices, pedagogy, in drug and disease testing, biogenetics, cloning, and so on. Surveillance is only one of its strategies, but certainly a key one, and one particularly organized around the function of sterilization.

Sterility, we could say, is the biological analog of transparency (Baudrillard 1993b: 61). Here, the cancellation of the surface refers to the cancellation of the body, i.e., the unclean body as a site of contamination, germs, and viruses, the slate on which are written the signs and symptoms of dying. Foucault, again, was the first to refer to the development of a medical "gaze," which included, among other things, the performance of autopsies as tools of medical classification, instruction, and diagnosis in the seventeenth century. From this point on, surveillance is inextricably linked with a technics of death, but as a means of fostering life, and the medical model of observation becomes a generalizable form of power. Open up a few corpses, so the saying went, probe beneath the surface of the flesh, make the body transparent, for a glimpse of the truth of disease and origins of illness, for the ultimate causes of death, so that life itself can be protected, enhanced, and rationally ordered.

If simulation in one sense constitutes a kind of frontier toward which the technologies of surveillance develop, then the effort to construct a genetic map of the human body marks the most recent phase of that development. The human genome project, as it is dubbed, promises, in suitably mythic form, no less than to break the code of life (Duster 1989; Nelkin and Tancredi 1989; Wingerson 1990). Knowledge of relevant sequences in the structure of the genetic code is equivalent, in this dream, to absolute foreknowledge of the course of a life from the moment of its conception (and before!). At that point, biomedical surveillance approaches its limit, and the driving value is sterility – an aseptic life, predictable, clean, medically speaking, which can be tailored, cybernetically and ergonomically "retrofitted," to appropriate kinds of work environments, targeted for preventative and therapeutic forms of intervention (screened for susceptibilities and dispositions of all sorts). Methods that bring biosurveillance tools into contact with genome research are the ultimate cyborg technologies, and their aim, their imaginary destiny, is the final resolution of the opposition between life and death (life, at last, as a pure function of its code, its fantastic hyperrealization in cloning, genetic "cleansing," total body prostheses). In the older forms of medical surveillance, and in surveillance generally, this tension is never fully resolved. Life remains the limit of death, the living subject observes the dead body, which it "survives." Control functions in one direction, from observer to observed, from the gaze to its object.[12] The new technologies, which simulate in addition to merely observing bodies, blur the boundary between organic and inorganic forms, i.e., between the living and the dead – the cyborg apparatus establishes itself at the most microscopic levels here (applications of basic biochemical and chromosomal research on the plane of cellular development).

All this has to do with sterility, because it develops against the background of the fight against disease, the battle against contamination (an imaginary battle of epic proportions from the very beginning). Not just reproduction of the real, but clean reproduction, is the first and highest goal of simulation technology. Each new development is cleaner than its previous incarnation. Consider the figure of the clone (the ultimate sci-fi development of genetic engineering) versus an existing (audio) simulation technology like compact disks (CDs). Just like CDs eliminate the "noise" of vinyl records (noise associated with recording and playback), cloning eliminates the "noise" of living, working bodies. CDs last forever (they don't wear out as easily, so we're told); they sound real, even better than real (so we're told). The clone doesn't wear out either, at least not exactly (it is replaceable with an identical copy). In that sense, it's better than the real thing (body), too. CDs are clean, clones are clean. Both are prosthetic, prophylactic technologies. The CD is (in its imaginary) not only a cleaner reproduction of sound, but how the ear "really" hears (if necessary, it will even simulate noise to reproduce that experience exactly);[13] the clone is not only a cleaner reproduction of life, but how the body "really" works (thinks, acts, remembers). And we could even imagine clones designed to reproduce accurately the diseases of the body, perhaps only better timed to be less disruptive to one's plans. For CDs and clones – and all these technologies of duplication and repetition – sterility *can* mean the simulation of decay (programmed, "clean" noise, clean levels of contamination, excess), because simulation, after all, like surveillance, aims for the real, and *that can be anything*, even what corrupts it.

If surveillance functions to produce sterile environments, its simulation is necessary to carry that function to its highest level – perfect disinfection (which of course, is impossible – perfection is not a possibility, but a delusion of these technologies). The simulation of medical and biosurveillance is a kind of last-chance, impossible solution to the inevitable decay of the flesh. The problem is to produce an absolutely sterile zone that is at the same time alive, and will support life indefinitely. It would be a zone that unites complete prosthesis with total prophylaxis. Baudrillard (1986; 1985) refers to the "bubble-boy," the famous child born without immunities who had to live out his life behind clear plastic in a filtered environment, which functioned for him as a kind of external immune system (all simulation technology erodes the line between inside and outside, here between internal body organs – lymph nodes – and external confinement areas). For Baudrillard, the bubble-boy is a metaphor for a prophylactic order, and the fundamental uncertainties which that order raises for the meaning of the distinction between life and death. The bubble-boy eventually died, but in one sense he was already too clean ever to be alive in the first place. Here, the body (child) is both observed *and* simulated – or simulated in a perfectly observed and controlled, i.e., surveilled, environment. "Human" contact can only take place across the transparent membrane (or surface) that separates the boy from the "outside" world. In the imaginary development of this technology, the membrane itself would disappear, it would "shrink-wrap" on his body and be totally transparent. The technology of protection for the boy would become so faultless that it would become unnoticeable to him (and everyone else), allow him to move around, to interact in a "normal" fashion with other "normal" people, totally uninhibited by his "prosthesis," which for him and others would be like a second skin (surface). This boy would then be perfectly cyborgian, his (invisible) apparatus protecting him *from* the world while allowing him completely unfettered contact *with/in* that world, *as if* nothing was different, *as if* nothing had changed, *as if* he were human and healthy and new, *as if everything were normal.* But what are "human" and "healthy" and "normal" to mean here? What does a "sterile" environment mean in this imaginary solution to a body that has no inherent immunities, which in fact is its own worst threat to its immunity (think only of AIDS or cancer, the body's own attack on itself).[14] At the limit of the sterile zone, supported by a system of continuous observation, of full enclosure of the space of the body, the body itself is no longer a body, no longer either dead or alive (who could seriously call the bubble-boy's existence a "life"?). Rather, it is more a death-in-life or a life-in-death. Or rather still, it is simply cyborgian, an attribute of existence at the threshold of the dissolution of the border between life and death. The surveillance of the body pushed to a limit of transmutation, fully technologized, that now miraculously again takes on the appearance of real life (the bubble-boy, just like any normal boy). And who would know the difference?

Breaks and flows

All biomachinic assemblages are series of breaks and flows (shifts in activity, motion, energy, speed), and the surveillance-simulation assemblage is no exception. The machinic language I use here (assemblages, apparatuses) doesn't, however, refer to mechanism in the classical sense of external causes and effects, but is more akin to the complex, rhizomatic linkages that Deleuze and Guattari describe in *Anti-Oedipus* as "desiring machines" (1977: 1ff.).[15] Here, object relations are viewed "machinically" as immanent, quasi-causal connections that function through the initiation of starts and stops. The eye connects to the breast that connects to a mouth that breaks its flow of milk, which in turn connects in ever widening and contracting spirals to other machines (hand, throat, anus, mommy-daddy, systems of knowledge, the psychoanalytic machine, the social machine), creating still further breaks and flows, ever branching and looping series, in the production of desire. Desiring-machines, in their conception, are not defined by the fact that they "work," but rather by the fact of their continuously breaking down, i.e., by the interruption and diversion of flows, sending them along new paths, down different channels. The hand grasps a hoe that breaks a surface, draws a furrow, channels a flow of water, cuts in again, releases itself. One conversation breaks into another, forms a new series, until it in turn is interrupted. The screen breaks the gaze and hooks up to a keyboard that connects to the fingers. The cyborg of science fiction is like these kinds of desiring-machine – a human–machine interface, a series of energy/information exchange points or switches, or more accurately, an unbounded, branching surface of relays and flow exchanges (pleasure, desire, knowledge, power) where human energies are informated and information is embodied, recoded, and sent off in other directions.

Surveillance technology, we have said, works on the time of movement; it records flows of events (motions, sounds, rhythms, performances), translates activities (of bodies, persons, groups, nations, populations, whatever) into information to more conveniently control them – to enhance them, speed them up, slow them down, repeat them, knock them off course, cancel them (like a motion sensor activates an alarm, chasing away an intruder; like a microphone records a sound to play it back later; like a computer file stores and transmits data on the progress of a disease). Induce a break in order to redirect a flow. Sometimes, the flow of activities or events changes velocity under observation (surveillance produces a reaction, a different trajectory or speed, as in our patrol car example). Here, the observer "interferes" in the observation, modifies the observed conditions, like Heisenberg's uncertainty principle. Or sometimes the flow is simply arrested or fixed, the activity comes to an end, is extinguished or absorbed, making room for other, more controlled flows. All surveillance, in any case, operates on this principle: break a flow by recording it – surveillance is, at this first level of operation, the *recording machine* (the apparatus for the production of records).[16]

Now the simulation of surveillance works on second-order flows – recording plus *reconfiguring*. It doesn't operate at the level of activities/events but already at the level of their documentation or record (of informated activity), i.e., it is an operation *on* the recording surface, on the medium of recording itself. Simulation, we have already suggested, aims to dismantle surfaces, and the surface of recording – the surveillance machinery itself – is no exception. Either the recording surface is rendered transparent, it is hidden, disguised, or otherwise made invisible. Or it is so completely reconfigured that it becomes superfluous. In the former case, simulation *supports* the surveillance function (by hiding the "flaws" of the recording surface, it generates an apparent reality – the CD, for instance, reproduces the concert hall in your living room). In the latter case, however, simulation *subverts* that function, but then immediately redoubles it at higher level. Here, the *program*, not the recording, reproduces the concert hall – computer-generated sounds, to extend the example, can eliminate the recording function altogether (what's the point, if programmed music sounds the same or even superior to "recorded" music?). What we have here is surveillance in its pure form, the desire/dream-form of perception (watching, hearing, feeling), that is, the *creation* of flows, and breaks in flows, and not merely their observation, indeed, not even their "reproduction," but the ecstasy and radically consumptive pleasure of absolutely, without remainder, absorbing the real – real becoming, real movement and change – into simulation. Full front-end flow control – no more performances to monitor, no more "surprises" in production. (What goes for the move from CDs to programmed sound goes also for medical surveillance's evolution to recombinant genetic technologies, from diagnosis and therapeutics to actuarials and cloning, the totally surprise-free body.) This, as I have begun to argue, is the utopian or imaginary function of the simulation of surveillance, to solve, in a sense, the problems associated with how to scan flows of activity (a practice that is always to an extent hit or miss, a matter of chance). Simulation instead guarantees to surveillance apparatuses certain flows in advance, and to that extent, does away with the need for more traditional, "reactive" strategies of monitoring, in favor of designing hyper-scanned envelopes that wrap around the observer and generate all possible flows.

The simulation of surveillance is the *repetition of recording* (at its limit, repetition *in advance* of recording, pure repetition). Probably the best and most common example is the xerox machine. Here the scanning device is also a mechanical copier, a duplicator. The technology is crude today, but we could imagine the perfect xerox of the future: it would eliminate the scanner altogether – or more accurately, it would disperse the scanning function to a multiplicity of centers (data sites, PCs) – and be a pure copier. We can easily imagine xeroxes wired to computers that scan files and electronically transmit them to be xeroxed, wherever and whenever. Indeed, this technology already exists (fax modems are an early development here, and it is only a matter of time before the fax assumes all the general copying functions of the old xerox technology).

If we consider it apart from simulation, surveillance is haunted by the problem of the original (or the origin), just as it was with the real and the true. The apparatus aims to uncover the source, the origin, of appearances. When surveillance connects to simulation, all this changes. The xerox, in its ideal, imaginary form, is indifferent to originals or copies, what's real and what's not – it turns everything into copies. Or better, everything, for it, is already a copy, already done with, a reproduction, *already over*. Any original only exists, for the xerox, *to* copy, and thus, for all it cares, *as* a copy. The original *will have been* its repetition (its perfect repetition, if the technology is perfect). This is also the kind of perverse thinking behind cloning, where the imaginaries of hard and wet reproductive technologies (cybernetic and genetic engineering) converge in a solution to the problems of medical surveillance (the need, for example, to scan for certain diseases, over the entire life course). Clones are *already* scanned (for disease or whatever other traits you can think of), their genes configured in advance. Surveillance identifies and tracks differences. But it makes no sense really to "track" a clone; the logic of sameness and difference, the categories of copy and original, are of no help to us; we can always number the copies to identify them, but which particular copy is one, which two, etc., is finally a matter of indifference. In the dream of recombinant genetic technology, "original" genetic material isn't altered. Instead, already altered genetic material is replicated (but in a way that also cancels the sense of "altered," because alteration is defined in terms of a norm). The clone, too, is of the paradoxical order of the will-have-been, the future past – it is the child-parent.

Flows and breaks, surveillance into its simulation: in the case of the xerox, the optical-scanning assemblage breaks the flow of passing documents to record them as discrete instances which are in turn reconverted into flows by the simulation-copying machinery, which is broken by an operator-machine, a power supply-machine, a reader-machine, a society-machine, and so on. The xerox connects scanning and copying mechanisms (and operators!) in the most intimate fashion. The image of the moving text is recorded, but here the operation of recording is in itself the first movement in the production of simulation. This is in fact true of any technology of surveillance – if it records what it observes, it also simulates. Documents, files, copies, reproductions: all simulations. The surveillance camera and microphone, we could say, in addition to being simple *monitors*, are also recorders, parts of an apparatus of the production of recording, means of capture and entrapment of images-signs, methods of doubling and redoubling their object, and in that precise sense they are also simulators. Common sense tries to tell us that this is not an accurate way of looking at things, that simulation has to do only with the projection or reproduction of images-signs, their display across a surface, not their capture. But common sense is mistaken here. The production of recording is always already a kind of simulation; it is making a copy, and making a copy is always the interruption of a flow or a movement, the creation of a new flow as reproduction. In the same way, simulations are always records (even if what they record is only another record, one that has no original). The copy is always the document of an event or object, regardless of whether that event or object is itself a copy. The two functions are so intermingled as to be virtually inseparable. They form part of a single assemblage, a single machinery of breaks and flows.

It is useless, in this sense, to try to conceive of surveillance, in any form, in isolation from simulation. One can analyze modern surveillance, as many writers have, in terms of specific technologies or practices of supervision (e.g., anything from electronic sensing to state espionage), but unless this gets connected to an analysis of how what is supervised is recorded, and how recording becomes the second-level site of repetition and reconfiguration technologies, one hasn't really grasped how the machine works, nor how social control functions in telematic societies.

The imaginary that annihilates the image

I have said that this is not just a book about the way certain technologies *are*, but about the way they *will have been*, their imaginary. In Lacan's work (1981: 227ff.), the discourse of the imaginary is organized under the figure of the mirror, whose surface reflection is the source of a fundamental misrecognition (the self as other). For us, the screen is a better figure of the imaginary in simulated systems. Here, the question is not about reflection off a surface, but about *inhabiting* the surface, not about misrecognition, but an implosion of self into other along that surface. Baudrillard (1993b: 54) writes: "We lived once in a world where the realm of the imaginary was governed by the mirror, by dividing one into two, by otherness and alienation. Today that realm is the realm of the screen, of interfaces and duplication ... All our machines are screens, and the interactivity of humans has been replaced by the interactivity of screens." For Althusser (1971: 52), who follows Lacan, the "imaginary is that image or representation of reality which masks the historical and material conditions of life."[17] Here too, however, the imaginary is the site of a fundamental division or alienation, between the real and its other, its representation or false image. But for us, the so-called false image of telematic societies simply *is* the material order, and it is not false at all, but a simulacrum, truer than true, more real than real, the hallmarks of the virtual.

The imaginary, as it's used here, is not a psychic figure or an ideology, but a temporal orientation – the future-past – a biomachinic logic, and a virtual-material regime. The imaginary is "the impossible" real, a "miraculous" event (the "miracle" of perfect virtual realities, perfect doubles, not copies, but more like immaculate conceptions!).[18] We could summarize all this in a formula with three steps. The imaginary – the impossible – of surveillance is perfect exposure. The imaginary of simulation is the perfect double. Finally, the imaginary of the simulation of surveillance is the *perfect doubling of exposure*, absolute virtual reality. (Ask yourself, who sees in virtual reality? VR, in its imaginary, miraculous form, is perfect, total vicarious experience.)

We are talking about an imaginary of pure, unlimited control, control as it approaches its highest state. That, in its simplest terms, is the *utopia* of telematic orders – the promised land of ultra-informated, ultra-capitalized, and ultra-cloned societies. Limitless surveillance, perfect simulation. It is also the *endgame* of those societies, literally, a game of ends – the end of politics, privacy, the social, power, history, war, sexuality, the end of control itself. Here, however, the ends of things are also their perverse beginnings, in the way your genetic code is a like a menu of ways to die (pick your disease); in the way virtual reality is the end of one space and the beginning of another, cyberspace; in the way everything about you can be stored on disk and projected over electronic nets, where "you" disappear, or rather implode into a second, surrogate, digital self – an end and a beginning with no end or beginning, endlessly replayable, always already played, always already *over* (and over and over again). In these worlds, we have to talk about ecstasies, not just strategies, of control, hypervision and info-power, the ether-police.[19] We have to talk about tele-spies, spaces of absolute vision and the implosion of linear time. We need, in short, a different language to describe the modern cybernetization of power and discipline. For us, the imaginary is a zone of fantastic solutions – solutions to the limits of disciplinary power in normalizing societies, to the limits of Labor and Capital in a postindustrial economy, to the degeneration and decay of the social itself at the end of the twentieth century – a zone in which societies simulate, in the most creatively alien ways, their own means of control, that launch their technologies of policing into electronic orbit and dream of discipline as a matter of genetic engineering. The simulation of surveillance is an imaginary solution to all the problems of discipline in postindustrial societies (all its imperfections, its inefficiencies, its inability to record everything, see everything, be everywhere, all the time!). From now on, the hypercontrol of virtual systems will be the order of things.

Virtual systems are our compensation for society in ruins, a return on a loss. In the United States, that means society strangling on its own excess production of waste, the industrial and cultural dead zones of twentieth-century Capital. It is an order that is no longer precisely social at all, since its very operation subverts the experiential, communicative, and cognitive horizons of the social, and erodes the gaps in time and space, the radical otherness, that were always the conditions of sociality. (When communication times are reduced to zero, what happens to communication? When the "other" is always onscreen, what happens to socialization and the social relation?) Today, a new wasteland is being forged for us, a new "social," where all experience is instantaneous, simultaneous, vicarious, and priced to sell. For all that, telematic societies are not societies of the present, of "today." Nor are they exactly societies of some imminent future, just around the corner (I make no predictions in this book). They are, rather, societies of the "future-past," of the "soon-to-be-but-already-over-present," whose code antedates and is superior to them in every way. The telematic imaginary is about society *after* society, but where after also means *before*, about the criss-crossed, inverted hypertemporality of informated societies and their methods of supervision – the fantasy of cybernetic rule, the regime of the code. It is about an imaginary of power – of perfectly disciplined societies – and also the end of that imaginary, or rather, its infinite reproduction in simulation (the virtual reality experience does not require an imagination – it is a surrogate imagination).[20]

In one sense, the endgame of telematic societies has nothing to do with ends at all because the game always already is over; like a hologram, each move contains the entire game; all variations are accounted for in advance at each step. At the same time there are an infinity of ends, since these societies can simulate any end (even the end of the world, a favorite computer scenario of military strategists preparing for World War III). They are black holes, which can absorb any meaning, any image or sign, where everything about the game is radically uncertain, not least of all *who the players really are and what they really do.* In telematic societies, the players are cyborgs, wired flesh, the observers are all observed, the controllers all controlled. In this zone, who watches, who supervises, who polices, who disciplines, all these activities and the persons who perform them are strictly open questions, as everyone gets caught up indifferently and equivalently in the simulation-surveillance assemblage.

An endgame can be the most ecstatic, most dangerous time of the game, a time of great sacrifices, perverse strategies, and sudden reversals of fortune. At the same time, the life-and-death stakes offered up everyday in telematic societies – over the mass media, in the bio-wars against viral infections and genetic "mistakes," in the electromagnetic wars of the global military machine – these stakes are entirely banal, and precisely to the extent they are mass mediated. Death has no meaning in them, which is not to say that it doesn't happen or that they don't produce it, and on a mass scale. (The Gulf War, a virtual, computerized, "televisual" war if there ever was one, produced incredible numbers of casualties on the Iraqi side.) Telematic societies belong to the order of *deadly fictions,* fantastic but lethal worlds; in their most extreme form (from which all others derive), they trade mass, meaningless death for the *imagination,* the ultra-inflated desire, of pure control and unlimited surveillance.[21]

This is an ironic utopia, and not simply because unlimited surveillance is impossible, *but because it is actual only in simulation.* Today that means that it is actual only in systems of instantaneous digital communication – not communication as a means of producing understanding, but in the sense of the *unmediated immediacy* of remote places and times, of absolute command over speed and distance, of instant access to other, once invisible, inaudible, untouchable, and *unreal* worlds. Virtual reality, again, is the new paradigm here; at the same time, it is no more than one way of materializing dreams of instantaneous time- and space-travel among many, some of which have been around a long time (a digital form of mysticism, of self-, body-, or spirit-projection). Virtual reality, again, is an imaginary solution to the *limits of perceptual control.* Here, by definition, one sees/feels (or will see/feel, given enough repetitions) all there is to see and feel. But this also signals the end of both imagination and the power of perception, which in the last instance are given over entirely to the operations of simulation. With simulation, one needs neither power nor imagination (all that's already taken care of! – the couch potato syndrome). In virtual systems, you can be there yesterday, log on, and touch someone (anyone, everyone); your origin equals your destination. No imagination necessary, at least that is the ideal, that everything is fully explicit, "obscene," in the literal, not the moral, sense of that term. These, in essence, are the "solutions" simulation throws up to our own finitude, the imagination of harnessing forces beyond our control. As solutions, they are certainly never perfect. In one sense, they do not even "aim" for perfection, but instead already embody it. Virtual reality machines are, in their imaginary development, supposed to give you the perfect illusion of going wherever you want to go on time (or anytime). But perfection is only relative to the specificity of instructions and the sophistication of hardware – or soon, to the "wetware," the coded surface of contact between organs (fingers, eyes, brains) and machines (keyboards, screens, processing units, electronic files). The paradox of this utopia is that it is both fully realized and completely artificial at the same time.

Simulated surveillance is the mundane form of control one exerts, for instance, channel cruising the television on the remote, playing a video game, or working on a computer. Or rehearsing a battlefield operation onscreen, or recombining DNA, or splicing a gene – all imaginary solutions to the limits of vision, to our capacity to expose objects to vision, to experience and manipulate them and touch them and set them in some kind of order with some kind of meaning. This is not, I have suggested, "really" control at all, or rather, it is something more than control, control pushed to a threshold where it reverses itself. Who or what controls the video machine, one can ask. The programmer? The player? The machine? The electric company? All of these? Certainly, you want to say, the machine has to be plugged in, one can still walk away when the game has run its course. But a break in one connection means little in a vast and growing network of connections. One only walks away to take up another game later, plug in somewhere else. In the imaginary, the "machine" is always on even if you disconnect, there are layers upon layers of games, nested infinitely into one another, so that the isolated game is only a passing zone of intensity in a more generally simulated field into which we are all gradually being absorbed (the biotelematic field – TVs–telephones–fax–computers–CDs–microwaves–sensors–ergonomics–cliometrics–genetic probes–hardware–software–wetware). To resist absorption here would mean resisting not only the entire network of connections, but overcoming their imaginary, and that means subverting somehow the very dream-desire of absolute control that governs these technologies.

To simulate surveillance is to break down and reconfigure the latter's conditions of possibility. Surveillance, we now know, has limits: time and distance, speed, each of these constrains perception (vision, hearing, touch) and communication. We shall look further into how the development of surveillance technologies is in the first instance about seeing faster and farther, more closely, more distinctly, from all perspectives, with greater contrast and clarity; and about seeing now, immediately (if not sooner!), simultaneously with the event or object seen (if not before!). Simulation is the next step in the logic of this development. Where surveillance is impossible, simulation steps in (virtual systems often compensate for an inability to exercise control through observation – this is only our patrol car example again). This solution does not make the problem of spatial and temporal limits go away, but at least it offers the temporary ecstasy of their transcendence (virtual reality is a form of escape).[22]

Of course, simulation considered on its own is a technology for exceeding limits of all sorts. Anything, we have said, can be simulated (not only surveillance) – this is really what virtual systems are all about in their imaginary, the capacity to simulate anything (space, time, events, objects, experiences, whatever). By definition, the imaginary that fuels contemporary simulation technology is about the end of limits, about the end of the imaginary itself. Just jack into the system and you are there, really, instantly, everywhere you want to be (as the logo for Visa goes) – "you're" not imagining this, it's being imagined for you. By whom ... ? That, we know by now, is not the right question.

Instant information on anything in all places at all times. Instant "projection," or rather "introjection" of any space and any time. To this we could add the imaginary of modern genetics and the technologies of the (disappearing) body – life and death translated by a common code, the life course known (i.e., simulated) in advance, everything secure, safe, sterile, no risks, no hazards, the life that precedes life. Even life and death are no longer limits to each other in this brave new world; the boundary that separates one from the other is permeable, or no longer exists at all. There's no "who" in this order, either. This is the view from everywhere, and from nowhere, too.

All this is, in a special sense, quite Hegelian, and thus a very "modern" kind of imaginary – the transcendence of limits of time, space, life and death, and the body. There is really nothing "postmodern" about it. The simulation of surveillance, in its late twentieth-century guise, in many ways is still all about the Absolute Subject at the end of history. Plug in and you are there, or *there is here* (tele-presence technologies, telecommunications connections that bring libraries, markets, entertainment, *whatever*, into your home and make your home a potential *anywhere and nowhere, anytime and no time*); press a button and time can reverse itself (playback technologies playing havoc with linear, forward

time); hit a key and create your own world, in which you are fully interactive, a simulated time and space, the Absolute Subject as the Absolute
Object, consciousness as information saturation, retinal imaging, dream
projection (like in Wim Wenders's film, *Until the End of the World*, in
which a technology for translating one's dreams onto video acts like a
kind of addictive drug, an image-capture device for the protagonists'
brains that brings them hypnotic pleasures, a pleasurable, and deadly,
stupor). What drives these sci-fi techno-images is the breathless sense of
calling up new worlds, inhabiting them, destroying them, traveling anywhere, immediately, in absolute control of one's destination and destiny.
That's the delusion, anyway, and the idea is to make it perfect. In the
future, so the theory goes, when you travel somewhere in virtual reality,
you *might as well* be there, because there is the same in simulation as it
is in "reality."

Simulation, when it is applied to the technologies of perceptual control (surveillance), produces some of the most sublime paradoxes of time.
Perception *has no time* in simulation (at least that is what the technology aims for); it can be any time, past, present, or future. Relive the event,
or see it (again) for the first time. The controls on your videocassette
player are really time-travel controls (fast forward, reverse, slow
advance). Simulated time is a time all its own. (What is the time of a
video game, of a flight simulator? What is the time of the genetic code?)
Simulated control aims for a transcendence of time, in the same sense as
the Hegelian Subject stands, literally, at the end of time. There is nothing at all mysterious in this development. Even the older surveillance
technologies were about overcoming time – to see faster, to interpret
instantaneously, to react immediately, to throw light on the dark zones
of temporality, where information lags behind the event, where space is
an obstacle to supervision and mastery – these are the elements of a control based on surveillance, and they are nothing new. In simulation, by
contrast, one merely manufactures the spaces and time over which one
exerts control. The result is a perfectly controlled environment, or better,
an environment that has no need for control, that is just control, pure
and simple.

In another sense, all this is strictly un-Hegelian (see Bogard 1994:
328ff.). In the most obvious sense, transcendence, the Absolute Subject,
the end of time, all these things for Hegel were still a human, and not a
telematic, affair. Hegel's absolute is still a matter of finitude, human
being. Now, however, it's about the cyborg, the clone, the jacked-in
informated data cowboy, an engineered mutant at the amorphous border between life and death. The marriage of bodies to coded information

systems may be Hegelian-inspired but is not really part of the Hegelian imaginary, where Hegel could still set *himself* up as the culmination of history. No longer: Hegel today would have to wear his virtual gear and have his own personal genetic identification chip hot-wired to his frontal lobes – a sim-cyborg Hegel, absolute, but only within the strictly defined and programmed sphere of his technical apparatus.

Hegel would have critiqued simulation as a "bad infinity," endless rep-etition – in our terms, repetition in advance. A simulation is just a scene duplicated from a model. The sequence of images in a video game may vary from game to game, depending on the skill and reactions of the player, but all the elements are programmed. A simulation does not "transcend" what it simulates; if it replicates "real" scenes, it doesn't, for all that, transcend the real; the same is true for time and space. Hyperspace/hypertime may be "superior" to real space and time (higher definition, greater plasticity, infinite repeatability), but only in the imag-inary. Modulations of virtual spacetime happen according to instructions that are formulated to account for the potentially random actions of an operator (in a video game, if the interaction is too random, the game ends quickly). Each game played, however different in content – sequences of images, times of play, etc. – is formally an exact replica of any other game. And this is true across games. One video game, in a formal sense, does not really differ from another – they are all just variations on basic computer code. The imaginary of virtual technology may be Hegelian, viz., that of transcendence, but its mundane reality is a field of often crude technical approximations of space and time (monitors, screens, plastic, prosthetics). The system is only Hegelian if it can surpass itself, in the sense that it can reproduce an object, event, or image perfectly. Can we imagine such a technology? The short answer is that at least we have to try, if we are to understand anything about the forces that orga-nize telematic societies today. We have to imagine that technology in the most paradoxical way, both as not existing (never existing, something improbable or impossible) and as having always existed deep within our technological past. The only ground for that kind of reflection is the imaginary of the technology itself, as it drives its own development and operation. Anything, I have said, can be simulated. That is the bizarre utopia of a fully realized technology of repetition.

3

Social control for the 1990s

The forces of surveillance which once served the integration and reproduction of Capital in the industrial period are everywhere today in the
process of disappearing. As I've argued, they are being absorbed into the
forces of simulation, which do not so much follow as precede them in
time, like a program precedes its "run," or provides the formal instructions for its operation. That has two implications for how we examine
the simulation of surveillance. First, we focus on the technical processes
that anticipate surveillance, specifically those that *prepare* the observer,
not just the process of observation itself. Computer profiles, to return to
a previous example, generate objects *for* surveillance – they instruct or
train the observer in what to watch and how to watch for it. Police, psy-
chiatrists, educators, physicians, to name just a few groups, increasingly
use profile technology for early or pre-identification of various traits
within preselected populations – if you match enough elements of the
profile, you could become a target, even before any trait has manifested
itself. Second, we examine those processes which *double* surveillance, that
"stand in" for it, and at the same time, reduce its risks and inefficiencies.
Profiling, to stay with this example, has become a popular technology
with police because it frees them from the time-consuming and sometimes
hazardous duties of surveillance, in effect downloading this function onto
a computer. The computer scans information on the network for profile
anomalies and selects targets, and the police can focus their energies on
apprehension. In the imaginary of this strategy, you go directly from profile to arrest. Direct, "hands-on" surveillance, if you will, is bypassed or
short-circuited; it's already done, or at least on automatic. Having to
watch or wait for an infraction is a thing of the past, if you're a police
officer. Or for the onset of a disease, if you're a physician; a learning dis-
order, if you're an educator; the movement of an enemy, if you're a sol-

dier. Genetic profiles, intelligence profiles, psychiatric profiles, military force profiles. These are the new "eyes" of the authorities at the end of the twentieth century. And profiling is only small corner of a picture that includes modeling, matching, scenario construction, artificial intelligence, cloning and other forms of genetic engineering, virtual reality, counter-espionage, electronic work, sex, privacy, war. In all, the formal operations are similar. To prepare the observer, to train the observer to see, and in the last instance, *to be* the observer's eyes, this is the imaginary of the simulation of surveillance.

What appears to us first as a historical evolution of surveillance technology – ever more sophisticated means of watching, recording, etc. – from our point of view is just the progressive realization of this imaginary. There, the whole development of the apparatus is laid out in advance, and it is nothing less than perfect surveillance, surveillance raised to the highest power, where nothing escapes the gaze. Everything already observed, absolute foreknowledge of events grounded in the possession of the codes which generate them. Historically, the discovery of basic codes is the final step in the process of surveillance. Code-breaking always involves the most concentrated forms of observation and recording, analysis and trial combinations, finding the key for controlling complex flows and breaks of information and activity. The code is always the last thing to be recorded. Or better, it is now the *first* thing to produce records, a hyperrecord, a formalization of records, a kind of distillation of future events, events that now (will) have (had) a meaning, an intelligibility and calculability (that in effect they will have had all along). Once the code is broken, time passes from the order of history to the order of precession, from recording to prerecording, recording in advance. Once the code is broken – genetic, linguistic, economic, social, whatever – the order it henceforth establishes becomes intelligible and programmable.

Control, then, is passing from a logistics of inspection or perception (to use Virilio's concept [1989]), to a logistics of *pro*spection, from watching to anticipation, from surveillance to its simulation. From computers to cloning to war games, control no longer means discipline as an effect of observation, but observation as an effect of virtualization. What you get (design, engineer, program, model) is what you see (hear, touch). Prescanning, fore-sight, assessment against and precession from codes. All this has been termed, somewhat misleadingly, the "new surveillance" (G. Marx 1986; G. Marx 1988; Giddens 1990: 59; Giddens 1987: 154ff., 174ff.; Dandeker 1990).[1] In fact, as I've said, there is nothing really "new" about contemporary surveillance methods – surveillance has been and always will be about discovering the reality and truth behind appearances (surfaces). To this end, it is always willing to place itself in the service of appearances (disguise, ruse, deception). The sense that surveillance is entering a new phase arises in part from all the possibilities that modern info- and biotechnologies create for instantaneous, automatic control. But all these technologies really do is allow the surveillance apparatus to function efficiently at its limit, more quietly, more invisibly, more quickly. They do that by simulating (appearing as) the observer (codes are just tools for sorting out appearances, they are "informated eyes"). From the standpoint of their imaginary, there is no difference between a surveillance camera, a computer profile, and a military decoy. They all double an observer or mode of observation. The problem with most current accounts of surveillance is that they ignore how it is linked from the very beginning with strategies of doubling and repetition, anticipating and training, of simulating perception. Today it is not about the "new surveillance" at all, an idea too much inspired by Orwellian nightmares of the future. It's about simulated surveillance, the disappearance of the observer into the screen, and that's an old idea indeed.

It does seem, however, that the electronic revolution has given events a different twist. Sol Yurick (1985: 1) writes that, in the information age, "perceptions of reality are once again being *distorted* by the insertion of a vast new mediational system into an already multiplexed, historically accreted maze of mediations." Forced to live in and through information-processing technology, people and social relations are converted into electronic impulses, their actions and transactions ceaselessly filtered, screened, and modulated by a vast network of monitoring and projection apparatuses whose linkages are still poorly understood. Mainframes and PCs, automated tellers, barcodes, vision systems, faxes, xeroxes, telephones, microwave relays, electromagnetic sensors, video games, expert systems. Processing information at the speed of light, transcending the constraints of time and distance, these devices increasingly supplement and substitute for the slow, localized process-control technologies of the industrial period (Hagedoorn et al. 1988).

But the new mediational system Yurick refers to is not precisely a "distortion" of perception. Here we are no longer talking simply about seeing better, but seeing *before* seeing, seeing as a kind of absolute "knowledge," for lack of a better term.[2] In an age of information, "whole nations, their economies, their peoples, their resources, their land, can be simulated and displayed on some electronic input/output device" (Yurick 1985: 3). We are not dealing here with a distortion – an idea still laboring under the sign of ideology and false representation – but an *apotheosis* of perception, a transfiguration, moreover, of mythic proportions.

Instantaneous, universal information, interlinked databases storing everything on every conceivable subject (Godfrey and Parkhill 1979: 1). Codes of life and death, communication, sublime power and knowledge. This is the (ancient) dream and the epistemological utopia of surveillance, its incarnation as hypersurveillance: total control in the form of ultra-smooth access to information (images, meanings, persons, bodies, truth). For this dream – and that is all it is – surveillance is willing to sever all of its ties to "reality" in favor of the "inflated reality" of simulation. *Realize* the image. In the sci-fi landscape of an electronic civilization, sim-ulations transfix the gaze of the observer, an observer who no longer, properly speaking, *has* a gaze. The code, the screen, the surface of appearance, these are now the "gaze," a bio-electronic sensorium. In this utopia, the observer *sacrifices* his own gaze to the gods of simulation – gods ruling over *the perfect appearances of another world (the virtual world), another time (the future past).*

First the organic, then the machine scale of control in this process is lost. On the terrain of simulation, the order of perception – the gaze – is no longer human or machine-like, but cyborgian, the hypercontrol of the human machine (Haraway 1985). That at any rate would be the uncon-scious wish of today's cybernetic, visionic engineers: the apotheosis of the power of perception. The god of surveillance is a virtual reality techni-cian's cyborg dream.

Visionics

Take, for instance, what the military – usually ahead of everyone else in these matters – refers to as the low/fast problem (Edwards and Mayer 1990). Today, successful penetration of an enemy's airspace depends on the ability of pilots to fly high-performance aircraft of numbing techni-cal complexity at extremely low altitudes and very high speed. Navigating as low as fifty feet off the ground to avoid detection, these pilots have to rely heavily on visual cues from the stream of scenery that passes by their canopies at 500 knots. The smallest distraction or miscalculation at such speeds can be fatal, a problem compounded by the pilot's confinement to a highly artificial environment where the erosion of his direct percep-tual control is already at a very advanced stage. As Paul Virilio (1989: 84) describes a pilot of one of these aircraft: "Looking up, he sees the digital display (opto-electric or holographic) of the windscreen collima-tor; looking down, the radar screen, the onboard computer, the radio and the video screen, which enables him to follow the terrain with its four or five simultaneous targets, and to monitor his self-navigating missiles fitted with a camera or infra-red guidance system." Add to this the constant chatter over the radio, everyone, including the enemy, talking at once, shouting directions and commands as targets draw closer and the dangerous confusion of battle sets in. To prepare pilots for these oversaturated conditions where precise scanning of terrain features is so important, the military has typically relied on extensive – and expensive – outdoor training exercises under conditions designed to approximate actual combat.

Recently in Germany, environmental and public safety concerns, combined with significant cuts in military budgets, have placed pressure on the military to reduce the number of operational low/fast training flights. The air force has responded to this pressure with increased funding for research on sophisticated visionic systems – polygon-image generators – that would faithfully simulate the visual conditions of low/fast flight. Using these simulators, pilots can be trained to scan and react to important visual cues under a variety of different flying conditions without ever having to leave the security of their bases. If these systems can be perfected, i.e., eventually substitute for actual training missions with only minimal distortions of "real" conditions of flight and combat, they will garner their corporate developers huge profits and reward the military machine by pacifying public concerns and smoothing out public relations: environmental and safety concerns would be defused (deflected away from the low/fast issue at least), and pilots would, arguably, be equally or even better prepared for actual combat situations at less cost. We know that current propaganda from the state–military–industrial complex is about the "leaner, cleaner, meaner military machine" in an age of "reduced tensions" (viz., the so-called end of the Cold War). In part, the new generation of visionic simulators is designed to make this possible.

Of course, cockpit simulators have been in use for many years, although not for low/fast training, where a number of technical imaging problems still remain to be overcome. The military has always been interested in the technologies of simulation and perception which, as much if not more than missiles, guns, and soldiers, are weapons of war. The next chapter will take up this topic in more depth. Visionic systems are only one of numerous examples that could be drawn from both inside and outside the military to illustrate a general point about the contemporary relation of surveillance and simulation. If the aviator's perceptual control – his ability to react to visual cues at very fast speeds – was already disintegrating in the already highly artificial, instrument-intensive conditions of actual flight, the virtual landscape of the new visionic simulators at first appears only to complete this movement of de-realization. But in fact, simulation *reconfigures* perceptual control at a higher level, in the synthesis of pilot and screen. Visionic systems aim for completely integrated, risk-free control environments, which substitute for control based on the pilot's conditioned – and increasingly limited – ability to scan a real, but information-saturated, scene. The gaze of the aviator, his last source of control over the machine, now connects to devices that produce only simulated effects (like the joystick of any video game). In simulation, the pilot no longer "flies" the aircraft, nor does the aircraft "fly him." Instead, there is an "ecstasy of control," a delusional effect of complete, perfect, and absolute control, whose basis is that control no longer arises from external relations (pilot to plane to landscape), but instead is fully integrated in the closed circuit of aviator, inputs, and screens. All that is required to achieve perfect control is practice, i.e., *submission to training* (or rather, "sim-training," to note that the type of discipline or exercise involved is the same as that required to achieve a perfect score on an electronic game).

Submission to simulated training is a concession surveillant power makes to realize its imaginary of absolute control – if not mastery of "real" situations, then at least mastery of the game, of the real in replication. Of course, military flight simulators are still used to condition pilots to perform more efficiently in "real" situations. But the utopian trend is unmistakable. Power functions more smoothly, it encounters less resistance and is less prone to miscalculation and error in completely informated, "disembodied" environments. The current phase of visionic systems is only another, and relatively small, step in the eventual elimination not only of the pilot from the aircraft but of the warrior from the theater of battle – his replacement with completely automated weapons controlled remotely from C3I (command, control, communication, and intelligence) centers where combat decisions are referred to the scenarios of expert systems (computer war models, artificial intelligence) (see Lehner 1989). The gaze of the warrior increasingly falls on the simulated battlefield, the wall of video screens that instantly informs him of the combat situation and forewarns him of all the possible consequences of a particular strategy or course of action.

TV and the Holodeck

Visionic systems – vision simulators, virtual reality devices, etc. – represent an evolution of televisual technology, one paradoxically directed toward its eventual disappearance. What guides the technical development of TV is the progressive erasure of the *distance* between viewer and screen, image and event. This, as I've suggested, is not done in order to *create an illusion* for the viewer of being discreetly present – unobtrusively on the scene – at an event (the experience of being a covert witness to the events on the screen), but, on the contrary, to eliminate that illusion by rendering the artifice – the *technical support and staging* – of the image invisible, undetectable. To eliminate, that is, through technical means, the distorting, disconcerting effects of the technology itself (here, the screen and the camera), which signal that what is being watched is "only" a reproduction, a "mere appearance." (This project, of course, is not unique to television, but informs the history of all recording and reproduction technologies). To make the image indistinguishable from – no, even better than – the scene. Perfect TV would be like the Holodeck on *Star Trek: The Next Generation* – a surrounding, "noiseless" projection that is fully interactive and produces images indistinguishable from the "real" thing. In the twenty-fourth century world of the Holodeck, one "enters" the televisual apparatus, and the room is transformed by voice command into a perfect simulation of space and time which transcends the material limits of projection. The "TV" (i.e., the *room*) disappears and is replaced by a new sim-territory, bounded now from the *inside*. No more screen, no more camera, no more TV or room, no more projection surface, a new geography spreads out before the gaze. The Holodeck eliminates the "illusion of being there" by not only making the technology "appear to disappear," but in some sense "really" disappear. You gaze directly onto the (interactively programmed) scene. No technical mediation (camera, screen) that is detectable (since everything here is *perfectly, universally* mediated – unmediated immediacy, technology approaches its limit). Instead, a hyperlogistics of perceptual control (the perfectly prepared environment for testing, training, instructing, drilling). Perception and simulation here are fully interactive, "in sync" (the active/passive polarity of conventional TV implodes in an ecstasy of hypercontrol). The gaze, the observing subject, disappears – together with its "object" and its raison d'etre – in being elevated to a higher form. *You are there, you are the TV*, as Baudrillard says (1983b: 53). No longer the illusion of being on the scene, but a perfect transparency of the screen, a perfect dissolution of the body. You *are* the scene. Regardless of whether or when such systems will ever come about – they are, in fact, impossible – this is the project of TV and informs the technical development of the new visionic systems. To eliminate the distraction of the technology itself by making its images more and more real, more real than real. No more of television's falsification of the real, its staging of illusions, but a higher form of falsification, the perfect, instantaneous implosion of distance and time, of the difference between being here and being there, being now and being anytime. A mere fiction? Or a real project into which enormous material resources are today thrown (high-definition television, virtual reality, tele-presencing, neural imaging research, integrated visionic systems, war replicators)?

The gaze

I want to argue, perhaps somewhat controversially, that a concept of simulated surveillance is already implicit, though undeveloped, in the work of Foucault, whose critiques of the medical "gaze" in *Birth of the Clinic* (1975) and of panopticism in *Discipline and Punish* (1979) evoke images of surface transparencies and dissolving, disappearing bodies. Foucault, it is true, hardly mentions simulation in these books, but the idea is there, nonetheless, just below the surface of the text, complicit in the work of "normalizing observation," but also silently subverting that work, so to speak, from the inside. In *Birth of the Clinic*, Foucault describes a logistics of the gaze in terms remarkably similar to how I have characterized simulation, as "preparing" environments for training or organizing perception. Around the middle of the eighteenth century, medical clinics begin to use dissection as a technique of instructing students in anatomical knowledge and diagnostic skills – an entire science of pathological anatomy was built up around procuring corpses to cut open and display to medical observation. The corpse is not just a dead body, but an object of pedagogical interest, an instrument for teaching others how to decipher the operations of the living body in its depth. From this time forward, the living body will owe its life to a knowledge and a practice of death. Foucault's work certainly isn't the first to evoke the morbid, nightmarish qualities of this vision. "To examine the causes of life, we must first have recourse to death," confesses Victor in Mary Shelley's *Frankenstein* ([1818] 1992: 53). "To this end I devoted myself wholeheartedly to the study of anatomy." Already in 1818, when *Frankenstein* was published, Victor's "workshop of filthy creation" shares a certain imaginary with the clinic, one that has to do with surveiling the body, certainly, but also one that ultimately dreams of replacing it with a superior product, a "double" that would eliminate, once and for all, all its troubling and worrisome "defects." Anatomy, that imaginary says, is not just about observing dead bodies (or body parts), but about creating new, better forms of life from them. And anatomical knowledge, the goal of clinical experience itself, will become superfluous after it becomes possible to construct the perfect body – i.e., the immortal, beautiful, technically flawless body. The myth of the clinic, then, is nothing less than the end of the real body – i.e., the body that gets sick and dies, the body that decays – and thus the end of its "truth," too. Foucault writes how, in the eighteenth century, this myth was born contemporaneously with the clinics, nourished by Enlightenment ideals and the imaginary of medical power. Contemporary society still labors under the myth of a free, detached, and purifying gaze which, by virtue of its capacity to probe beneath the surface of the flesh and read the signs of disease, will someday finally eradicate human suffering, foretelling a time when medicine disappears along with its object. This myth, Foucault writes, is rooted in a deep "convergence between the requirements of liberal political ideology and those of medical technology" that occurs in the years prior to the French Revolution. At that time,

liberty [becomes] the vital unfettered force of the truth. It must, therefore, have a world in which the gaze, free of all obstacle, is no longer subject to the immediate law of truth: the gaze is not faithful to truth, nor subject to it, without asserting, at the same time, a supreme mastery: the gaze is a gaze that dominates; and although it also knows how to subject itself, it dominates its masters

(Foucault 1975: 39)

The truth of the body, the whole aim of clinical surveillance, is already subverted at the beginning by a higher aim, one in which the body disappears (see Ostrander 1987). In its place, a simulated body, a simulated gaze – clinical perception is absorbed into its hideous creation (in *Frankenstein*, it is the inhuman gaze of the monster – Victor's own gaze reflected back at him – that causes Victor to flee and marks the end of his "medical" power).

For Foucault (1975: 115, 120), the clinical gaze is not passive but violent. "To look in order to know, to show in order to teach, is not this a tacit form of violence, all the more abusive for its silence, upon a sick body that demands to be comforted, not displayed. Can pain be a spectacle? Not only can it be, it must be ..." (Foucault 1975: 84). And this spectacle would be justified in the name not only of scientific progress, but of compassion for the poor who made up the majority of the medical clinic's non-paying clients, people who nonetheless would pay "interest" for their hospitalization – an objective interest for the science that uses them as a means of instruction, a vital interest for the upper classes who relied for their own well-being on the enumeration, docility, and minimal health of the masses.

From the beginning, modern medical perception is an individualizing as well as totalizing violence; the dead body is dissected, its parts examined, the smallest details are recorded. And in turn, each living body is a unique set of coordinates, scanned, marked, documented, verified, and identified. But the body is also located in a population, a grid of other bodies and diseases, where it becomes a "case" or an instance of movements that cross the surface of the *social* body. The clinic, Foucault writes, was probably the first attempt to order a science on the exercise and decisions of organized perception (Foucault 1975: 89). It was the site of an *expressible* as well as visible body, around which an increasingly professionalized biomedical discourse could be mobilized in the nineteenth century. Its tools were not just body probes, but emerging instruments of statistical analyses, the aggregation and manipulation of information. Early on, the State took an active interest in the kinds of information the clinics generated, to monitor and project trends in the population, births and deaths, public health and sanitation, their relation to productivity at work, in school – a whole info-bio-politics of the masses with an eye for maintaining social control. Already here, at the start of the modern age, we begin to sense in Foucault how the "real" body as a focus of the normalizing gaze is surreptitiously doubled by the body as information, codes, probabilities – alongside the surveilled body, beside the corpse as a means of training students in diagnostic and surgical skills, yet another figure of the body double emerges and grows in the technological assemblages that develop down to the present day, a clean, sterilized body, a shadow figure inhabiting files and data dumps, a statistico-actuarial artifact that in the twentieth century becomes the means for linking political, scientific, and corporate-insurial discourses into a web of total domination.

Bodies that can be surveilled can be informated, and bodies that can be informated can be reduced to codes – in medicine, we have noted, this is the ongoing work of what has been imperiously dubbed the human genome project. But this is only the visible edge of an imaginary that runs deep in telematic societies. Today, medical informating is only one aspect of a general overcoding of the body that occurs on all levels of the culture, a perversely excessive concern with body function and image that marks *panic* over the body's growing obsolescence (Kroker and Kroker 1987: 20ff.). Rather than the rough violence of the clinical gaze, which displayed without shame the disintegration of the natural body, we are presented with the smooth violence of reconstructed, renovated bodies, brought back from the dead – designer bodies, cyborg bodies, sim-bodies. Health screens, computer-enhanced diagnostic equipment, cryogenics, DNA research, artificial organs and transplants, sex without secretions (condoms), plastic surgery, and cosmetics, even the craze for aerobic conditioning and body "sculpting," all reflect the current hysteria which surrounds the body today, experienced as a horrific site of disease and toxicity and death. We could say that the imaginary of the flawless body has escaped the clinic and become a cultural obsession. Why? Because today, the natural body appears increasingly threatened with extinction. At the limit of medical power, the dead body returns – only this time it returns perversely as a phantom body, a body of codes, screens, information, signs. The pace of the body's disappearance is only matched by the pace of its hyperrealization. Is this the new surveillance? Rather, it is surveillance in its highest, most intense form: not a passive and detached gaze (as Foucault already knew), but an active, violent project to produce a prosthetic body that stands in for the natural body, which everywhere today lies in ruins.

In *Discipline and Punish* (1979), Foucault would extend his concern with the violence of the gaze to a genuine logistics of the physical environment – to the "architecture" – of surveillance: walls, spaces, openings and closures, breaks and flows of light and darkness. Although Foucault used the term *surveiller* in the French title of this book, he made it clear that its sense was not always equivalent to the English infinitive, but closer to the meaning of *to discipline*. Much of the contemporary debate with Foucault, we have said, has revolved around his thesis in this work that western societies can be characterized as "disciplinarian," and that discipline, as a strategy for normalizing individual conduct or administering the affairs of social collectivities, has now become the general formula for domination in these societies.

Rather than start from a universal formula for discipline, Foucault describes a profusion of minor techniques, of the most diverse origin and application, and asks how, over a period extending from the seventeenth century to the early nineteenth century, they come to produce something like such a formula, a "blueprint of a general method" of domination. In *Discipline and Punish*, Foucault traces three converging historical developments that look both backward to and forward from *The Birth of the Clinic*: the birth of a detailed "political anatomy" of the body, the diffusion of a mechanics of normalization and individualization, and panoptic surveillance. Beginning in the seventeenth century and continuing throughout the eighteenth century, a number of forces coalesce around the body to increase its power and capacity for work. A whole microphysics of distributing spaces, serializing movements, combining and ranking behaviors is organized on an unprecedented scale to transform bodies and their relations into a generalized productive machinery – obedient, economical, and efficient. Supplementing these is a whole set of techniques for training the individual to conform to a norm, utilizing "corrective mechanisms" that coerce by means of continuous examination and hierarchical observation. Behind everything, we've already seen, looms the figure of the Panopticon, Bentham's ideal prison or "inspection house," whose concrete operation depends on an art and mechanics of discreet surveillance, but whose formal principle – and perhaps here it comes closest to an abstract formula for discipline – *is to impose a particular form of conduct on a human multiplicity* (Foucault 1979: 205; also Deleuze 1988: 34).

Foucault says that the Panopticon is a schema or "diagram" of the forces that individualize persons, differentiating and separating them from a confused mass of bodies, composing and realigning their relations, and turning them into a productive order. It is a

pure architectural and optical system: ... a figure of political technology that may and must be detached from any specific use.

It is polyvalent in its applications; it serves to reform prisoners, but also to treat patients, to instruct schoolchildren, to confine the insane, to supervise workers, to put beggars and idlers to work. It is a type of location of bodies in space, a distribution of individuals in relation to one another, of hierarchical organization, of disposition of centres and channels of power, of definition of the instruments and modes of intervention of power, which can be implemented in hospitals, workshops, schools, prisons.   (Foucault 1979: 205)

The panoptic diagram thus becomes something like a general "model" of the disciplines, the "map" of what Foucault will come to call a disciplinary society (terms, I think, already suggestive of the forces of simulation that inhabit the margins of his text).

Panopticism emerges in the late eighteenth century and early nineteenth century as a generalizable response to the problems of control posed by deviance, crime, insanity, ignorance, and disease in modern urbanizing societies. For Foucault, Panopticism is both a mechanism of supervision and a strategy of truth. As a mechanism of supervision, it operates by means of discreet surveillance within a fixed place, recording the slightest movements and changes in attitude. As a strategy of truth, it probes below the surface of the body and "brands" it, knows it by marking it off from other bodies according to a binary logic (separating healthy from diseased, sane from insane, delinquent from normal, young from old, etc.) (Foucault 1979: 199).

As a disciplinary apparatus, Foucault writes, the Panopticon reverses all the principles of confinement which applied to the dungeon (deprivation of light and the hiding of the "prisoner") except enclosure (ibid.: 200). It is a system of light, a systematic play of visibilities and invisibilities facilitated by the architectural arrangement of its parts and whose ideal is absolute transparency. Its major effect is to induce within those relegated to its cells a reflective consciousness of their permanent, or more accurately, always potential, visibility. A single observer stationed in the central guardtower of Bentham's Panopticon could efficiently monitor the entire group of prisoners confined along its periphery. The tower functions indifferently to mask both the observer's presence or absence, its windows fitted with screens and blinders that allow seeing out but not seeing in. Although it is continually visible to the inmates from their cells, they are unable to verify, and are thus perpetually uncertain about, the fact of their observation. Thus, in terms of its actual effects, the exercise of power within the Panopticon is rendered invisible and non-corporeal; ideally, those confined within would not have to be continually supervised by a human observer – the presence of the tower and its windows alone would be sufficient to insure their docility. Foucault notes that the Panopticon is therefore "light" in another sense. Because inmates virtually police themselves in panoptic contexts, power can "throw off its weight" (all overt use of power would be unnecessary). Panopticism would assure the automatic and subtle functioning of power insofar as the observed are "caught up in a power situation of which they themselves are the bearers" (1979: 201).

Here the figure of the Panopticon is already haunted by a parallel figure of simulation. Surveillance, we are told, is "discreet," unobtrusive, camouflaged, unverifiable – all elements of artifice designed into an architectural arrangement of spaces to produce real effects of discipline. Eventually this will lead, by means of its perfection, to the elimination of the Panopticon itself. At least this is the essential fantasy that guides its development. Already in Bentham there is the recognition that the technology of surveillance functions by subtly subverting itself, not simply by creating an "illusion" of observation with what is essentially a blind apparatus (the central tower), but a frictionless mechanism of self-observation and "participatory" policing in which the central tower is increasingly reduced to a supplement, a "mere" sign or signal of the power to discipline, a counterfeit. In the final analysis, it is superfluous. Thus, from the beginning, the panoptic mechanism, in fact the entire arrangement of panoptic space, is haunted by its double – its "immaterial" form – a simulation of power which secretly works to dismantle the old inefficient technology of control while simultaneously refashioning it in a purer, less confined, less obtrusive, yet more inflated form. With simulation, the still relatively crude form of panoptic surveillance first manifests the possibility of escaping the limits of *place*.

Model deviants

Following Foucault, criminologist Stanley Cohen (1985; 1979) notes how the current system of deviancy control had its origins in the great transformations of power that took place at the end of the eighteenth century. Those transformations included the development of a centralized, bureaucratic state apparatus for the control of crime and the care of dependency; the differentiation of deviant and dependent populations each with its corresponding field of scientific knowledge and expertise; the increased segregation of deviants and dependents from the general population and their confinement to special treatment facilities. Today, however, the consensus that had once formed around the desirability of segregating and confining these groups (in prisons, asylums, etc.) appears to have broken down in favor of more decentralized, dispersed forms of social control, what Cohen calls the "second Great Transformation." Cohen cites as an example of this the proliferation of community-based corrections facilities, diversionary programs, halfway houses, and prevention centers that began with the so-called "decarceration" movement of the 1960s in the United States. At that time, liberal reformers perceived the "diversion" of delinquents into these programs as a humanistic response to failures of the criminal justice system, which, they claimed, was poorly designed to rehabilitate offenders and instead did much to produce them. Cohen (1979: 343), however, recognizes here an alibi for increased surveillance of the population, for new forms of intervention that supplement, not abolish, centralized state control and retain, in disguised form, all the coercive features once associated with confinement and the old tactics of segregation and exclusion. The discretionary and screening powers of the state in determining deviance and dependency have been formalized and disseminated throughout the larger society, and the net of surveillance widens and its mesh becomes finer to include those who, had the new facilities or programs not been available, would either have been dealt with in traditional ways (such as prison, parole, etc.) or not processed through the system at all (1979: 348).

Cohen argues that the increased dispersion and decentralization of surveillance has been accompanied by an ironic blurring of distinctions, both normative and geographic – between guilty and innocent, freedom and captivity, confinement and release, inside and outside. These distinctions still meant something in the nineteenth century. But today,

under the ideology of a society that "cares," we have instead constructed a "correctional continuum"; instead of having prisons and the outside,
"free" world, we have ever finer-grained classification and treatment
schemes that, as they begin to entangle more and more of the population, end up finally blurring the very lines between delinquent and non-
delinquent, deviant and normal, sane and insane (Cohen 1979: 344; also
1985: 57).

Although Cohen limits himself to a critique of the *ideology* of decarceration here, showing how this merely conceals the real (and ironic) dispersion of carceral mechanisms into the wider society, what he describes
is, expressed *positively*, a *simulacrum of control* – not merely a "dispersion" of disciplinary tactics into the wider society, but a *simulation* of the
forms of surveillance that characterized the last great transformation of
social control at the end of the eighteenth century. At times Cohen recognizes that his geographic metaphor of "dispersion" itself conceals a
strategy of simulation, as when he describes how so-called community
"halfway" houses are often more rigorous in terms of their surveillance
demands than traditional prisons: "What is likely is that projects that are
genuine alternatives to incarceration have to make a trade-off between
treatment goals (which favor the integrated community setting) and security goals which favor isolation. The trade-off under these conditions will
tend to favor security – resulting in programs which *simulate* or mimic
the very features of the institution they set out to replace" (Cohen 1979:
351; my italic). The new facilities outdo even the prisons as sites for generating information: research projects, tracking, screening, compiling
dossiers, categorizing behaviors, profiling, and preventive deterrence
replace punishment and become ends in themselves.

In another place, Cohen writes of how the ideology of "community
control" has canceled the distinction between public and private modes
of surveillance (groups like Neighborhood Watch, for instance, turn us
all into police) (1979: 353). Often seen as a return to earlier forms of
social control where the community was responsible for policing itself –
Gemeinschaft societies – in fact what is involved is the simulation of these
forms of control. In a confused way that signals his desire to move
beyond the critique of ideology, Cohen acknowledges this very fact in
denying it: "today's forms of peacekeeping by the community are not
quite the same as those golden days of 'mutual responsibility.' Closed circuit television, two-way radios, vigilante patrols and police decoys hardly simulate life in a pre-industrial village. *This is not for want of trying*"
(1979: 355; my italic).

Had he followed his intuition here, Cohen would have focused his analysis on the simulation of surveillance rather than the ideology of surveillance. An ideological analysis of surveillance reveals only the subjective irony of a society that professes to care for its members but in fact universally betrays them, a homogeneous society of watchers. A simulational analysis of surveillance, on the other hand, reveals the *objective irony* of a society beyond caring, beyond betrayal, which now functions solely to reproduce and perfect its information-processing capabilities, its modeling and gaming skills, its talents for encryption and decryption. Who is captured or who "falls through the cracks" in such a system is of secondary importance. Surveillance today is not so much a question of halfway houses and detention centers, as it is, with Yurick, of the conversion of persons and social relations into the universal ether of information, which is their simulation. And this is what provokes Cohen (1985: 86) to remark finally that the new mechanisms of control require no justification other than themselves: "there is hardly any point in asking about success [of these mechanisms], this is not the object of the enterprise. Research is done on the classification system itself – working out a continuum of community-basedness [with] prediction tables or screening devices." It takes little imagination to project this out to its fantastic conclusion, the not-so-distant future of the simulated logistics of deviancy control. Henceforth, everyone will be screened at a very young age – genetically, chemically, psychologically – for their deviant or dependent "dispositions" (or whatever dispositions you like). This information will then be compared with criminological profiles or matched to other preexisting records, stored in a form easily retrieved to deal with any conceivable problem when it (predictably!) arises. A case of the model – the simulacrum – of deviance preceding the reality; and of surveillance, the logistics of the gaze, converting to simulation.

The test

In *Cancer Ward* (1968: 221), Alexander Solzhenitsyn wrote:

As every man goes through life he fills in a number of forms for the record, each containing a number of questions ... There are thus hundreds of little threads radiating from every man, millions of threads in all. If these threads were suddenly to become visible, the whole sky would look like a spider's web, and if they materialized as rubber bands, buses, trams and even people would all lose the ability to move, and the wind would be unable to carry torn-up newspapers or autumn leaves along the streets of the city. They are not visible, they are not material, but every man is constantly aware of their existence ... Each man, permanently aware of his own invisible threads, naturally develops a respect for the people who manipulate the threads.

We have already noted how, in the United States alone, billions of records on the activities and histories of individuals and groups are stored in various departments and agencies of the federal government, the majority of them computerized.[3] There have been periodic calls for the creation of a national databank to store and coordinate all this information. Even though no such databank actually exists today, it makes increasingly little difference. In fact, the trend, spurred on by the tremendous growth in the numbers of interlinked personal computers over the last decade, is toward a de facto, *decentralized* national database. And federal records are, of course, only a small part of the picture. They do not include information generated by state and local agencies (such as law enforcement, licensing bureaus, community services, taxation, etc.). In the private sphere, banks, utilities, and marketing organizations own vast stores of information on persons, much of which is shared or used for matching and profiling purposes. The five largest credit firms (such as TRW, "the tomorrow people"!) hold an estimated 150–200 million individual credit records, with the name, address, name of spouse, workplace, salary, credit history, tax and legal history, bankruptcy claims, etc., of each individual. Computer-generated statistics form the basis of work evaluation on 4–6 million office and sales workers (primarily women). These are probably very conservative estimates given the current rate at which businesses are computerized, and in any case do not include information collected by corporations through drug-testing programs, polygraphs, charting of employment histories, salary histories, records of dismissals, and so on.

If we add to this the vast electronic monitoring capacities of the modern military and state espionage apparatuses, the information-generating capacities of colleges, universities, and scientific research institutions (the latter exploring new technologies like genetic screening and brain-wave scanning), and remind ourselves of the global dimensions of the electronic media, it is no surprise that surveillance has become a central concern for the theory and history of social control.

The problem is that, again, none of this is precisely "surveillance" any longer, but rather surveillance in its most hyperinflated, simulated form; not an architecture of inspection, an arrangement of space and light, a play of visibilities, as with the Panopticon, but, as Baudrillard (1983b: 143) has called it, a "simulacrum of spaces" – it would be difficult to find a better metaphor for virtual systems – the superficial depth, the cold steel luminescence of the display screen.

End of the old illusions of relief, perspective and depth (spatial and psychological) bound to the perception of an object: now it is the entire optic, the view become operational on the surface of things, it is the look become molecular code of the object.[4]

Not simply the gaze that probes beneath the surface of bodies, but the informated, ultra-mediated bodies themselves, whose pathologies and performances are so many genomic modulations, variations on a uniform code of life and death.

This is not at all to say that panoptic and electronic surveillance are distinct forms of social control with no point of contact. On the contrary, as I've argued, nothing fundamental changes with the electronification of surveillance. With the proliferation of electronic sensors, codes, and databases, with information availability in "real-time," all that happens is that the Panopticon becomes a Superpanopticon (Poster 1990: 85ff.)[5] – a doubling and redoubling of surveillance, a shifting of its operations onto a simulated, informated plane, a metastasis of the gaze that no longer probes the individual body but instead now "leukemizes" the entire social body.

Baudrillard cites three general orders of appearance since the Renaissance (Baudrillard 1983b: 101ff.). First, the order of *counterfeit* in the "classical" era, based on the natural law of value, where the sign is first emancipated from the feudal bonds of rank and caste. The order of counterfeit is the beginning of the modern age and its core problematic of Nature (of reality versus appearance), the birth of fashion and the bourgeoisie, and of the mechanical conception of man.

Following this, the order of *production*, the so-called "industrial" period of the eighteenth and nineteenth centuries, based on the commercial law of value (exchange) and the transition from the principle of equivalence to the principle of seriality (mechanical reproduction). The order of production is the age of the *robotic* conception of man (culminating in the figure of the assembly-line worker) and also the origin of the modern media of communication and control (telegraph, telephone, photography).

The present period, according to Baudrillard, is the order of simulation, based on the structural law of value, the age of control by the "code" (that which allows encryption and decryption, which "translates," which interprets or enables interpretation, controls an operation, which *models and tests*). The order of simulation signals the abolition of all referential finalities that governed earlier periods (God, Nature, Man, History, Society). References now refer only in and to simulations. Nothing flows *toward* its end anymore, but *from* its end, i.e., its simulation; reality no longer "tests" its model, but rather the reverse. Precession of simulacra. The model – the simulation – now tests reality, becomes the "signifier of reference" (Baudrillard 1983b: 101). "Practically and historically, this signifies the substitution of social control by the *end* (and by a more or less dialectical *providence* which surveys the accomplishment of this *end*) for social control by anticipation, simulation, and programming, and indeterminate mutation directed by the code ..." And all this marks a change "from a capitalist-productivist society to a neo-capitalist cybernetic order that aims now at total control" (1983b: 111).

With simulation, Baudrillard suggests, we enter a universe of binary structures – models, games, tests, tree diagrams, flow charts, polls – whose principle is no longer, as in the industrial period, seriality and reproducibility, but operationality and digitality. The real is not what can be reproduced utilizing a model; the real is that which is always already reproduced, already a simulacrum, without original. The order of simulation marks the end of modernity's fascination with *signs* (their destiny, their repression, their deep meaning), just as it is the dissolution of the Renaissance problem of the real and its appearance. Henceforth, there is nothing but *signals or a process of signalization without direction or depth*, an informational nexus from which everything else flows, everything reduced to the digital, binary structure of the code: question:answer, yes:no, true:false, 0:1. In simulation, space is no longer linear and objective, but microcellular and digital, comprising the infinite generation of electronic impulses (1983b: 105).

For Baudrillard, simulacra, including simulation, are *orders* – orders of appearance, to be sure, but nonetheless orders. "Simulacra are not only a game played with signs. They imply social rapports and social power." They are schemes in which the "internal coherence of a system is already at work" (1983b: 88, 90). Although at times he *opposes* simulation to power (i.e., to disciplinary and panoptic power as Foucault has described it), and thus falls back into the dialectical logic he desires to abandon as a remnant of the era of production, in other places he clearly has in mind what I have called the simulation of surveillance, of the *apotheosis* (not negation) of panoptic control, which still allows us to speak meaningfully of not only the simulation of power but the *power of simulation*, i.e., of the hyperdisciplinary effects of simulation as productive of a (hyperreal) social order. Simulation is not at all the opposite of power, but another mode of its exercise, in fact its most elevated and most paradoxical mode. It is not identical to artifice or the opposite of the real, or something that has no consequence in the order of power relations. Rather, simulation produces effects of discipline by virtue of a *transfiguration of discipline*, by imposing a higher, more devious, order of discipline that, as Baudrillard himself has said, aims at total control, complete, ecstatic manipulation, and this not through artifice or illusion, but by keeping the relation between the artificial and the real indeterminate, in a state of continual suspense and uncertainty.

Surveillance and simulation connect for Baudrillard in the *test* ("test" itself connoting a monitored training that already links it to the concepts of "discipline" and the "calculating gaze"). Tests are simulated methods of control in the sense that the question posed by the test *calls forth* – anticipates – its answer, designates it in advance (1983b: 117). But tests are obviously also tools of the surveillance apparatus. They are "probes." Foucault (1979: 184) also refers to the importance of tests. He notes how, in the nineteenth century, the *examination* combines the earlier techniques of an observing hierarchy and normalizing judgment to qualify, classify, and punish. The examination imposes an "economy of visibility," and introduces individuality into the field of documentation, into a network of writing (today we would say into a web of information and databases). Examination – testing – transforms each individual into a case, to be filed and compared with other cases (ibid.: 191). Even here, an early form of "programming" is involved that assures each "case" its place in the network of signals (information), which reduces the heterogeneity of possible responses to match the homogeneous textual space of the file. Already, examination, insofar as it records and reorders the effects of its administration, involves a measure of simulation.

Let us return to our example of the flight simulator and examine its imaginary. There, none of the pilot's responses to what he sees occurs "outside" the simulation ("inside" and "outside" in effect lose their sense here), all moves are possible only as moves in reference to the informated space of the simulator. But those responses are still "examined." They are "measured," and measured moreover with the *ironic* precision that only absorption in an environment which prespecifies all possible forms of response can provide. The pilot becomes qualified to fly low/fast missions as only simulation can qualify, viz., by transforming the pilot into an integrated part of the machine that trains him, into a cyborg. The integrated circuit of the simulator plays off a vertiginous cancellation of the distance between active subject and passive object, between what the pilot sees and what he is shown, between what he does to the apparatus and what the apparatus does to him. In the simulator, he scans – surveils – what in effect *would be* his own visual field (if he "really" flew the mission), which now in turn is projected back to him as an "exercise," a *challenge* to his performance that is simultaneously a seduction of absolute control. Like any video game addict, the pilot *sim-learns*, is sim-trained to sim-fly the simulator, challenged to beat the machine and thereby master the flying conditions simulated by the machine. But who is master here, who's in charge, man or machine, and where is the privileged point of the gaze, the locus of its power? In fact, one can speak of mastery and the gaze only within the *total context of the simulated environment*, of control only as an ecstasy of power, an ecstasy of the gaze, within the cyborgian framework of the simulator.

This is only the most obvious example of how discipline gets hyperized in an electronically simulated environment. But it is the same each time we fill out a form, participate in a statistical study or public opinion poll, conduct an electronic transaction, are subjected to computer monitoring at work, or hook into, in any of these or other ways, an electronic database. We are being subtly tested, challenged to "higher" performance by a seductive image of ultimate control. Just fill out these forms and (re)take control of your life! Solzhenitsyn, it turns out, only saw half the picture. Not only do you wind up submitting to those who control the system of information, the network of databases. More and more, you *are* what you enter into a computer, you *are* the electronic transactions you make, you *are* public opinion, you *are* the endless forms you fill out, in the same sense that pilot response in the above example is already an integral element of training. This doesn't exactly mean, as we've seen, that you thereby monitor and control yourself, that you *participate* in your own discipline. But neither are you passively controlled by the test. Instead, the test generates a self-contained hyperdisciplinary context, a *model control environment or climate*. The active:passive, participatory:non-participatory distinctions, along with those of subject and object, here and there, all these polar oppositions disappear in favor of the hyperspace of total control. At least, that's the imaginary.

If the secret wish of surveillance is absolute control, the test grants it, but in the paradoxical form of simulated control, total control in exchange for equally total submission to the conditions of the test. Control, that is, within a simulated space (the "space" of the simulator, the "space" of poll and the form, the "space" of electronic transactions and databases). But does this control, being purely informated, ever really touch ground? Baudrillard (1983b: 127) says it is a "fiction whose index of refraction in any reality ... is nil. This is even what gives models [tests, games, etc.] their *forcefulness*. But also it is this which only leaves them, as truth, the paranoid projection tests of a case, or of a group which dreams of a miraculous correspondence of the real to their models, and therefore of an absolute manipulation." A "fiction," perhaps; but a fiction difficult to separate from fact, whose effects are *indiscernibly real.*

Electronic surveillance and testing are only higher forms of the examination, elevated forms of discipline. Whereas before discipline was an art of distributing bodies in space, of ranking and classifying cases, of imposing repetitive and graduated tasks, of individualization, now it is an art of moving information through cyberspace, of testing cases against classificatory schemes, of imposing a total task environment, of matching information collected on individuals to computer-generated profiles. Everywhere the technology of surveillance has been streamlined, everywhere made to overcome the barriers which confined it to a particular territory or time. Ironically, this has meant its simulation, the sacrifice of its effects in the Real in exchange for absolute power in the Hyperreal.

The "new surveillance"?

Surveillance without walls, towers, guards – electronic remote sensing, real-time transmission/reception capability, cybernetic control. No longer mediated by an architecture, no longer bound to a territory, surveillance becomes the equivalent of the mediascape itself – the "simulated" territory, the entire electronic media assemblage. As Virilio (1989: 115) says, "Space is no longer in geography, it's in electronics. Unity is in the terminals." Panopticism is a strategy of place, one that makes it possible for the gaze to transform alien forces into objects that can be observed, measured, and included in its scope of vision. Panoptic control is a matter of constructing visible locales, of extending perception beyond visible horizons. It reduces temporal relations to spatial relations. The organization of temporal practices into routines, tasks, scheduled events, etc., is rendered possible through the arrangement of places, the establishment of locations via an "architecture" that enhances the possibilities of the exercise of disciplinary power.

Today all this is changing, as we move from a geopolitics based on the division of space and the distribution of territory to a dromo-politics based on the absolutization of speed. It is no surprise that absolute speed is first of all a military imaginary. In war, existing observation machines become obsolete the moment one's adversary invents a faster observation machine. Making the observation machine faster, making distance disappear: this telematic idea has guided the development of surveillance technology up to the present generation of orbital spy satellites and beyond. Today, the speed at which information flows negates the effects and the problems of distance; images of remote events are accessible onscreen, computer enhanced, in real-time, instantaneously. Better, remote events are programmable onscreen, in *sim*-time, without reference to anything but their code. The whole idea of remote (or close, for that matter) is nonsensical in simulated environments.

It's easy to see why modern technologies of observation have been termed the "new surveillance." Panoptic power has always aimed at overcoming the inhibiting effects of distance, to enhance control by exposing what before was inaccessible to vision. In the project of erasing distance, modern electronic surveillance first appears as only a refinement of equipment and an extension of strategic principles developed in the past – today remote sensors have replaced the localized technologies of observation, providing instantaneous access to information over an infinitely expanded territory.

But the progressive erasure of distance has irreversibly transformed surveillance, not into the "new" surveillance, a concept which glosses over the most important logistical features of modern observational technologies and relapses into the strategic thought of an earlier age, but surveillance as its own simulation.[6] Now it is no longer simply a matter of the speed at which information is gained to defeat an enemy, no longer, to return to our military example, a matter of becoming informed of an adversary's actions (intentions, desires) before he can become similarly informed. Now one can *simulate* a space of control, project an indefinite number of courses of action, train for each possibility, and react immediately with preprogrammed responses to the "actual" course of events (which is *already* over and through a simulacrum). With simulation, sight and fore-sight, actual and virtual begin to merge (Virilio 1989: 3). Surveillance, approaching the hyperspeed of simulation – where information is not *gathered*, but *projected* – becomes prepanoptic, scanning a scene that has no object, that is not simply a scene, but the seamless unity of terminal and operator, subject and object of surveillance. Increasingly, the technological enlargement of the field of perceptual control, the erasure of distance in the speed of electronic information has pushed surveillance beyond the very limits of speed toward the purest forms of anticipation.

This is what the gaze is becoming. The dialectic of control and resistance made possible by architecture, the oscillation of visibility and invisibility, is increasingly overcome in the perfection – the hereness, the pure affirmation – of the simulated gaze. The gaze is no longer invisibly on the scene; it is the *total* scene. It no longer merely watches, it is not exterior, calculating and detached. It is perhaps not really a "gaze" at all, but a kind of "informed touch," since the whole environment is transparent and hyperperceptual. (Again, this is not *just* science fiction. The project of modern electronics to substitute a hyperperceptual experience for an original perception is unmistakable. Visual technology, as any videophile knows, aims at images that are not simply indistinguishable from the original, but cleaner, more present, more enveloping and "available." The same is true of audiophile technology, sound recording, and playback equipment, etc.)

Certainly, there is no doubt that surveillance is ubiquitous today. Public and private, corporate, state, military, scientific institutions: surveillance is a central, constitutive feature of all modern organizations. More individuals are targets of surveillance than at any other point in history. What these facts fail to capture is the imaginary of surveillance, and that is an imaginary of its own simulation, its own operation at the limit of its powers. Surveillance develops from an arrangement of spaces and visibilities to a simulacrum of spaces and times. From the control of territory and distance to the mastery of self-organizing, self-scaling, fractal landscapes. From examination within a context of writing to the binary form of the test within the ethereal space of information. These changes mark both the totalization of the global apparatus of surveillance (all information in all places) and its operation at the limit, its passing into its own simulation. Simulation technologies now aim for the hyperization of the very polarities which historically constituted the limit conditions of surveillance – visible:invisible, interior:exterior, watcher:watched, here:there, active:passive. Vertiginous, turbulent forms of polarization, where poles incessantly verge on implosion in an ecstasy of feedback and feedforward.

We must, then, develop a new critical discourse of social control, one that accounts for the operation of a system that depends less and less on the normalization of practices within the confines of a place – the factory, the office, the hospital, the school, the market – and which now operates universally via a complex qualitative, temporal process that brings into play modeling, gaming, forecasting, testing, all ways of electronically mediated feeling and perceiving. Increasingly, virtual realities, artificial intelligence, expert systems, sever us from older forms of control and project that control – refashioned, smoothed, and streamlined – onto the plane of simulation. And increasingly, we need to view social control less as a function of supervision and monitoring (though these forms still coexist alongside the newer methods), and more as a paradoxical inflation of these processes, which without negating them both surpasses and completes them. The "new" surveillance, that is, is a higher and purer form of supervision.

4

Sensors, jammers, and the military simulacrum

Support and subversion

There are many technologies of social control in telematic societies, but surveillance and simulation are perhaps the most generalized and diffuse forms, ordering multiple realms of human activity and experience. Surveillance includes those methods of "ocular" control, scanning-selection mechanisms of the most diverse sorts, which command objects and events by means of their *exposure*. "Ocular," of course, is only a metaphor here, a reminder of surveillance's etymological ties to vision (to observing, watching, gazing, staring), and to seeing as a technology of truth and power (overseeing, supervising, overlooking). Today, we have seen, surveillance is mostly a matter of electronic monitoring and information technologies – remote sensing devices, barcodes, computer-enhanced imaging techniques, bioscanning equipment, and so on – its connection to human vision (and the other senses) thoroughly mediated by *machineries* for recording and manipulating data.

Simulation, on the other hand, refers to a diverse practice of appearances, a technology of similarities and simultaneities that commands objects or events by doubling or otherwise *repeating* them. Models, games, codes, and tests are all paradigms of simulation, of initiating or governing series of repetitions, and all, as we have seen, are powerful technologies of control. Simulation also has an "ocular" sense, that of the false or deceptive appearance; hence its long association with decoys, feints, mock-ups, and other distractive or diversionary maneuvers.

But I have argued that simulations are not *simply* false. Rather, their power derives from how well they nullify their falsity, from how "real" they appear. In the realm of appearances, the aim of simulation is to transgress the true:false dichotomy altogether by dissolving the gap between an object or event and its double. Like surveillance, the visual (or perceptual) element in simulation has been thoroughly caught up in a wave of modern infotech – virtual reality, visionics, holographics, ergonomics, high-definition TV, digital reproduction technologies of all sorts. Or rather, human perception is *integrated* today as one more component in an elaborate cybernetic machinery for the replication of objects and events.

We have seen how in present-day societies, the relations between these two generalized forms of control are very complex, the distinctions and points of contact between them difficult to specify. One usually appears with the other, often, but not necessarily, in the same technology or social practice. Surveillance cameras, for instance, both simulate the human gaze and are methods of exposure; or espionage, which from the very beginning has been both an art of unconcealment (seeing behind surfaces) and a strategy of appearances. To oversimplify matters somewhat, we could say that the relations between practices of surveillance and simulation are both complementary and conflictual, both *relations of support or enablement* and *relations of subversion*. That is, between these two groups of practices, whatever their specific technical, political, historical, or social forms, there exist reciprocal strategic dependencies and evasions, ways of supplementing and reinforcing or, conversely, eluding the other's means of control. Some examples follow.

As a support of surveillance, simulation produces those disorienting effects of the oscillation of presence and absence – i.e., uncertainty regarding its locus, its modes of operation, its intent, and so forth – which are the source of its (surveillance's) power. The first rule of surveillance is *discretion*, to show only what is practical or necessary for its efficient operation, the remainder being left secret. The second rule, closely related to the first, is to be *covert* – be here while appearing to be somewhere else, at this moment while in fact operating before or later, seen but not recognized or identified. It is the play of these conditions – and the tension between them – that defines the paradoxical space-time of surveillance, its command of location and duration, as it were, from the "outside," out of view, while nevertheless remaining a kind of "presence." Surveillance is always linked in complex ways to those forms of ruse and deception which, in supporting the exercise of power, present power to be something else, elsewhere, not what it seems.

Thus the observation tower at the center of Bentham's Panopticon, which commands a view of all the cells along its periphery, is a figure that simulates a condition of continuous observation, but which, because prisoners cannot verify whether or not guards are stationed behind its walls, in fact renders continuity of supervision unnecessary. Watching, or not watching? The face of the guardtower is like an absent eye, but whose absence is masked. Or just the opposite: it is a perfect, uninterrupted gaze, always present, unblinking. Presence, absence – what's the difference? The effect, the docility of the prisoner, is the same. Simulation here supports the ocular function of surveillance, even if it renders that function superfluous (the "mask" lets the machine relax; the guards, for all it matters, can go home). If we follow Foucault, this marvelous, abstract machinery of power, refined and perfected in an efficient penitentiary technique, now assembles a multiplicity of social relations in the modern age, and reproduces in the thousand mundane routines of everyday life the deep collusion that has always existed between a method of supervision and the ways in which it secrets itself (Foucault 1979: 205).

This relation operates in reverse: surveillance also supports simulation. Simulations are copies – at least in their lower-order forms – and copies are produced from originals exposed to observation or measurement. Again, the xerox is the readiest example here, the scanning operation functioning as the first step in the process of replication – scan, record, duplicate. But other kinds of simulation, like the statistical models used in public opinion polling, population analyses, genetic research, criminology, and so on, also depend on elaborate perception-induction mechanisms (surveys, experiments, tests) to gather and sort information derived from "original" material (attitudes and opinions, living conditions, diseases and deaths, arrests and convictions). In panoptic settings in general, simulations and simulacra can proliferate, as visual fields are structured by the observation-machine in ways that allow for various codings and displays (panoptic prisoners, e.g., are always "model" prisoners, and the guardtower itself is what they model themselves on – they become their own surveillors). Finally, decoys, fakes, and counterfeits – all second-order simulacra – operate in analogous ways, insofar as they replicate objects or events which first have been subjected to detailed observation and inspection.

Simulation, however, also aims to free itself from this dependence on an "original," and at the same time to break its ties to the apparatus of observation. It does this by perfecting its appearance of genuineness or authenticity, eliminating the gap between itself and what it models. Simulation, in short, resists detection as any kind of decoy, mask, mockup, or double resists its exposure. The better the copy, the less chance of its recognition as a copy. Here simulation, far from a support of surveillance, is the practice of its subversion, the elusion of all modes of inspection that attempt to assert their control over space and time, all exercises of power that work to verify, identify, and fix. History is replete with examples of the creation of fake locales, blind spots, ambivalent regions within the general space of supervision, of "autonomous times" within the regulated, sequential structure of human activity – all the myriad ways persons have devised to elude observation and control by means of simulating their presence or their performance. De Certeau (1984: xiii ff.), whom we will discuss in the next chapter, has, for example, drawn our attention to those ingenious ways indigenous peoples foil the efforts of their colonizers to control them, not by outright revolt or refusal, but by appropriating the cultural practices of their oppressors after their own fashion and traditions – in effect subverting the system in appearing to conform with it, in simulating the very mode of their supervision. Or how factory laborers manage to find the "time," in a practice known in France as *la perruque*, to work for themselves even as they appear to be doing the bidding of their employers, by means of an elaborate and rich tradition of elusion – staging, to use Paul Virilio's (1980) term, their "disappearance" beneath the very eyes of the authorities.

Finally, surveillance subverts simulation as any technology designed to penetrate appearances or surfaces will resist being fooled or seduced by them. The gaze generally opts for what's real. It goes for what it can see and touch over what "merely appears" (see Baudrillard 1983b: 41). In general, simulation is a challenge to surveillance because it threatens to unhinge the conventional oppositions between the real and the apparent, between directed (controlled) and autonomous (free) time, fixed and mobile spaces, crucial distinctions for an order based upon ocular forms of control. In relation to surveillance, simulation is like *the gaze that returns the gaze*, like a *stare* that syphons off the power of the other's stare by repeating or doubling it, and that thus becomes, discreetly, covertly, something more than a gaze (the best way to neutralize the observer is to look back with the same, or even greater, intensity). In that return of the gaze, a "moment out of time" is created, where differences of power are canceled in the virtual space of an endless repetition. I have been arguing that the most important aspects of contemporary social control are those found in those circumstances where surveillance is simulated, where it dissolves into pure repetition. This dissolution, however, is also its paradoxical transfiguration, surveillance's simultaneous disappearance and elevation to the realm of simulacra, where it dreams of absolute control.

Each of these four categories of relations – reversible relations of support and subversion – between two diffuse technologies of control is a way of viewing the deployment of power relations in telematic, information-based societies, how an apparatus that controls by exposure connects to an image-machine that controls by its command of appearances. These societies, addicted to infotech, are "surveillance-simulation societies." In them, the observation-machine is integrated to a technology that refashions it, if you will, after its own image. Fueled by developments in silicon technology that in the last third of the twentieth century have continually pushed at the limits of technical "explicitness" – enhancing the speed and efficiency of communications, the clarity and presence of images – simulation and surveillance are paradoxical rivals in a contest that today increasingly favors the former. The evidence for this is everywhere. It ranges from the current explosion of and interest in the development of simulation technologies in fields as diverse as attitude research, product quality control, computer consulting, visionics, and fractal imaging, to the modeling of human behavior, affect, and cognition. Nowhere, however, is this development more apparent than in the military forces of postindustrial nations. There, simulation is rapidly becoming a preferred mode of combat training, is extensively employed in deterrence strategy, in camouflage, espionage, and war-gaming, and has begun to replace the battlefield warrior with a new breed of fighter, the "cyborg soldier," a shrinking speck of human consciousness at the center of an array of electronic screens, image enhancers, replicators, bioscanners, pills, prosthetics, and artificial intelligence systems (Gray 1989).

The terms may be relatively modern (in fact, dating back only to the nineteenth century), but simulation and surveillance have long military histories, from the origins of the first intelligence services in ancient Egypt, Babylonia, and Persia (Dvornik 1974), to contemporary stealth equipment, the sophisticated sensing and jamming technologies used in electromagnetic combat, to cybernetic weapons targeting and guidance systems. And from their strategic applications in war, where they are first developed, the technologies of simulation and surveillance have always found their way into the wider society – today, as means of controlling deviants, regulating work, educating children, as diverse forms of pleasure and entertainment. At the end of this century, military control is rapidly becoming a paradigm of social control, as battlefield technology is ever more routinely and successfully adapted to between-war uses. Did we say "between-war"? In fact, postindustrial, postmodern societies have become thoroughly militarized societies where the distinction between civilian and soldier, soldier and machine, war and peace is increasingly blurred by the mass diffusion of infotech (de Landa 1991), where distant wars are flashed instantly across our television screens, where battlefield engagements are replicated by electronic toys and games, and where supercomputer technologies developed for annihilating an enemy are ironically promoted as tools of global friendship and communication.

The observation-machine

Alongside the "war-machine," there has always existed an ocular (and later optical and electro-optical) "watching-machine" capable of providing soldiers, and particularly commanders, with a visual perspective on the military action underway. From the original watchtower ... to remote-sensing satellites, one and the same function has been indefinitely repeated, the eye's function being the function of a weapon. However great the area of the battlefield, it is necessary to have the fastest possible access to pictures of the enemy's forces and reserves. Seeing and foreseeing therefore tend to merge so closely that the actual can no longer be distinguished from the potential. Military actions take place "out of view," with radio-electrical images substituting in real time for a now failing optical vision.   (Virilio 1989: 3)

Virilio's words capture almost perfectly the transition, in military terms, from surveillance to simulation. But one needs to add that military actions increasingly take place not just out of view, but "out of time" of actual combat. War today is as much a matter of simulation as it is of battlefield engagement. In the Persian Gulf War, conducted under the sign of the United States's purge of the legacy of Vietnam, preparing for the war consumed far more time than its brief four-day execution. It was preceded by months of war-gaming, modeling, constructing combat scenarios, satellite targeting, training soldiers for a high-tech encounter that included the possible use of advanced chemical and biological weapons, probing the world political scene for support, and preparing the general public for the inevitability of conflict. Virtually every aspect of the war – economic, social, cultural, psychological, and not just "military" – was played out in advance, no contingency was taken for granted.

Even the war itself, the actual fighting, in a literal sense, took place "out of time," in simulation (Baudrillard 1991; Kellner 1992). Both for those who watched it at home on their TVs and for the soldiers who fought it, it was the first technically sophisticated video-computer war, the first large-scale opportunity to try out all the elaborate wartech that an opulent Pentagon had developed during the high-rolling years of the Reagan administration. The images of missiles impacting their Iraqi targets that fighter pilots saw on their cockpit screens were not just "real-time" images. They were simulations, stand-ins for the events on the ground, rendered comprehensible only in reproduction, and, as all simulations in war, they compensated not only for the distances over which modern combat is waged, bringing things into view that must take place out of view, but corrected also for the time, the speed of modern war, in order to slow things down (to replay them, "pause" them), to manage the sheer pace of battle which today has begun to escape human control. Where the virtual simultaneity of events on the battlefield threatens to overload the decision capabilities of soldiers and their commanders, their machines – i.e., their on-board computers, radar and image enhancers, expert system consultants, and so on – now come to their aid, reducing the complexity of the rapidly changing battle situations to which they must react. Simulation simplifies and sorts out this virtual simultaneity, brings the chaos of modern war paradoxically back into "time," not the real time of events, but the simulated, "timeless" time of their reproduction, their onscreen, computer-enhanced image. That is, it indeed supports the increasingly failing vision of the war-machine, but it does so on its own terms. In the long term, it may mean the elimination of the human soldier, the original "observation-machine" in war, from the field of battle, as his functions are increasingly replaced and executed by computer simulations. For now and the near future, it means investment in and development of cyborg warriors, soldiers who for all practical purposes are man–machine interfaces – prosthetic enhancements of the ocular-optical functions of the war apparatus – designed to operate fearlessly on the lightning fast, information-saturated, and increasingly uncertain terrain of combat.

"Technology," Lyman Bryson once wrote, "is explicitness" (in McLuhan 1964: 56). The new simulated warrior currently being planned by the military is supposed to reduce the fog surrounding contemporary war. Plugged into expert systems that will coordinate battlefield communications, analyze and sort information, generate options, even make autonomous decisions, military commanders will have an instant picture of the battlefield updated at regular intervals and projected against the latest scenarios. Via satellites connected to sophisticated computer-enhancement technologies, they will "see" the battle as it unfolds, project its development, issue without delay orders to their forces in the field. All this, with the support of modern recording equipment, can be instantly replayed, re-analyzed in an effortless search for information that might have been "overlooked." This Promethean space of virtual war – with its computer-generated images of enemy movements, the instant analysis and summary – lays everything out in integrated modular form, imparts a "sense" of directionality to a chaotic scene where "real" information goes in all directions at once, and across a space of conflict whose destructive potential is unmatched in history. Here, in the electronic command and coordination centers of modern military forces, the war raging "outside" regains an element of closure and containment. By means of its simulation, war once again becomes "visible," discussible, "slower," the decisions on its course, even in this cyborgian environment, brought back, ironically, to their "human" scale. This is its *seduction*, of course, because computers and simulation technologies do not "really" slow down the pace of war, or place it under more explicit control. If anything, by speeding decisions and expanding the volume of information, they contribute to its further acceleration and chaotic development. Military simulations, like all simulations, claim to do something they don't, to control the war outside. The object of this electronic transfiguration is to carry war to very limit of its *disappearance*, that is, to conduct the battle in its entirety "inside," in the simulated, secured time-space of the command bunker.

This military dream (for that is what it is) of the disappearing war, the war over before it is fought, all its uncertainties and indiscernible qualities brought "inside" and placed under rational control, is as old as the desire to avoid the killing ground of battle. In the fifth century BC, Sun Tzu claimed the key to success in war was foreknowledge (Tzu 1963: 145). Armed with quick and accurate information on the status of the enemy, coordinated by a central command with a clear set of objectives, victory could be achieved with minimal losses to *all* (and not just friendly) forces. Today armies everywhere are investing heavily in new simulation technologies to realize this dream. Increasing importance is attached to research on various applications of artificial intelligence, from Strategic Defense research to so-called "pilot's associates" (computer decision aids for pilots of modern aircraft), from applications of chaos theory to battlefield management systems (Athanasiou 1989). Newer branches of AI research, those involving optical pattern recognition, are exploring the possibilities of "machine-vision" systems that might be used for various combat and non-combat functions that are now done by human soldiers – collecting the dead from the battlefield, for example.

Many scientists believe that the potential of these battlefield management systems has been severely overestimated. The military, however, sees things differently – in their view, AI can reduce casualties, simplify strategic decision-making, train soldiers for combat contingencies, and coordinate massive amounts of information generated by sophisticated electronic sensors and communications devices. Integrated with the newest image-enhancement technologies for observing the enemy under adverse conditions (at night, in bad weather, etc.), AI promises to shorten the time of war, to enable its conduct at a distance and out of harm's way, to transfer the war, that is, to the security of a completely controlled cybernetic environment. The contradictions and paradoxes of this project have apparently escaped military planners. The battlefield, it turns out, has not been brought inside, the war outside has not been brought under rational control, casualties (overall) have not been reduced (if anything, AI research promises a more deadly battlefield). Instead, "inside" and "outside" have lost their sense as the virtual observation-machine has gained autonomy over all aspects of combat and its preparation, from the battlefield to the command bunker to the generation of public opinion. And war itself has grown more deadly, more unpredictable, despite the evolution of a host of simulation-surveillance technologies designed to make it disappear, to make it impossible. But this, of course, is an old story.

"War is perhaps impossible: it continues nonetheless everywhere you look" (Baudrillard and Lotringer 1987: 111). In fact, nuclear war appears to be the only "impossible" war, completely relegated to simulation since World War II – endlessly updated scenarios of deterrence, estimations of first- and second-strike capabilities, psychological games of threat and counter-threat, geopolitical maneuvering. Nuclear war is virtual war *par excellence*, war generated entirely with models, pure war, not "unthinkable," to recall Herman Kahn's words (1984), but thought out and articulated to the point of its disappearance. At the same time, other, more "conventional," wars – wars of national liberation, civil wars, insurgency, counter-insurgency, terrorism, border disputes, environmental war, religious and racial conflicts – continue unabated at an accelerated pace (Gray 1989: 44).

But aren't these wars, too, becoming "impossible"? Modern weapons engineering is outpacing the skills of combat soldiers. As the speed and deadly force of weapons is multiplied, the drive is on to engineer the human combatant to operate fearlessly in a territory he can no longer see and can barely comprehend. In developments that are still in their infancy, cyborg soldiers are being trained on visionic simulators that replicate battle conditions, outfitted in electronic headgear that filters and translates incoming information, plugged into computer "associates" that flash out decision options (or automate decisions altogether), all mechanical interfaces *ergonomically* designed for maximum comfort and efficiency, molded to the body. Video war-games for use between missions to relieve stress, video chaplains for spiritual preparation. And the modern cyborg soldier will have all the latest high-tech drugs to focus his mind on his objective and eliminate fatigue, without the numbing fear that develops in a situation where the enemy is invisible. Anti-viral and anti-bacterial vaccines, chemicals to retard nausea and control various other body functions, skin-graft sprays for burns, miniaturized sensors to warn of chemical or biological attack. In perhaps the most fantastic developments of all, military biocybernetic research is exploring direct brain–computer, neuron to silicon, connections, the goal being to "develop biochips that can be activated by hormones and neural electrical stimulation and which can, in turn, initiate hormonal and mental behavior in humans. It is hoped that such human–machine integration will result in quicker reaction times, better communication, improved control and greater reliability" (Gray 1989: 53).

Here we reach a point where the simulation machine and the surveillance machine converge in a cyborg apparatus under the paradoxical sign of the end of war. Welded to a machinery that once again brings the chaos of combat back into (electro-optical) view and (digitalized, preserved) time, the psychocybernetic warrior fights on a virtual killing ground, where death is the blue-gray static on a video screen, signifying the target has been killed.

Virtual spies

If the enemy can be seen, he can be killed. It is the same if he can be blinded or otherwise rendered unable to see. Observation and its elusion, from the very beginning, constitute the strategy and the paradox of war, where material carnage is brought into alignment with the immaterial force of appearances. For Sun Tzu, it was a simple matter of *identification*. Every warlord, he writes, must know the *names* of his enemies – the garrison commander and his bodyguards, the staff officers, the gatekeepers, and ushers – and their affairs in minute detail. He must discover the enemy's condition, resources and weaknesses without revealing his own. Seen for who he *is*, in his nakedness, the enemy becomes the object of a calculation that aims to surprise him at the precise moment his defense slackens (Tzu 1963: 147ff.). Behind this strategy are all the maxims of the control of military force: get an overview of the field of battle, strike faster than your enemy can react – disorient his perception and freeze his lines of communication, blind and deafen him, cut out his tongue, and sever his nerve centers, before he can engage his forces and retaliate.

For his own part, Sun Tzu recommended the wise use of spies: inside and double agents, who are paid to feign loyalty to their leaders; agents who are intelligent but can act stupid, strong at heart but seem dull, who can gain access to a sovereign's intimates, then betray them. Agents whose talents for (mis)representation and the alteration of appearances allow them to live and return with valuable knowledge. But also agents who, if necessary, are expendable, deliberately supplied false information, who become sacrifices to the very technology of ruse and deception that is their stock in trade.

Spy technology has changed dramatically in the last half-century. Simulation, long in the service of covert intelligence, is rapidly coming to subvert a faltering apparatus of observation. Intelligence work today is compartmentalized, mechanized, and inscribed with scientific-sounding acronyms – ACOUSTINT (acoustic intelligence), ELINT (electronic intelligence), FSINT (foreign instrumentation signals intelligence), RDSS (rapidly deployable surveillance systems), etc. (Der Derian 1990: 304). The human agent is increasingly threatened with extinction, unable to function efficiently in the hyperinformated space of battle, doubled by machines, used only to fill in for what can't be covered by technical means, or integrated as one more component into mechanical and electronic monitoring systems, digital photo-enhancement equipment, miniaturized microwave listening devices, and so forth. In an age of satellite surveillance and remote sensing, when political and physical borders no longer serve as obstacles to gathering intelligence, when the secrecy once guaranteed by these borders is virtually impossible to maintain, spying has become a circular (indeed, *orbital*) game of watchers watching watchers, or as Dürrenmatt (1988) has described it, "observing the observers of the observers,"[1] and traditional distinctions, like that between intelligence and counter-intelligence, have begun to break down in the universal circulation of information. Like the cyborg soldier, the modern .spy functions within a closed loop of technologies ostensibly designed to manage the speed and scope of modern war. The latest reconnaissance tools, it is claimed, do what human spies have for centuries been unable to do, viz., serve up images and messages in "real-time," that is, without the delay or distortion that plagued covert intelligence work in the past, and without risk to human life. Geopolitical events around the world will pour across the screens and into the computers of intelligence analysts "as they happen," as the distance which once served as an obstacle to reliable and timely information contracts to the point of its disappearance in the simultaneity of those events and their reproduction.

Or so it appears. Modern espionage technology does not so much capture events in the moment they occur – the ocular myth of instantaneous exposure and communication – as divert flows of information obtained through electro-optical and electro-acoustic means through a computational assemblage which selects, sorts, files, and projects back that information according to a preexisting set of criteria. Contemporary espionage, like modern war in general, takes place in the virtual reality of simulation, cyborg sensors linked to supercomputers that map out the entire array of geopolitical options in advance. Information is not communicated in "real-time" (which is as absurd as saying the events reproduced on an electronic screen occur in "real-space"), but in virtual, purely constructed time (and space), where events unfold according to an immanent, self-contained logic, an immaterial logic of appearances.

War and its preparation have always been this struggle for an immaterial, "spiritual" advantage – for the view which commands the space of conflict by virtue of its comprehensiveness and accuracy; for the disguise of one's own forces, invisibility, indiscernibility, mastery over appearances. "The history of the battlefield," Virilio writes, "is the history of radically changing fields of perception" (Virilio 1989: 7). Today, this struggle is waged in the neutral, "timeless" ether of information, where perception is no longer on a human scale, where cyborg soldiers and spies, armed with an array of electronic sensors and jammers, battle for control of the electromagnetic spectrum.

The electromagnetic spectrum is the channel through which information passes, is, in fact, information itself. Virtually the entire spectrum – radio waves, visible light, ultraviolet radiation – is used in modern war and its preparation (which today amount to the same thing) (de Landa 1991: 179ff.). It is as much a weapon as any explosive device. Skillful "policing" of the spectrum, according to contemporary military thinking, will allow targets to be quickly and efficiently destroyed, and speed victory without crippling losses of life.[2] Such predictions, of course, have been borne out more for the winners than the losers of this kind of combat. Once again, the military myth of the disappearing war intrudes into the conduct of electromagnetic battle. Speed does not guarantee a bloodless battle. Quite the opposite. As Neil Munro (1991) has noted, the same disjunction that existed for war in the past applies to electronic, panspectral war: either you're quick, or you're dead.

The problem, of course, is to gather information on the enemy without revealing one's own status. Some older electronic surveillance technologies, like radar, are "noisy" (or "active," in military terms). That is, they emit signals that can be identified and targeted by the enemy (in war, one person's noise is another's information). Accordingly, much current military research centers around the development of "passive" sensors – high-resolution telescopes used in satellites, image enhancers, thermal viewers, and ultraviolet and microwave technologies – designed to leave no discernible trace of their operation.

These technologies are supported in turn by a host of electronic "counter-" and "counter-countermeasures" (both active and passive) engineered to destroy or confuse the enemy's surveillance system, his ability to receive and transmit messages. The list of these measures, many of which employ simulation techniques, is extensive: anti-radar missiles; sophisticated noise jamming or so-called "smart noise" techniques (which garble messages by *mimicking* them); deception jamming (broadcasting false revealing or misleading information, rumors, etc.); "expendable" jammers (like radar decoys, simulated-surveillance technologies designed to deceive the enemy's own countermeasure forces into attacking); computer viruses; "stealth" techniques (which minimize electronic "signatures," and which we will discuss below); high-energy laser pulses that not only "blind" electronic sensors, but destroy the retinas of enemy soldiers; and a host of "communications security" measures to protect the integrity of messages (spread-spectrum transmission, radio silence, encryption, frequency diversity, and so forth).

For every technology of surveillance, a parallel technology of simulation; for every effort to observe, a method of disguising or foiling observation; a crypto-technology – all are efforts to control flows and breaks of information and thus the outcome of battle. In modern electronic combat, it is increasingly difficult to differentiate these functions, as all messages slip into the homogeneous space of information, as it becomes virtually impossible to extract any meaning from the random flux of images. And as the same weapons systems are utilized for both purposes. Here monitoring assemblages are planted as decoys, the same technology that exposes and targets an object (e.g., lasers) can also be used to blind, communications codes are altered so rapidly that encrypted and decrypted messages start to look identical, and electronic counter-countermeasures begin to disrupt or replicate friendly communications. In electromagnetic battle, the sheer quantity of sensors and jammers, and of the information they transmit, can generate great confusion. Military commanders are finding it impossible to decide, given the shrinking time frames in which modern electronic combat decisions must be made, whether to jam an enemy signal or attempt to decipher it (Munro 1991: 108). Is it true or false, noise or information? This space of undecidability, in which communication and meaning is lost in the chaos of information saturation, is a function of the simulation of modern war, where the need to know, to "see," the conditions of battle not only as they happen but before they occur, has generated instead the infinitesimal difference of events and their electronic replication, the implosion of the virtual and the actual battlefield. Today they are the same (similar, simultaneous, simulacra). Electromagnetic war *is* video-game war, the first real taste of which came in the Persian Gulf, where everything is not only "seen" but "seen beforehand"; where everything is programmed and managed, but where paradoxically the war "outside" becomes indiscernible from the war "inside," both now out of sight, out of time, out of control – and more deadly than ever.

The military simulacrum

In war, "what is perceived is already lost" (Virilio 1989: 4). Knowing this, the military has traditionally invested heavily in technologies designed to foil the detection of its forces. Military deception – camouflage, concealment, diversion, night raids – has an ancient history, and despite all its technological and scientific sophistication, the military, in its perpetual preparation for combat, has never really broken with its prescientific past, its fascination with spectacle, smoke-screens, and sleight of hand, staging appearances and disappearances in order to elude (subvert) the enemy's gaze, to distract or divert his attention, to thwart his calculations and cloud his judgment.

In the twentieth century, such deceptive "counter-surveillance" measures – often designed to *reinforce* the surveillance capabilities of friendly forces – have ranged from the widespread adoption of khaki uniforms by the British in World War I (khaki is Urdu for "mud"), to figure-ground experiments (e.g., the "dazzle" painted ships and planes of World War II) and isoluminescent techniques (such as arranging aircraft lights to mimic background stars), to various kinds of decoy weapons (fake tanks, artillery, radar installations), and even entire simulated military bases. Electromagnetic warfare research is busily devising methods to evade detection by enemy infrared heat sensors, targeting by laser guidance systems, and so on. Recent concentration on so-called "stealth" technologies, such as the B-2 bomber and the latest generation of fighter aircraft, architecturally engineered to reduce radar cross-section signatures, is only one more development in this long history of deception.

But it is a development, nonetheless, with far-reaching consequences. Virilio (1989: 4) has argued perceptively that the military's increasing reliance on stealth technologies signals an inversion of the deterrence principle which has served as the basis for international relations for decades, since effective deterrence is based on the *publicity* of forces, whereas modern stealth weaponry can function only in an environment of cynical secrecy and uncertainty. Deterrence, that is, can no longer be supported by *displays* of military strength or superiority – especially those involving threats to use nuclear weapons, which for years now have been dismissed as not credible. While old ways of thinking die hard in the military, current thought is beginning to move beyond a conventional strategy of deterrence which, grounded in the calculation and optimization of utilities, emphasizes the notion of credible threats: "If you do, or don't do, this, it will cost you dearly" – which can be backed up with visible proof. "Credible" deterrence resorts to spectacles of military power supported by principle of truth (viz., the demonstrability of that power), and which are reinforced by a multiplicity of unconcealment practices involving verification of the strength of enemy forces, counter-surveillance/counter-verification measures, and the public show of forces ("saber-rattling"). Military spectacles of this kind today are rapidly being absorbed into simulation, where the strategies of truth and unconcealment – to reveal the enemy's display of force for what it *is*, to display one's own forces for what they *are* – are giving way to a strategy of doubling, of the production of imperceptible differences the effect of which is to create a radical uncertainty regarding power's use or non-use, its truth or falsity, reality or appearance, presence or absence. This is what stealth technology, and military simulation technology in general, does. It is a technology of power that controls not through its organization of space and time, but through their replication – to produce the effect of being here but not here, now but not now, to leave a virtual and perpetual question mark in the mind of the enemy. And it completely inverts a theory and practice of deterrence necessarily grounded in the stable opposition of these categories.

Secrecy has always surrounded the military effort to deter the enemy or deny him his objectives; a threat proven to be not credible is no longer a threat. But the new technologies of war – stealth, communications jamming and encryption, electronic decoys – aim at far more (and far less!) than secrecy. (For all the secrecy that surrounded the development of the Stealth bomber, it has been almost obscenely visible in other ways, in televised public relations attempts to secure congressional funding, to persuade the American public of its feasibility and value, and to parade US wartech to potential buyers abroad.) If stealth can be made to work, it produces *indecisiveness*, and indecisiveness produces *time*. Less time for the enemy to react, more time (breathing time!) for friendly forces to target and strike. Like all forms of military simulation, stealth aims to slow or otherwise control the pace of events (at least for one's own forces), to manage a situation of threat. This, of course, links it to more conventional forms of deterrence. It too is part of the military imagination, the dream to make war disappear, to "freeze" it, make it *stop*. It is a myth, because the military believes the simulated war will *end* the real war, simply by repeating its images. What the military seems unable to appreciate is that the simulated war *is* the real war; at least this is where the technology, admittedly still in its early stages, promises to lead us.

Part of the problem is that we, and the military, still define war as the limited *time of battle,* that span when casualties occur, when soldiers and civilians die, cities are destroyed. But in fact combat marks just a brief spasm of death in a game of death that precedes it and passes through it, "out of time," traverses it in the timeless space of simulation, in endless technological *preparation* for war (combat training, public relations, military "exercises," stealth, video battle games, GI Joes, Top Guns, virtual reality headgear, and, of course, continuous, omnipresent electronic surveillance). This is the daily, quotidian, "peacetime" *replication* of the war machine, technological preparation for a fight that consumes the energy of entire cultures, and turns us all into soldier-civilian-cyborgs.

Despite all this, deterrence is not over, only transfigured, to satisfy the changed conditions of war. Once based on publicity, now it functions through indecision and uncertainty, as once-simplistic bipolar models (superpower deterrence scenarios) are replaced by more complicated, "realistic" models utilizing multiple variables (perhaps reflecting changes in the Soviet bloc, eastern Europe, etc.), fuzzy logics, psychological models of threat, variable decision options, probable outcomes (see George and Smoke 1974). Deterrence, no stranger to simulation and display in the past, now threatens to identify itself with it fully, as hostilities develop, threats are delivered, battles rage, nations and their economies are laid to waste, all this endlessly repeated on the electronic screens and in the supercomputers of the military information machine.

Deterrence and preparation

In all these examples of military practice and technology, surveillance and simulation link together in complex and reciprocal relations of reinforcement and subversion. In multiple ways, simulation supports a logistics of military perception; it fashions a "techno-environment" where observation is (ideally) controlled and risk-free, where battle, which increasingly takes place out of human view, is brought back to vision via electronic reproduction, as information. In doing so, it redefines – and "plays" with – the time of combat, slowing it, putting it on rewind, replaying it, fast-forwarding, pausing it for a closer look, storing it for future reference (war as videotape). Simulation converts the war into data and thereby attempts to manage the perceptual nightmare modern battle has become – to react to its numbing speed, the explosion of communications, sensory and cognitive overload. It aims to remedy the failings of the military observation-machine, failings generated in part by the very complexity of that machine, by rendering its object *explicit* once again. Once more war comes into view and into time, but now the time and view of simulation, a "reconstructed" space-time, no longer "combat," but sim-war, cyborg war, a war of electronic sensors and jammers.

All this is gradually and subtly subverting the observation machine, as surely as a technology of replication, elusion, and mimicry subverts a technology of exposure. Perhaps it is too early to know, but in the war of sensors and jammers, the jammers may be winning. The Persian Gulf War was an indication of just how far this technology has evolved in the years since Vietnam, and how important it has become in modern war and its preparation. Stealth weaponry, electronic decoys, simulated training, mock exercises, precombat targeting, weapons programming, scenario construction, battlefield management – all of these factors seem to have been important in the speedy destruction of Iraqi surveillance, communications, and control functions by US-led forces in the Persian Gulf. In a movement contrary to what it was designed for, however, simulation technology is also increasing the "fog" of war, making it more difficult for military personnel to separate artifice from reality, true from false appearances, friendly (or neutral) from hostile forces – that is, disrupting the functions of the military surveillance apparatus. Der Derian (1990: 301), for example, thinks that the excessiveness of combat training and the automation of sophisticated weapons systems (to speed decisions, to more rapidly verify, identify, target, and fire on enemy forces) may have in part been responsible for the shooting down of a civilian Iraqi airbus by the USS *Vincennes* several years ago. Other such "accidents" appear to be on the rise, as friendly forces are increasingly mistaken for the enemy in combat, as hostile and friendly communications become more difficult to differentiate, as the volume of information increases, and as the preprogrammed inflexibility of battle plans overpowers a "reality" that no longer conforms to them in the rapidly changing space-time of battle.

De Certeau (1984) reminds us that wherever the effort to command a space of activity by means of its *exposure* has developed, there has evolved, alongside and against it, an art of inhabiting those "noplaces," those inscrutable, free zones where the watchers are blind, the authorities powerless to act, those spaces "outside time" that resist the imposed directionality of the temporal order and seek to create a separate, free, "timeless" time. At the same time, that art – simulation – is the target of a reappropriation that seeks, in the end, to annihilate it. Simulation is the "target" of surveillance, that is, what it desires to expose and whose processes – the elusion of its spatio-temporal order – it seeks to control. As Sloterdyck (1987: 330ff.) has observed, in the ocular framework of modernity, surveillance is first fashioned as a weapon in the *war against appearances* – a strategy of truth, against everything that presents itself as something else; against, above all, what *disappears* from beneath the gaze of power.

But present-day war is far more than that. For some time now, the military has been fashioning the disappearance of war *in general*, into the homogeneous ether of information. This is not the kind of disappearance that simply aims to elude the enemy's apparatuses of observation, but a paradoxical project that involves raising the entire technology of surveillance to a new level of explicitness, the explicitness of high-resolution electronic imaging, remote sensing, digital enhancement, and integrating those "ocular" technologies with cybernetic equipment, robotics, supercomputers, battlefield artificial intelligence, and a host of similar devices that convert the *war which passes* into the *war that is continually preserved*, updated, revised, played back, repeated, reduced to its "essentials." Present-day war technology, to borrow an image from Deleuze (1989: 68ff.), is like a "crystal" that indiscernibly splits the time of battle in two – the images of battle "as it happens" (on the electronic screens of the surveillance assemblage), and the battle "preserved in repetition" (in the software and circuitry of the simulation assemblage). Ultimately, they are the "same" battle. An uneasy and paradoxical alliance of info-technologies that enhances the cyborgian confusion of the real and unreal that clings to contemporary war.

Today, military imperatives – speed, stealth, control of information – are widely diffused in the culture of postmodern societies. The real and the unreal are not the only distinction to have been blurred by the evolution of war technology. Increasingly, the distinction between the military and other institutions has become just as clouded. This is not a new development. De Landa (1991: 229) writes that:

From the sixteenth century on, drill and discipline were used to turn mercenaries into obedient cogs of the war machine. These military methods were later imported into the civilian world by schools and hospitals. To that extent, tactics, the art of creating machines using men and weapons as components, permanently affected nonmilitary institutions. But it would be wrong to suppose that military influence was exercised solely at the tactical level. At the level of logistics, the problems of military procurement and supply shaped the urban environment in the age of siege warfare and continue to shape the world of economics to the present day. Logistic considerations regarding the procurement of manpower are behind the drive to get humans out of the loop. And the methods the military developed to shorten the chain of command were later exported, through people like Frederick Taylor, to the civilian sector, ... [evolving] into what is known as "management science."

Today, as in the past, military infotech is routinely transformed into "civilian" infotech, simulation and surveillance technologies originally applied to problems of military force increasingly find their way into police work, the labor market, medical and legal institutions, recreation and entertainment realms (video games, war-toys, computer software), and so on. This is also one of the ways war and the military machine "disappear" today: into the wider network of social relations to become a generalized technology of power. The fantasies of military power – victory without cost, the view from the high ground, absolute mastery of time – increasingly organize social production and consumption, as the war economy is transformed into the general economy of nations. As more of the population of postindustrial societies is directly or indirectly involved in military work and functions, as the social identity of individuals is increasingly militarized, the more blurred the conventional distinctions between peacetime and wartime, civilian and soldier, enemy and friend become.

Modern war, as Virilio (1983) correctly saw, is *preparation* for war. The world's military forces do battle with each other every day in simulation, in "fake" exercises, in the endless procurement and testing of military hardware, in forecasting deterrence outcomes, in monitoring and jamming each other's communications, in exploring the ways to be stealthy. Global surveillance of geopolitical events and the world's system of weapons is continuous; supercomputers never stop analyzing and revising this information, planning for military contingencies. "Real" war, when it inevitably comes, is just business as usual, that is, a training ground for – and a simulation of – the *next war* (just as Vietnam, the first true electronic war, was a "preparation" for the Gulf War, a lesson, for some future general or president, in how *not* to conduct the next war).[3]

War as continuous, omnipresent, its sign infusing every relation, and every relation a repetition of war. War transported out of time into simulation. Disappearing war, its material force converted into bits of information, flashes of electronic light, social relations. Television war, scripted war, deterrent war, calculated, "line-drawn-in-the-sand," already-played-out war. This is the military *simulacrum*. A simulacrum, writes Foucault (1988), is a sign that is "at once prophetic and ironic:

hanging from a future that it repeats in advance, and which will repeat it in turn, in broad daylight. It says this, then that, or rather it already said, without our knowing, both this and that ... In its essence, [the simulacrum says] everything simultaneously and ceaselessly simulating something other than what it says. It presents an image that depends on an ever receding truth ..." The military simulacrum is a "double," a generalized figure that refers back to a model of military power that it duplicates, and which is bound to a historical expression that is never completed. War, in its effort to disappear (never entirely successful) – to locate and seize once and for all the source of its power – repeats itself in a movement that continuously alters its nature to become what it always has been, viz., a crude means of domination. Today, war finds its mode of disappearance, its escape from the killing ground, and its means of domination in the electronic simulation of war, that is, of itself, in the transfiguration of the ocular battlefield into the "timeless," managed realm of information. Here, the simulation machine and the surveillance machine support and subvert one another in a game of reversal and paradox that transports death from its isolated, enclosed space, out of view, out of control, into the homes, and onto the screens of an electronic society.

5

Simulation, surveillance, and cyborg work

Simulated work and the limits of exploitation

For Marx, the critique of labor was, among other things, a critique of its exploitation by Capital. Today, however, we need a critique of *simulated labor*, because the simulation of labor is the present condition of its exploitation – or rather, of its *hyperexploitation*, since the traditional means of exploiting labor have reached their limit. Marx had already formulated this limit in his concept of "living, productive labor." Living labor, in Marx, is in fact the limit of Capital itself, both its necessary condition (as the sole source of surplus value) and its final negation (the victory of the laboring classes). In its effort to transcend this condition, and thereby escape its historical destiny, Capital seeks nothing less than the death of living labor. That end is always deferred, however, given that the death of living labor, at least in the sense of annihilating the totality of productive value, also means the death of Capital. Capital's strategic goal, then, is to devise means of exploiting labor to the maximum, short of killing both labor and itself in the process. In Marx's time and until recently, that meant rationalizing, mechanizing, and closely supervising the labor process, to hold down the costs of production and increase productivity. Today, it means much the same thing, but in a much higher register. In telematic societies, the project is to exchange living labor for simulated labor, or what I call "cyborg work," which doesn't mean just work using computers, but the informatization and virtualization of the entire work environment. Cyborg work, in one sense, is the last, best solution for Capital to the problem of its fatal dependence on living labor. In fact, it's the perfect answer for the inability of Capital to annihilate Labor altogether – living labor (miraculously!) can be transformed into something that is itself neither living nor dead. Finally, it's the only solution for a system strangling on its own excess production of dead labor (accumulated Capital), and one, as it turns out, that absorbs Capital into the virtual order right along with Labor (how else, since for Marx they are already just two sides of the same coin?). No more evil exploitation, no more exploited masses, just a clean, positive functionality, a seamless integration of organic and telematic systems.

Exploitation was a strategy better suited to the industrial period of Capital, when the worker had to be *disciplined* (Foucault 1979).[1] Today, it is more a matter of finding ways to jack the worker in, make him or her just one more switch or relay in a growing cybernetic assemblage. This signals a dramatic intensification of the control of labor at the end of the twentieth century, a grand extension of the practice of synchronizing human labor to the rhythms of machines. As labor slides into its simulation in the postindustrial era, so do all the disciplinary methods that were once used to exploit it – the close supervision and inspection of work, meticulous, detailed organization of worktime and workspace, ranking and serializing productive tasks, the alignment and integration of laboring bodies into workforces. These methods are not discarded, but reconfigured and totalized by new information technologies and bio-logics. Worktimes, in this dreamland of hyperproduction, become "any-time-whatevers" (days/nights, weekends, holidays, vacations), workspaces "any-place-whatevers" (factories, homes, offices, cars, planes, sidewalks – the "cellular revolution"). Supervision, but "in advance" – just enter your code. Today, we are crossing the threshold of informated labor, which is also hyperdisciplined labor, and the cyborg is its new "body."

In saying this, we don't have to deny what remains true in Marx's critique. Labor in a postindustrial economy is still exploited, to be sure, still the same old endless drudgery and extortion – *even more so*. The low-paying, eyeball-numbing, stress-inducing jobs in today's computer sweatshops are only one example of how contemporary labor gets exploited to its limit (Attewell 1987; Garson 1988). At the same time, however, the "sweatshop" imagery as a general metaphor for postindustrial labor conditions is misleading and conceals a paradox. The new jobs of the information age point far beyond simple drudge work, which in the past could at least still be said to have a meaning (the production of some use-value), as well as some relatively fixed or bounded coordinates (the workplace, the working day/week). Instead, they are today just one part of a more generalized drudgery that now extends beyond the job, just as "the job" extends beyond the drudgery of a particular place, time, or project (and begins to intrude into almost every sphere of everyday life) (Negri 1991; LeFebvre 1991; Black 1987). What this amounts to is a radical *rematerialization* of the labor process made possible by its conversion into information – now labor resurfaces everywhere and anywhere the telematic network reaches. We'll return to this below. For now, we can say, contra Marx, that Capital in one sense no longer exploits labor at all, because *real* labor, i.e., labor corresponding to any coherent finality – to utility, to meaningful time or sense of place, to value itself – is dead, or at least disappearing as a distinct, discernible form; it is mixing and bleeding into everything else, and what remains after this infusion is only a simulacrum of labor, a "puppet-reference" of its former utility, which serves only to postpone its disappearance altogether. Today, it's becoming more apparent that labor can serve any utility – particularly those forms of labor whose only absolutely necessary qualification is the ability to punch an electronic keyboard or enter a password – a fact which testifies to its more general uselessness.[2] This in turn represents a kind of perverted liberation of labor, one in which it is granted a reprieve to exist in a twilight zone of disenchanted, virtual forms. In this sense, the exploitation of labor was only a historical *preparation* for its simulation, which takes over when labor finally has been *exploited to death*, or as close to it as possible, its utility finally exhausted; the industrial sweatshop, drudge labor, was merely the first approximation in the development of a bio-informatic-telematic assemblage – the virtual sweatshop, if you will – that now redoubles the labor process on a higher level, in the effort to push back, one last time, the limit of its exploitation.

That limit, again, is living labor (or the collective worker, which Marx opposed to the collective forces of Capital and the commodity-form). Beyond it lies the imaginary of cyborg work, the brave new world of ultra-surveilled, silicon-enhanced production – informated offices and factories, home workstations, electronic supervisors, robo-clerks, virtual markets, hypermalls that never close. In fact, cyborg work hyperizes even production itself, to the extent that production, as the creation of new values, corresponded in Marx to the very essence of living labor. The new configurations of informated work carry Marx's idea of overproduction to its extreme – not just the production of things, or even signs of things, but the simulation of production itself. Today, it is information that makes production, and thus living labor, possible. Or rather, information is what virtualizes production, sends it into orbit. Before anything circulates, before any market opens, one must first plug in and log on. If today it is hard to picture how thoroughly information technology will transform the way we work, tomorrow it will be the *un*informated workplace that will be difficult to imagine, and everything that is produced will first be reproduced in information, and that includes the worker himself

(increasingly programmed, bioscanned, background-checked, creden-
tialed, career-tracked, insured, disinsured, and trained to push buttons
that run machines that automatically and continuously monitor his or
her performance).

The cyborg worker is the virtual form of living, productive labor, production in the mode of its self-organization. If living labor was the target of diverse disciplinary mechanisms supporting capital formation in
the industrial period, then cyborg work is targeted only by itself, a fully
self-organized, self-referential mode of control. Cyborg work is the discipline of living labor shifted into hyperdrive, the bionic, wetware answer
to the diminishing returns of exploited labor to industrial-commodity
capital at the end of the twentieth century. Just when we thought more
discipline was impossible, along comes the information age. Foucault's
vision of a million tiny theaters of judgment dispersed across the entire
surface of modern societies has come true with a vengeance. The cyborg
worker – a shorthand concept for all the multiple ways in which organic energy is harnessed and disseminated along informational nets to form
self-regulating systems – represents the radical *collapse* of disciplined
(normalized, surveilled) production as a dialectic of control – in the
cyborg workplace, production *is* control, and control *is* production, and
both are information. At the same time, production and control, workplace and worktime, Labor and Capital, no longer have a definitive
meaning or location in this environment, but rather dissolve into a homogeneous medium which sustains only superficial and indiscernible differences (now any time is worktime, any place a workplace, any time
productive time, no more gap between work and play, work and home,
work and whatever). The cyborg worker, the dream of Capital at the limits of its development, works round the clock and online everywhere.

Capital and labor unlimited

In a discussion of commodities in the *Grundrisse*, Marx (1973: 272)
defines living labor as

non-objectified labor ... *labor* as subjectivity ... which is *present in time*. If it is to
be present in time, alive, then it can be present only as the *living subject*, in which
it exists as capacity, as possibility; hence, as *worker* ... *as value-creating, productive labor.*

Capital, in contrast, is *dead labor* or, in the language of the *Grundrisse*,
labor "present in space" as opposed to time, "past labor" preserved as
exchange-value in the commodity. In Marx, the accumulation of com-

modities is the piling up of dead, past labor, a process limited only by the impossibility of a completely unrestrained expenditure of the labor force. The most abusive systems of exploitation in history are those that simply work people (slaves, soldiers, prisoners) to death that wear them out, then discard them as so much waste or refuse. For Marx, this is the general condition to which Capital, if unchecked, would reduce the entire working class – not much better than dead. If it could extract surplus value from a dead form, capital would dispense with the worker – with living labor – altogether, which for it is always nothing more than another *cost of production*. It would pile up dead forms – that is, *itself* – to infinity. Instead, Capital is forced at every stage of its development to recognize the worker as the only source of added value and to devise minimal means to sustain him. And that's why labor organized by Capital is always a deterred death, a graduated, measured violence against the worker (understood collectively), a managed economy of "little deaths," even as the logic of Capital propels it toward a totalization of death. *Engineering* the death of living labor, always however with an eye to reproducing it minimally, is Capital's constant preoccupation. Indeed, it is Capital's *own* labor, *to which it also seeks a definitive solution* (as Marx knew, Capital itself has no desire to labor). If today that project takes the form of simulating labor, it is to insure that it is no longer a threat for Capital, i.e., a movement that seeks Capital's negation. In accomplishing that, Capital's own labor (the oppressive labor of management, surveillance, discipline, exploitation) comes to an end.

Marx's writings contain many images of Capital as a death-machine or killing ground of labor. There are the references to the worker as a weapon – Capital's "reserve army" of the unemployed, even before being objects of exchange, are a store of projectile bodies, human "munitions" for use in the "war" of production (the competitive war among capitalists). Or again, various intimations of the "cannibalized" worker, a figure of sacrifice and transfiguration: parallel to its role as a force of production, Capital *consumes* living labor and converts it into abstract, fetishized labor (exchange-value). Labor, in turn, is sacrificed to the high gods of capitalist production – money and profit – as a guarantee of its own continued survival. Labor, in Marx, is what is *lost* to life, what is given up in order to live (life, for Marx, always begins outside work, in the public houses, at home, in bed).[3] Capital's consumption of living labor has a limit, too. In cannibalizing labor, Capital cannibalizes itself. Ultimately, Capital cannot incorporate (digest, excrete) the *totality* of labor, even if that is precisely what it desires to do. It must therefore fetter itself, not only as the abstract point toward which all the forces of production converge, but as a consumptive, parasitic force that converts living to dead labor. The totalization of dead labor (excreta) leaves nothing for Capital, itself embodied in the dead labor of machines, to consume – it is the outer limit of Capital and capitalist exploitation, the horizon where it confronts the spectre of its own death (by starvation). It is in the effort to transgress this limit, to consume the totality of living labor, that capital simulates labor, and in so doing begins the transition from a material productive order to a rematerialized, informated order of simulation, a cyborg order. While it can, the system will consume and live off information, the virtual body of the worker. As we have said, it is a fatal strategy for Capital, one whose developments Capital cannot contain, and which finally prove overwhelming for it. Ultimately, Capital itself is pulled into the cyborg order – eventually, the informated body of labor doesn't feed it as much as it, along with Labor, feeds information.

It can be argued that the cyborg worker emerges at a particular historical juncture that corresponds to the crises of industrialism in the United States and western Europe in the late twentieth century, but it is not, strictly speaking, an historical figure; it is, more precisely, a paradoxical figure whose future is already in one sense its history, whose code delineates every function that it *will have carried out* in advance. It is not labor in the present (as Marx would have it, who also identifies "the present" with time). Instead, it is virtual labor: labor in the mode of its "future-past," whose past is its future and vice versa, labor "out of time" (the linear, blocked time of production) – each individual worker a clone, each one's development a function of a code that precedes his birth and coordinates his production until he dies (the telemated, genetically engineered workforce) (Bogard 1994). Cyborgs can be designed to simulate conscious or intelligent human labor but, as we have seen for all simulated objects, they can never be more than their code. Technically, a cyborg doesn't "work" at all; it *operates*. That it "works," that it "produces," is only the effect of a prior operationalization that is directed in the first instance only back toward itself. Production requires an external, i.e., human input. Cyborg work is self-organizing. Had Marx lived into the age of information technology and bio-power, he would have noted that cyborgs are not really "workers" at all. They are *prosthetic* objects – figures of a more general prosthetization of organic life and society – and they send the old organic:inorganic, alive:dead dualisms of the traditional critique of political economy into postindustrial orbit. Neither humans nor machines, they are, in today's terms, electronic media–body connections, biodigital circuits of varying complexity and scope, ergonomic alignments of organs, screens, and switches. For industrial Capital in ruins at the end of the century, i.e., for a system suffocating its own accumulation of waste – dead labor, rusting machines, polluted languages, all the detritus of capitalist consumption – they are utopian figures portending clean, instantaneous, telematic control of the labor process, the final solution to the problem posed by living labor, by *labor as such*. Think only of all the hype today surrounding information technology – how easy and convenient it makes life (not work at all!), how accessible it makes everything (signs, images, products), how potentially "liberating" it is (freeing workers to become their own managers, for "reskilling" the workforce, reducing bureaucratic hierarchy and red tape) (Zuboff 1988), how environmentally friendly and clean it is (the paperless office, the home office, no more drive to work, etc.). Ultimately, these developments, we are told, are supposed to signal the end of the struggle between Labor and Capital itself, the end of exploitation and alienation, as informated technology takes over production and leaves more time and energy for all of us to enjoy life's pleasures (our home offices, our cellular phones, our televisions!). In this fantasy, all the problems of industrial Capital and exploited Labor dissolve, fade away forever in the uniform medium of electronic impulses.

We are now beginning to experience the effects of this utopia and they are not at all what we imagined. As it turns out, labor does not die or get easier, doesn't fade away, but rather returns with a vengeance, and in its most obscene forms, in the pure operationalism of cyborg work. Rather than a paradise of leisure and free time, cyborg work turns out to be more work than ever. In fact, it is *only* work, or work is only it, which amounts to the same thing. Cyberwork doesn't so much liberate work as raise the tedium factor of labor to truly creative levels, work whose sheer emptiness is only intensified by its monumental sameness and repetitiveness – enter, edit, format, store in memory, repeat operation. No matter what other skills you might possess, these are the ones that matter first and most, and what increasingly occupy your time. Keyed into a universal system of information, everyone can be a worker, and everyone a boss. You can choose the time of work (the myth of "flex-time"), but all times are equally work. Cyborgs, in short, signal not the end but rather the *exorbitance* of the relations between Capital and Labor, pure ecstasies of exploitation and discipline which erupt today even at the most microcellular levels of experience. They are points of concentration of forces around problems that relate to the *genetic* control of labor, bio-engineered to fit the job, generated by codes and systems of controlled feedback. Cyborg workers herald, at the close of the industrial period, not just the disappearance but the resurrection of both Capital and Labor as disenchanted simulacra, in the ultra-saturated, hyperspace/hypertime of information.

In an order of simulation, the problem of the limit of living labor undergoes a fantastic mutation. Cyborg labor, we have said, is neither living nor dead, but a mixture of living and dead forms. In science fiction or fantasy, which contemporary work increasingly resembles, the cyborg is a miraculous, impossible assemblage, an electric body or an intelligent machine. It is not an autonomous subject, but one component in a larger unity composed of identical elements (like monads or holographic pixels, each part contains, from its own singularized perspective, the whole). It is closely related to the robots and mechanical men of the industrial period of Capital (and to the automaton of the Renaissance era) and has analogs in various human–machine (tool) pairings throughout history, but it is properly a postindustrial figure. Its primary mode of analysis is *ergonomic* – the relations of power along the *points of contact* between the body and an informated surface, where the questions that are raised have to do with modular "fit," alignment, contour, pressure, smoothness of response, and from there to general systems design, communication loads and tolerances, receiver–operator interfaces, and so forth. The cyborgs of today's informated workplaces – the electronic offices, the automated factories, the computer "sweatshops" – are, in crude form at least, but already fully in terms of the logic of their development, wetware assemblages, machines wired into bodies plugged into machines to produce the *signs* (or rather the *signals*, the telematics) of living labor, the signals of production itself.

Cyborgs reopen a virtual timespace for work that would otherwise be dead (or exhausted), one in which all contingencies associated with production are modeled, modulated, and circuited directly through the body of the worker. The low-wage jobs in the computerized service sector of the economy are the most patent examples of modern cyborg work (telemarketing, reservations, operator assistance). These jobs are programmed, homogeneous, self-regulated, and, beneath all "clinical" signs of life, quite dead (or comatose, since they don't require a brain to do them). But ultimately, cyborg work spans all levels and sectors of the postindustrial economy and obeys no class distinctions or hierarchical divisions between manual and mental labor; blue-collar or white-collar occupations; staff or line. Labor that in any way today interfaces with modern bio- or infotech qualifies, to some extent, as cyborg work. Any kind of labor, i.e., potentially can be simulated, can be mediated by some form of biotelematic, simulation apparatus (teaching, medical work, even, in the case of AI technology, programming). This is also, we shall see below, what increasingly causes contemporary work to shade off into areas of experience that formerly were considered to be exterior to or separate from work – leisure and play, for example, or "domestic" life – as computerization and communication technologies transform the office or factory into an any-space- or any-time-whatever (at least, within the spatio-temporal constraints of the technology – wherever the central processing unit can be located), when every activity is potentially work and work fills every activity. Work unlimited, we could say, a formula for ultra-modern Capital.

To simulate living labor is something akin to taxidermy. It is to *preserve* a dead (or dying) form and restore it to a *semblance* of its former life, to selected aspects of its idealized past (like the stuffed animal dioramas in museums of natural history). In this sense, cyborg work closely resembles the older forms of commodity production, which (for Marx) preserves "past labor" as exchange value. What a cyborg "produces," however, is less a commodity than an immediate record or index of its performance – viz., information, that most mysterious and paradoxical commodity. (Information systems, in their imaginary form, are not really systems of exchange at all. One bit is as valueless, or valuable, as another. Think only of the "exchanges" that occur when you channel cruise the images on your TV, with the push of a button flipping between scenes of war, comedy, sales hypes, video-evangelists, pro wrestling – all pure equivalences. It may be possible to say that one image is "traded" for another, but it's still a fact that exchange systems rely at least on minimal differences in the value of the objects of exchange, i.e., differences in the needs they satisfy. The only "need" that gets satisfied in channel cruising, however, is the one for the stuporific, purely formal pleasure of circulation itself. The content of the images themselves, which would allow them to be placed within a system of equivalences, makes no difference.) In any case, cyborgs, to return to our thought, are apparatuses ruled not just by their pasts, but also by their futures, the records they *will have* generated from the codes that govern their virtual form of existence – their labor is always already "formatted." Like the preserved animals in the taxidermist's shop, or the startlingly "authentic" figures in museum dioramas, their overcoded postures and ideally portrayed environments will eventually become the sole standard for how we imagine their existence in "real" life, or rather, how that life would have been if it wasn't already (or soon-to-be) extinct. Cyborg work looks remarkably like the commodity production of the past (even more so!), but in fact is only its disenchanted, informated simulacrum.

This process has been in development for some time now. Political economy implicitly recognizes a primitive simulation dynamic in Capital in the reference to so-called "labor-saving" or time-saving technologies, technologies that can replicate a specific, measurable unit of the labor process. These technologies are perverse, however, in that they save labor-time only to free it for other and further tasks (not least among them building and servicing "labor-saving" machinery), closing the circle of work and prolonging labor's utility, such as it is, for Capital. The critique of political economy has long understood that labor is not really saved at all here – mechanization and automation in fact, force it into even greater expenditures than before. Juliet Schor (1991: 1), for example, has noted that despite dramatic increases in productivity as a result of technological innovation, the average American has not seen an increase in leisure or free time, but rather an addition of almost a full day to the working week in the last two decades.[4] This is only one aspect of a more general phenomenon, however. Periodic increases in productivity from the nineteenth century to middle of the twentieth century associated with technological change always meant more, not less, labor even for workers thrown out of jobs by machines. Conventional economic wisdom classifies unemployment as the opposite of work when it in fact is its most consuming form. Anyone who has had to work to find a job knows this – compiling documents, searching, the embarrassment of interviews, retraining, the consuming labor of living without an income. In capitalist economies, unemployment is always the *highest and most intense form*, and not just an effect, of exploited work.

The fact, then, that cyborg work is still work, just more of it, is not surprising. Recent studies of information and communications workers, for example, reveal high levels of stress, chronic fatigue and exhaustion, and other physical or mental problems. Most office workers know that computers do not save their labor or make their jobs easier at all, but rather multiply and compress the quantity of required tasks and intensify the passage of time (again, burn-out and stress are common complaints among these groups). The critique of political economy naturally tends to view such problems dialectically, as alienation, externality, and otherness. Here, "saving labor" is an ideology that masks the reality of machine domination and labor servitude. The imaginary of this system is much different, however. In this zone, a cyborg is a closed circuit; all its relations are internally structured. As a biomachinic assemblage, it cannot (even falsely) "save" someone's labor-time, since *someone* is already an integrated component of the whole. You can't save (or even *not* save) a cyborg worker. It can't be "liberated." Such concepts are meaningless today. Its labor is already saved, already liberated, stored in its files and codes. It *is* the liberation of labor, or rather the very consequence of its liberation, how labor that would be dead from overwork manages to carry on, despite the stress and burn-out. Without info-tech, we ask, who could possibly do all the work required? Without the biocybernetization of work, how could the worker survive in an intensely oversaturated environment? Recall the cyborg soldier – wired, pumped up with pharmeceuticals, hypertrained, scanned for imperfections – is this the future of work, how we now deal with the pressures of remaining productive, staying alive in an informated economy that increasingly squeezes our time and brains? The cyborg has its own "time," a simulated, virtual temporality which conforms to neither the "unnatural" rhythms of machines nor the "natural" rhythms of the body, but to the reversible, variable, interactive rhythms that run along their points of contact (the surface of the computer keyboard, for example, where touch is informated and projected on a screen to simulate the passage of thought). Cyborg work doesn't need to be saved, which is precisely why Capital turns to it in crises of industrial development. Cyborg workers don't die, they just go offline. They are like upgradable, plug-in modules, easily cloned, reproducible to infinity. For Capital, their "lives," their time, are a matter of complete indifference.

Simulation, surveillance, and *la perruque*

In *Simulations*, Baudrillard (1983b: 86) writes how in the Renaissance work already suffers the same destiny as the emancipated sign: both are liberated from prior systems of obligation, but only to produce a new order of general equivalents. With the collapse of the feudal order, "free" labor is systematically organized under the commercial law of value (free to exchange like any commodity). The "free worker" becomes an ideological figure of the system of production, a distortion or false appearance of political economy serving to mask the general *unfreedom* of work and its "real" function, as abstract exploited labor, in reproducing Capital. Baudrillard refers to such distortions, we have seen, as second-order simulacra (ideological formations), here the order of appearance proper to *production*, the "dominant scheme of the industrial era." Each order of appearance, for Baudrillard, absorbs the prior order and the form of value corresponding to it, and reconstitutes them as higher-order images (as "simulation references"). Thus, in Baudrillard, the law of *natural value*, which governs appearances in the Renaissance before the industrial revolution, is only a "simulation reference" of the subsequent law of *commercial value* – commodification, profit, accumulation – that dominates from the eighteenth century to the middle of the twentieth century. In the present order of appearance, it is the commercial law of value, and production itself, that exists only as a simulation reference. The evolution of third-order simulacra constitutes the regime of simulation proper (the reference to real production masking a permanently absent form), governed by the *structural* law of value and the emergence of a *hyperreal* economy. Here the dialectic of appearance (or illusion) and reality that generates the ideological formations of production gives way to the dominance of virtual forms. The technical logic of codes and models, clones and cyborgs, contributes to this general implosion, which is not exactly the end of political economy and production but, according to Baudrillard, their *transfiguration and apotheosis*: under the present (structural) law of value,

Capital no longer corresponds to the order of political economy; it uses simulation as a simulational model ... Hence, in a way, political economy is guaranteed a second life, in the framework of an apparatus where it loses all self-determination, but where it retains its efficacy as a reference of simulation.
(Baudrillard 1988a: 121)

Like the cyborg preserves dead labor, simulated production preserves Capital, but as its informated double. Capital, in Baudrillard, cannot contain simulation, which as a general dynamic subverts every determination, every limit, of political economy. When Capital turns to simulation, it is an indication that "real" production, that Capital itself, is on the way out, that now only the signs of production and Capital matter. The periodic value crises of production (overproduction, falling rate of profit) that had renewed Capital throughout the industrial period are over, having given birth to a telematic economy that now works by mimicking crises (all economic crises are first crises of information – market crashes, investment black holes, currency inflations and deflations, TV trade wars, all so many epiphenomena of the circulation and diffusion of digitalized forms). In Baudrillard's earlier formulations, this is the "political economy of the sign," the order of the sign-commodity. Later, however, the sign-form of production itself gives way to a pure process of signalization, a definitive apotheosis of production, its elevation to the realm of pure simulacrum. In telematic societies, cyborg work is not simply *un*productive, or even *non*-productive; it is, in fact, *ultra*-productive, production as information and information as production, one and the same. Information is what cyborgs "produce," and produce to excess. And information, in turn, is what produces cyborgs. For Capital, this is like a fantastic, wonderful dream, because it collapses the gap between production and control, between labor and the management of labor. Capital can rest easy, so it thinks; its work is over. Cyborg workers can be designed to produce, and produce *only*, the very measure of their production, viz., information; from output to input, the whole process is self-regulated and self-organizing, never having to touch ground. Cyborg labor frees production to fold back on and redouble itself.

But in one sense, this is also Capital's worst nightmare. The movement to close the gap between production and control also explodes the very principle on which Capital was founded, the alienation or externality of the product and the producer. Cyborg labor, in a paradoxical movement, *supports* capitalist production only to *subvert* historically sedimented relations of power in the workplace. When both product and producer become references in simulation, when work escapes the constraints of space and time and is free to rematerialize anywhere (as informated work is), when virtual production substitutes for production, control slips from the grasp of Capital. Social class differences don't matter in the least to the apparatuses of simulation; they serve worker and capitalist indifferently, and dominate them indifferently, too.

Simulation, then, is not solely Capital's prerogative, and certainly not its "private property." Working people, in fact, have always known how to reverse the poles of the control of labor using simulation. In France, they call this *la perruque*, "the wig," all those ingenious ways workers have devised to trick their employers or supervisors into thinking they are working, or that make their work less burdensome (de Certeau 1986: 185–192). *La perruque* can be almost any form of work, perhaps, we shall see, even informated, cyborg work itself. Its origins are ancient, dating back to the earliest forms of duping the Master; its most familiar forms (to us) correspond to second-, not third-order simulacra: disguises, masks, feints, decoys. It can be anything from a secretary writing personal letters on the boss's time to a delivery person using the employer's truck to move personal items to computer hacking (cyborg *la perruque?*). It presents itself as a kind of improvisation or *bricolage*, i.e., a making do with items that are designed or intended for other, more restricted, purposes, or that belong to someone else. It can transform certain features of work, such as its rhythm or everyday routine, into an occasion for subverting work's dominant cultural meaning (as, for example, when field workers sing traditional songs to accompany the monotonous tempo of harvest, and thus make work something *for them*). De Certeau notes that *la perruque* is different than simple theft or pilfering on the job, because nothing (or usually relatively little) of material value is stolen.

Instead, it is more like "looking busy," "looking productive," or "going through the motions at work," a kind of pretense or ruse, which also distinguishes it from simple slacking or the refusal of work. The wig is still "work," if work can be the "work" (effort) of not working (for someone else), the "work" of keeping up the appearances of work. It is the point where a job or a task becomes theater, or play, or reverie, or daydream, or any of a multiplicity of other things. The wig demands an equivalent, and perhaps even greater, investment of energy on the part of the worker (as a kind of supplement to his or her labor, that "accompanies" production). Although not productive per se, it takes place within an order of production and expends itself "acting out" that order. What matters to workers is that work appears strictly *confined* to the labor required by their employer or supervisor, that it replicates that labor in all its mandatory and observable details while simultaneously remaining wholly and radically other.[5] Work of this kind always exists in a state of tension, because the division between appearing to produce and really producing is unstable. This instability in turn reflects the power of *la perruque*. It silently accompanies the labor process like its hidden double. When skillfully performed, it is indistinguishable from the daily routines of the workplace, yet it quietly subverts those routines by feigning or mimicking their procedures.

La perruque, de Certeau says, diverts time on the job to the worker's personal use. More precisely, he claims that workers find ways to utilize their work*time* to resist the *spatial* control strategies of their employers or, more simply put, to elude workplace surveillance and discipline. These temporal maneuvers, which take advantage of contingencies within the architectural and political order of the workplace, take place "out of view," unnoticed by supervisors (or their optical-mechanical surrogates, cameras, listening devices, monitors). They form vanishing points within the general apparatus of surveillance, blind spots along the edge of work's visibility. Every worker learns these tactics on the job, how to *disappear* in a "timely way" beneath the passing gaze of the boss, how to project an image of working when he or she passes by, and they vary with the diverse nature of the tasks and schedules of surveillance. In multiple and contingent ways, *la perruque* "deterritorializes" the workplace and disrupts, at least temporarily, its grid of productive relations. Ultimately, it breaks the conventional identification of "work" and "place," opening a space (on the shop floor, in the office, on the assembly line) where creativity and play momentarily outwit the regimen of production.

But *la perruque* does not just occur "out of view" of workplace surveillance. It is not simply a temporal tactic of resistance set against a spatial strategy of supervision, but one that can operate directly on work-time itself.[6] It can, for instance, be an overexaggerated replication of the schedules of work. Sometimes perfect adherence to the schedules of production can subvert production, as in the old practice of "working to task," doing exactly what's required, no more, but no less either. Or again, workers often develop skills that allow them to simplify and complete assigned tasks in less than the scheduled time, or to give the impression that they take more, freeing time for themselves. Or they develop subroutines that cut across the established temporal series of the workplace, managing to get their own work done, finding ways to socialize with fellow workers, to relax the work pace, and to maximize breaktime, all the while getting the boss's work done, too. For someone skilled in *la perruque*, worktime becomes a little more like the natural rhythms of life, more livable, it has a more open and certainly more tolerable pulse (but not noticeably different to management!). *La perruque*, as it has developed in the industrial period, plays in innumerable ways with the *speed of work*, slowing it down, speeding it up, putting it on pause, varying its tempo. It makes the workday *pass* in such a way that it remains to some extent the worker's (even as s/he works for someone else). This is more than just stealing a few minutes here and there from the boss. And it is more than simply *using* worktime creatively (this way of speaking still relies too much on the old utilitarian-productivist language). It is, in the imaginary of things, about inhabiting a virtual worktime, one that doubles the time of the "job." That is, workers who practice "the wig" try to construct a secret *world of work's duration*, an invisible, "lost" dimension[7] alongside the exhausting world of sequential production. Although the worker inhabits it, and although in one sense it exists *for* the worker, in another this world of work really "belongs" to no one, and no one really controls it. In a basic way, it is fundamentally out of control altogether – for management, certainly, but in one sense for the worker, too, who is in no better position than the manager to draw the line between what is work and what is not. Instead, *la perruque* is a simulation game. If it's still work, it is also something more than work. When work is a game, is it still work? Yes and no. It's an open question. Or rather, it is up to the rules of the game – and not the "players" – to define what counts as work and what doesn't (or who is a worker or a manager, and who isn't). The wig is a game of self-enclosed signs, one of workers' many ways of covertly subverting the imperatives of production, which are always organized around a principle of reality – to be in *this* place at *this* time doing *this* task. This place, for *la perruque*, is at the same time somewhere else, another space. This task, in this series of tasks, is now a task in another series, but the two series, to anyone that observes them, are the same. In its highest forms, *la perruque* is not so much a struggle of Labor against Capital as a parody of Capital, the slightest exaggeration of its operations. It doesn't *visibly* alter production, but instead quietly breaks down the structures of meaning and power that relate production to work. One "produces," but it's not "work," or one "works," but doesn't really "produce" anything. One plays at work and works at play. Anyone who simulates work in these ways makes a mockery not just of production, *but of work itself*. Marx would never have been able to mock productive work in this way, so fundamental was its meaning to his conception of class struggle and revolution. It had to have a sense that, at the most basic level, was universal and fixed. *La perruque*, however, teaches us that the meaning of work can slide ever so gradually, that it is not fixed, that power in the workplace is a matter of the manipulation of infinitesimal differences, and above all, that the forces of simulation might be even greater than the forces of production.

Capital knows that production demands the *territorialization and temporalization* of work, i.e., the strategic deployment of tasks and the imposition of schedules; it imposes a "geography" and a rhythm-tempo of work. The classic struggle of the workplace, in this framework, is about who controls the space and time of work. *La perruque*, however, sets aside this struggle in favor of an effort to *reterritorialize and retemporalize* the media of control (see Deleuze and Guatarri 1987: 453–456). It simulates, not controls, space and time. "Control" happens without it (the work gets done, the work goes on). In doubling work in this covert and silent way, it erases the line between control and freedom, work and not-work, work and everything else. The worker who practices *la perruque* says: whatever else I'm doing at the time, in this place, I can make it appear like I'm working. Any place or time whatever can look like work, be work.

La perruque and cyborg work, we sense, have much in common. What distinguishes *la perruque* from cyborg work is not that the former is a strategy of Labor in the industrial period, the latter a strategy of Capital in the postindustrial age. Formally, strategically, in their subversive relation to production they are the same. In both, production becomes simulated production. In one sense, cyborg work is a postmodern mutation of *la perruque*, as third-order simulacra are of second-order simulacra. Cyborg work dispenses with Capital far more effectively than *la perruque* ever could. It converts Capital into information wholesale, where *la perruque* is more like a child's game with masks. And it dispenses with Labor far more efficiently than Capital could ever have accomplished on its own. Thus, perversely, cyborg work aims to fulfill the utopian dreams of both Labor *and* Capital – the end of production (even while maintaining the appearance of producing to excess), the end of work (even while work now accompanies us everywhere).

Hypersurveillance and the simulation of work – computers and the new diagnostics

Cyborg work is a function of hypersurveillance, i.e., extreme, excessive surveillance, pushed to its limit or line of totalization, unlimited control as a function of exposure. By definition, no aspect of cyborg work escapes the surveillance apparatus, because its own surveillance, a continuous record of its own operation, is, in effect, exactly what that work "produces." Filing an order, confirming a reservation, programming a task: any work accomplished via data entry leaves a trail, automatically. More, any work whose tasks can themselves be broken down and transformed into functions of coded instructions is surveilled even before it begins. This is really nothing new. It was already an explicit goal of Frederick Taylor's plans for the scientific management of production in the early part of the twentieth century, where the ideal worker would be someone who could be easily trained to conform to a highly coded, detailed, and prestructured pattern (Taylor 1984). For Taylor, the need for more reactive forms of surveillance or discipline would be minimized, since laborers from the beginning would be precisely matched for jobs. Or rather, the job itself, in the abstract, would have already been so perfectly specified, measured, and scientifically evaluated, so simplified to make for easy and efficient repetition, that the "work" of surveillance would be complete before the task was begun. Routine surveillance on the job, of course, might still be necessary, but less as a reactive measure and more as assurance of regular, smooth compliance with an abstract series of operations (profile) generated by a prior, rigorous method of observational control, i.e., with a preexisting "record" of the labor process.

Work has always been subject to supervision or "oversight," although the techniques of that supervision are as varied as the historical forms of labor and labor resistance. For each strategy of resistance, we can specify a complementary form of control, which both attempts to block that strategy and provokes new ones (Foucault noted how every exercise of power always generates countermeasures) (Foucault 1982: 225). For slacking off at work, new methods of worker accountability – quotas, quality checks, assembly lines, the labor contract; for arriving late or leaving early, time-clocks and schedules and work-forms; against worker alliances, networks of informers and supervisors; and against workers' jealous guarding of their knowledge of the details of work and their ownership of skills, mechanizing, dividing, informating, and coding the labor process as a whole. Despite the diversity of these strategies, there is a certain continuity in the logic of their evolution from earlier to postindustrial forms of surveillance, however, which, at its most basic level, is simply to *force work by holding it in view and fixing it in time*, and with these means to eliminate any *waste* of time and energy, to discipline and regiment the workforce into an efficient, productive machine. Throughout the industrial period, the apparatus of surveillance not only keeps work in view, it *informs* on work, i.e., discreetly records and deciphers its movements "from behind," "out of sight" (Capital, throughout its modern development, tracks the laborer in the most detailed but unobtrusive ways it can muster, keeping as many aspects of the labor process as possible visible and accessible, while its own operations remain covert). In industrial modes of production, every worker is surreptitiously tagged by the *sign* of his or her work, which functions like its silent double. "Good work," productive, efficient work, is not measured simply against the task itself, but against this ongoing record of its performance and how that record compares to a preestablished standard of production.

In its imaginary form, cyborg work represents nothing more than a radical intensification of these processes: surveillance now "saturates" work to the point of defining it. Instead of "informing" on work as it occurs, it "informates" work in advance, closing the gap between the activity and its sign. If it could, Capital would reconfigure the very "brain" of work. If it could only rewire the worker, all its problems – worker resistance, slacking, hiding, *la perruque*, whatever – would be solved. Rewiring would make the relations of surveillance a closed loop, or better, collapse those relations into a singular, concentrated point – no more external observation, no more hassle keeping the worker in view. In this imaginary, the product of labor is simultaneously its record, scanning is continuous and scales across multiple levels, from genetic to global work environments. In cyborg work, the program, which is nothing more than surveillance technology raised to its highest power, governs the routines of labor from the "inside." You don't like the way your employee is doing the job? Too many inefficiencies, too many uncertainties, not enough productivity? Just change the program, upgrade the system, or in the technological imaginary of these things, perhaps implant a new chip in the frontal lobes – break the old flow, create a new one.

Programmed work is just ultra-surveilled work – the older methods of surveillance continue to operate, indeed now with a kind of vengeance, but in simulation – codes, models, programs, chips, all these function far more effectively than cameras, microphones, certainly better than strategically placed supervisors, the eyes and ears and nose of the boss. Surveillance in the industrial workplace, in other words, suffers exactly the same postindustrial fate as exploitation, to which it is intimately related as a means to an end. In cyborg work, tracking the spatio-temporal dimensions of the labor process supernovas out into hypercontrol, radical control of work not by an agent but by abstract machineries of pre-contextualization and enframing, deterrence and simulation. But what does control mean here? In one sense, the evolution of cyborg work indicates a productive system fundamentally *out of control*, whose "normal functions" have become completely disordered, and in which any effort to intensify control only sends the system deeper into chaos (Marx already foresaw such downward spiraling processes operating in his theory of recurrent and ever more violent crises of Capital). Or just the opposite: control becomes so thoroughly integrated and wired into production today that it has become useless to speak about it as different from work at all – absolute, perfect, seamless control. In either case, control never touches the ground, never connects with anything real in either Labor or Capital, a self-perpetuating, cybernetic phenomenon, absorbed fully in the technologies of simulation.

This is the imaginary, anyway, but it is not so far removed from the facts as we might think. Contemporary workers, in general, are the most surveilled – watched, recorded, scanned, screened – in history. This is, of course, one major effect of the rapid computerization of work over the last two decades. Today computers generate, or are capable of generating, performance statistics on millions of workers across hundreds of occupations and every economic sector.[8] Every input, even a single keystroke, on a computer is a potential record of work performance (its efficiency, productivity, quality), location, or time. Every input is an isolated, preserved fragment of the worker's past (all of which are compiled and evaluated against a predesignated, ideal "work history"), which can be sorted with other bits of information and played back against various indices of the labor process that project its potential output and costs into the future. Even the *absence* of inputs can indicate performance characteristics (e.g., computer slacking). Hundreds of thousands of workers in both government and private industry are subjected to drug tests, have their prior work records scanned, are diagnosed for general health, intelligence, loyalty, family values, economic and psychological stability (through matches generated in searches of other databases), fitted to job profiles, placed on career tracks – or unemployment tracks – all in addition to routine, rigorous monitoring on the job. Together, all these records constitute what might be called a virtual scene of work, a simulacrum of the worker's "destiny." Simulation, we have said, is control from the end. The virtual scene of work is one where the end of work – who the worker *will have been*, what the worker *will have produced*, what path his or her career *will have taken* – governs the entire process before it begins. The future of work, on the other hand, becomes like some techno-eugenic dream. Is it possible to breed workers for specific tasks? Is it possible to decode the labor process so thoroughly, monitor it so completely that all its uncertainties are eliminated, to model it so perfectly that all the costs of developing, training, and preparing the labor force drop to zero?

These are the dreams of a surveillance machine evolving into an apparatus of simulation. The eye of the camera trained on a body connects to a videotape and from there to a screen; a DNA sample of the worker connects to an actuarial database to a screen; a keyboard to an electronic file (to a screen); a diagnostic test to a dossier to a profile, a transducer to a feedback device and, again, to a screen. A screen interfaces with an organic surface linked to a machinery of replication. These biomachinic linkages branch out and reverse and form other connections and cross-linkages, creating dense, multiple breaks and flows of information circuited through laboring bodies, and projected, at any selected point onto a display unit.[9] This is not just the future of work. It is already a fantastic description of the evolving informated workplace as it exists today, on the shop floor, in the automated office, the bureau, the factory, and soon, our own homes.

The cyborg worker is never an isolated unit, but a *bionetwork* composed of multiple and variable, alternating circuits, integrating molecular and molar environments. It is not just a machine-body, but a kind of mutant transformer, a bioscanner/biosorter in an assemblage of other scanners and sorters (surveillance-simulation relations). In one sense, it is useless to separate surveillance (scanning) and simulation (sorting, recording, playback) technologies in relation to cyborg work, because in the imaginary the two operations are so tightly integrated. We always find one with the other as interrelated elements of a general functionality – the surveillance apparatus supplies information, the simulation apparatus provides the screen on which that information is displayed, both joining together in electronic memory, i.e., in the file, the document, the electronic trace. Today, more than ever, work *is* its record, is absorbed into its moving record (or surface of recording),[10] into its (simulated, pre-served) past, and vice versa, as the worker's "product," information, is absorbed back into the passing present of work, as feedback and other modes of cybernetic control. We could think of cyborg work as a form of the recollection of work contemporaneous with the events it describes. In that way, it is like work's "afterlife" or double (work is already dead, over, past, virtual) but articulated on work that still "lives" and passes (is actual) in the present. Marx's opposition, in the *Grundrisse*, of living labor as labor in the *present*, to dead, *past* labor does not quite fit this changed situation, in which a preserved past (as record, information) occupies the same space and is simultaneous with a passing present (work, living labor). Cyborg work, in that sense, is different: in it, time splits in two along a line of interface, a point of contact that produces and records in the same operation, making the distinction and obliterat-ing it in the same movement. In cyborg work, even the "interface" between body and machine disappears in the abstraction of the *fit*, the de-sign, a molding of live and dead forms which aims for an *ergonomic perfection*, a perfect communication of energy between fingers and keys, eyes and screen, touch and movement in a simulated, virtual environ-ment. This "fit" is precisely hypersurveillance: automatic, *comfortable* control. Cyborg work, in short, is its *own* surveillance, in a process that has no end other than more surveillance, more records, more codes. But *who or what* surveils the cyborg worker is not a question here, as it might be from a Marxist perspective – these distinctions don't matter to the assemblage – only *how*, as an assemblage of identical biomechanical monads, it operates.

Again, I am referring only to a certain fictional logic or form of devel-opment, the projection of a fantastic future onto the present, and not to a set of empirical "facts." The technology of cyborg work, of hypersur-veillance and ergo-alignment of bodies to infotech assemblages, is still in its relative infancy. But the trend is also more pervasive than it might first appear (the "facts" constitute the zones around which we see this fiction circulate – anywhere phrases like "user-friendly" technology or "machines designed with you in mind" are used today, look for a cyborg). In less than two decades, these technologies have spread across the entire labor economy. Many traditional blue-collar occupations, in manufacturing, mining, and agriculture are rapidly moving to opera-tional forms of control (the new robotics, electronic imaging, cybernetic quality control, information systems, cellular communications networks, etc.) (Zuboff 1988; Garson 1988). As computers are introduced into these environments, work also generates more extensive, continuous records and is more subject to performance codification, more hooked into virtual image technologies and distanced from direct sensory inputs. Corporate managers and supervisors, too, are increasingly likely to find not only their performance but their tacit knowledge of organizational matters the object of electronic scans, as their work is computerized and simplified, and as computerized assistants, so-called "expert systems," are designed to simulate their traditional control and decision functions – planning, calculating costs, formulating options, and so on.

Computerization is only the beginning. Cyborgs, surveillance, hypersurveillance, and simulation also emerge as general themes in the "new diagnostics" of work, the use of medical screening and tests to select and biologically "Taylorize" the workforce. Substance-abuse tests, polygraphs, general lifestyle screens, and, most recently, genetic scans to determine susceptibility to disease or predisposition to adverse effects from work-related hazards (e.g., chemicals and other toxic materials) have supplemented traditional employment screens for relevant skills, experience, level of education, and the like (Nelkin and Tancredi 1989: 74–105). Modern diagnostic technology has extended and enhanced the power of professional medical knowledge over work, often blurring the line between health and production concerns, creating what we could call a medical–corporate simulacrum, a hyperspace of intensive biological examination and qualification that tracks the worker (read: simulates an ideal worker, free of actual or potential "defects") throughout the employment career (many large corporations now have their own in-house clinics and testing facilities, or retain their own medical staff). In conjunction with computerization, modern diagnostics is quietly "actuarializing" the work environment, redefining it in terms of risk probabilities, saturating it with biostatistical reason in order to detect and deter work-related problems before they occur. Many large employers are now also insurers and health-benefit providers – biological information on prospective employees is seen as a way to reduce costs (time wastage) and insure future productivity (e.g., workers who are discovered through genetic testing to have an inherited susceptibility to certain diseases may not be hired, to avoid the cost of future medical treatment). Such front-end, enveloping strategies represent the wave of simulation currently sweeping the contemporary work environment. An actuarial-biological model – a numerical index of health, a statistical prediction of risk – prepares the worker's entry into the workforce, and acts to determine his or her work trajectory. But that model in turn is dependent on extensive surveillance, on records generated in depth (the molecular-cellular constitution of the worker) as well as breadth (family medical histories, lifestyle indicators, etc.). Hypersurveillance, simulation of work: a *comprehensive* diagnosis, an exhaustive probe of the worker's past, ensures the ongoing reality, stability, presence of work. And its future, i.e., its insured replicability: the new diagnostics is nothing less than the first, fledgling effort to clone the worker, to guarantee his or her perfect and frictionless replaceability with an exact duplicate. In this sense, diagnostic technology, aimed at the most microscopic components of the body of the worker, represents the ultimate form of work simulation, one in which the body – prone to disease and all its attendant disruption of schedules and projects – is fully absorbed into the (in theory, immortal) cyborg assemblage. In appearance the future of work is, if only surreally, very much like work of the past, which, in a certain sense, it aims for, attempts to recover. Simulated work, cyborg "production," is designed to resemble a past when work still meant something, when there were still some real reasons left in working, an end or finality – political, social, economic – that would make sense of it. That's why it retains, distantly, something of the character of a craft, or even of primitive forms of labor, steeped in a paradoxical postindustrial techno-ritual (the sacrifice of the worker's body in order to resurrect it in a higher form). But it's too late – simulation has nothing to do with "real" time or "real" history, or primitive ritual, except in terms of their perverse postmodern replication, and only accelerates the final dissolution of these forms. Present and past, real and imaginary, are all the same to (perfect) simulation (and simulation always aims for perfection). The only workers, on this line of logic, will be cyborg workers, biomechanically perfect workers of a future already past, pretested to eliminate any chance of a mismatch or error, or to suit any whim, the way men and women, soon, will already know the complete medical "history" (read: "destiny") of their children in embryo.

The work simulacrum: cyborg work, *la perruque*, and the myth of control

Cyborg work marks the replication and diffusion of the workplace within the larger social environment, and that environment in the workplace, in the same way we already noted for military technology. It not only bio-engineers the workforce, it integrates formerly disconnected social fields that at one time were only tangentially related to work. The modern informated workplace might as well be the home, the school, the prison, the barracks, the clinic, or the church (all of which in turn now borrow extensively from the control tactics of the workplace). The effect is both radical and homogenizing, and extends beyond the fusion of corporate bureaucracy, systems engineering, and biotech. Today, work "disappears" as a specific locus of control only to reappear everywhere. In cyborg societies, even play or fun (leisure "time-off," exercise, vacations) takes on the features of work, a compulsive ordering of informated events and spaces, while work itself, in a number of modern mega-corporations, is increasingly "recreationalized" (sports, games, parties, and other morale-associational events are integrated seamlessly into the flow of work, ostensibly to improve productivity, efficiency, etc., but in fact as part of a larger project to finally cancel the difference between work and play, work and leisure). Or work is made to feel more like home, fellow workers like one's "family" (e.g., the paternalist protectionism of the Japanese corporate model, so-called "quality-circles") – just as home, thanks to silicon technology, is emerging as the workplace of the not-so-distant future, a space where one can continue to work after and before work, or that simply *becomes* the workplace (as information technology speeds up communication and eliminates the need to travel to work).

We mentioned earlier how simulation reterritorializes and retemporalizes work (envelops it in simulated space and time). Tasks that can be accomplished via a computer, over digital networks, can be performed anywhere, anytime; at least that is the plan. There is, again, a utopian image present here, of absolute control over work which is simultaneously the end of work, not only for the worker, but for Capital itself, insofar as *its* work of controlling labor would also come to an end (automatic control as the end of control). Work without leaving home, work at any time (driving a car, on vacation, in bed, on the toilet, etc.), plugged into a cellular video prosthesis (that also connects to shops, schools, churches, theaters, libraries, public forums, etc.). These multiple fusions make cyborg work a virtual paradise of paradoxes in space and time: the relative *mobility* of the workplace made possible by telematic technology corresponds to a relative *immobility* of the worker in relation (i.e., proximity) to that technology, technology that is designed to be a constant companion (lightweight, portable, user-friendly, comfortable, you can take it anywhere, or, in the coming revolution in virtual reality, simply wear it or have it installed somewhere in the body). Similarly, the temporal freedom offered by telematic technologies (release from the bounded work*day*, work*week*, schedules of all sorts, etc.) parallels the experience of "timelessness" of cyborg work, its paradoxically static, close-dimensioned quality, which it shares with all video and audio reproduction equipment, of producing any-time-whatevers within the virtual time of simulation, of simultaneous unfoldings and separations of time, past and present, record and event, in the dedifferentiation of real-time and sim-time.[11] Telematic technologies liberate the space and time of work only by virtue of their hypersurveillant features, i.e., their capacity to monitor tasks instantaneously and continuously over infinite distances, to track worktime as a totality, to constitute work as the very measure of its performance, to follow (surveil) it in order to model it. This is the *work simulacrum*. Today, work can be anywhere, anytime because, at its highest stage, it is designed *never to go offline*. Cyborg work is literally work "around and through the clock" and obeys the simplest rules – don't turn off the screen, don't unplug the apparatus (if you do, it will be recorded).

Cyborg work, we have suggested, generates multiple paradoxes of control. On one hand, it is about immanent, absolute control. This is its utopian dimension. I have argued that the cyborg apparatus itself, and all its relations, *is* the form of control and only the form of control. Norbert Wiener (1948) already knew this in the 1940s when he identified cybernetics with the science of control (prophetically, in both the animal and the machine, and thus a science of their connections). Wiener, of course, saw these as potentially open (learning) systems, but in its imaginary, cyborg work is a closed loop: the worker runs a machine that runs a worker that runs a machine, etc., in more or less broad circuits and branching logics. Programmed control here is total and diffuse, and passes through every node or branch of the system.

In its imaginary, in ways Wiener would never have anticipated, cyborg work is about the *disappearance* of control altogether, as structured differences that support control – visibility versus invisibility, presence versus absence, systems of hierarchy, rank, privilege, reward, etc. – are absorbed in simulation. In general, it is useless (or nonsense) to speak of control in assemblages which are pure functionality, in which all elements are equally indispensable and replaceable (modular systems), and where any *contact* with an assemblage (data entry) is automatically integrated into the loop, preserves another past, activates a profile, i.e., produces another cyborg.

Can such a totalizing system be overturned or subverted? Simulations, we have said, function to absorb their exterior, or fold that exterior back onto an interior that both encompasses and exhausts it. If subversion of this apparatus, and of cyborg work, can mean anything today, it is not a matter of simply reasserting control *over* it – outsurveilling the surveillor, so to speak – but in some sense of *disappearing inside it*, of making another fold, a double, reverse fold to re-encompass the encompassing interior, this time from within. If resistance still makes any sense for cyborg workers, it can only mean that they must learn to *simulate simu-*

lation, to vanish, somehow, within the totality of a hypersurveilled, informated system.

Such an idea perhaps is not as perplexing (or impossible) as it first sounds. It means, first of all, that perhaps there is a *la perruque*, an art of disappearance, of cyborg work, but at a higher level than the *la perruque* of industrial labor. Rather than turning the tables on the surveillance–disciplinary apparatus by means of a reverse strategy of managing visibility (presence in space and time), the hypersurveillance-simulation apparatus is subverted by a strategic art of simulated visibilities and flows in simulated space and time. Cyborg workers of all sorts perhaps already understand, or at least are beginning to understand, the problem – how does one create a zone of free time in a telematically engineered, programmed environment? In fact, that free zone can itself only be constituted within the already constituted zone of simulated space-time that is cyborg work. Telematic machinery, that is, must be operated creatively, in ways that subvert its operations from the inside while appearing to conform to them.

Can this be done? What is this *la perruque* of cyborg work, this revenge of cyborgs? As with other forms of elusion, the answer to that question is difficult to formulate and undoubtedly depends on features of specific operations or tasks. Various hacking and viral strategies, recodings, doublings, the staging of simulated readouts, electronic decoys, and other moves are certainly involved. Consider the following scenario. In a recent made-for-TV movie which played on a generic theme, a team of electronically sophisticated thieves foil a bank's security system by channeling their own images of how it appeared when it was empty (recorded directly from its surveillance cameras when it was closed) to the bank's guards, who are stationed in a room adjoining the lobby. They set off the bank's motion sensitive alarm systems with a small robotic device (planted under an ashtray on the floor) so many times in the space of a few hours that the police soon stop responding to the call (they eventually disconnect the warning system, in a variation of the "cry-wolf syndrome"). The success of the robbery depends here not on the incapacitation but rather the flawless operation of the security apparatus, on the thieves' ability to simulate its normal, everyday operations, effectively getting the system to subvert itself. Unlike industrial forms of *la perruque*, which generally function by concealing a presence – an activity which remains under the full view of the boss – this strategy worked by simulating an absence (practically, though, the two strategies are not that different). For the watcher (the surveillor), the camera doesn't lie – no one is in the bank. (At one point in the movie, an electrical problem causes the video monitors to return for a split second to their untampered images, and they capture a shadowy figure, one of the robbers as he passes in front of it, which abruptly disappears again a split second later as the simulated image returns. In the guard room, the security man witnesses the robber move across the screen, but he refuses to believe his eyes. How could the system malfunction? How could it generate a false image?)

Cyborg work, for all its appearance of being absolutely controlled, perhaps offers these kinds of opportunities for covert subversion of the apparatus, for disrupting it from the inside, as the very function of its normal mode of operation. If the apparatus can somehow be tricked into simulating its own output, this is what gains free space and time for its operator. In a curious way, what the operator desires is a machine that runs by itself, whose output and input functions double the operator's but without his presence, or more strongly, without his contact. The cyborg is reduced to a mere machine with only a simulated body, which now programs itself; the form of resistance thus utilizes the very logic of the system, its own operation, to subvert it. And here the dream of Labor and Capital to free themselves from any form of control, to escape their limits, converge in an autonomous technology to which neither has a responsibility, and which signals their mutual abandonment on the horizon of the end of work.

6

Privacy and hyperprivacy

Knowledge invents the secret.   Foucault, *Birth of the Clinic*

The secret, were there such, would be such that it could not be betrayed.
Baudrillard, *What Are You Doing After the Orgy?*

Hypercontrol and the secret

Who controls the codes in telematic societies? Who regulates the flow of
information, which information passes through and which doesn't, which
is public and which is private? If these questions seem important from a
political or legal point of view, they are the wrong questions if we want
to deconstruct the imaginary of modern information and biotechnology,
where the dream is one of pure control *without an agent*, and where the
"problem" of privacy, viz., its erosion and disappearance in surveillance
societies, is resolved by simulating it. Increasingly today, privacy has less
to do with "persons," "individuals," and "selves," less with secluded
spaces and being left alone, than with informated personalities and virtual territories. What is private, like everything else we have discussed in
this book, is becoming hyperreal, as "real" privacy, just like the "real"
agent, is systematically converted into data images and telematic constructs (Brown 1990: 75; Laudon 1986). In the imaginary of telematics,
privacy for all practical purposes is equivalent to publicity, because both
are functions of being online. There is no such thing as a private or public cyborg, since all cyborgs are just duplicates of one another. Real privacy and publicity implies difference, a certain distance or distinction
from the crowd. But in the fantastic logic of telematic societies, difference itself is just one more programmed effect of the code.

Information technology is always years ahead of privacy legislation,
which for the most part responds to the phenomenal growth of surveillance at the end of the twentieth century within a framework that remains
essentially modernist. In the United States, the law still regards privacy
largely in the way Warren and Brandeis defined it in 1890, as the right
to be left alone, rooted in the "principle of an inviolate personality"

(Office of Technology Assessment 1986: 11). It is precisely, however, the coherent, integrated personality, the individual as a subject (agent) with rights, obligations, etc., that is placed in question by the new virtual technologies. In the modern age, privacy as the "right of an inviolable personality" appears when the boundary between observer and observed is breached by panoptic technologies. With the revolution in computers and communications in hyperpanoptic societies, however, it has come to refer to the right to control access to information (Westin 1967: 39). In contemporary privacy law, access to persons, their private lives, their secrets, means access to the codes that govern their interpretation.[1] But what does "access" mean in the context of a technical imaginary where everything is already accessed, already visible? Panoptic societies exist by virtue of their capacity to manufacture secrets, to create the *illusion* of private space as the always accessible reality behind the screen of appearances. The "secret," as that which calls out, as it were, for its own unmasking, is only a fabrication of the surveillance apparatus. In telematic societies, this process is carried to its fantastic conclusion. There, if we can still speak about the secret at all, it is only in relation to a private space, a private person, that has been absorbed into the screen itself.[2]

Instead of asking *who* has control over codes, we should ask, then, how codes generate virtual agents and systems of control. And instead of linking control of codes to privacy, with all its modernist conceptual baggage about rights and access, we should link both to the postmodern production and consumption of images, to virtual secrets and unmaskings, to hyperprivacy. All virtual constructs, writes Baudrillard, tend toward their own implosion (Baudrillard 1993a: 4).[3] What is privacy in an imaginary realm where every communication is preceded by its password or cypher, where visibility and secrecy coincide, where everyone is a surveillor and everyone is plugged in, where everybody is a cyborg, where messages arrive before they are sent (and thus are always repetitive and immediately boring)? The answer is not that privacy in that realm no longer exists, but that it is rather an overbearing, excessive, omnipresent, overcoded reality. In the telematic imaginary, total privacy is fully consistent with total publicity. Perfect anonymity, absolute invisibility – just how different is that vision from one of the solitary electronic networker cruising the information highway, completely wired-in but completely alone, files locked by a singular, indecipherable password; or the citizen of the future (past!), equipped with a personal barcoded plastic card, definitive, positive identification enabling her access to all the world has to offer (money, credit, power, knowledge, pleasure), but also allowing instantaneous, automatic, precise tracking of all transactions by the "authorities." We can only admire the sheer perversity of these ideas: perfect security, perfect fortification, perfect control over incoming and outgoing information, the function of a similarly perfect and absolute individualization, the highest realization of surveillance society – everyone watched, everyone a watcher. This is the final solution to the modernist dialectic of publicity and privacy. Every *body* assigned its own unique code, which exactly, unambiguously marks (surveils) it, and at the same instant perfectly conceals and isolates it from every other body – radical difference (everyone a unique configuration of information) and sameness (all information translated by the code, each person a monad) all in one convenient operation, total uniqueness and total comparability, as the effect of simple variations in a universal schema. Absolute visibility as a condition and a guarantee of absolute anonymity. If privacy or publicity still exists here, it is only by virtue of a prior standardization (codification) that both cancels and invents their secret, by virtue, i.e., of their simulation.

Recently the US government proposed a plan that would require the computer industry to adopt a uniform encryption standard, built into a device called the Clipper chip, that would stop the proliferation of codes designed to insure the privacy of electronic conversations ("Cyberspace under Lock and Key" 1994). It also wants a law mandating new telecommunications conglomerates to install equipment that would allow it to listen in, in the interests, of course, of "national security" (whatever "national" means in an age of global communications). Predictably, the government's actions are meeting all kinds of resistance, both from manufacturers, who are concerned about their profits on the international electronics market – foreign governments presumably will not be interested in buying American computers equipped with miniature CIAs inside – as well as certain user groups, opposed to any interference with freedom of expression. During the early days of the Internet, the system operated fairly anarchically, and recent intimations of government surveillance are prompting numerous countermeasures. One Silicon Valley group called Cypherpunk wants to make powerful encryption devices available free to the public, distributed worldwide over the Net. They are talking about ways to make the government think that the Clipper technology has already been stolen, i.e., is no longer secret. (Basically Clipper scrambles communications with a mathematical code that requires two "keys," or numerical series, to unlock. The idea is that requiring two keys will prevent abuses, much like multiple codes entrusted to different individuals would be needed to launch a nuclear strike.) Computer hackers aren't waiting for the government or corporations to act. It is reported that some have already devised sophisticated encryption shareware that makes the Clipper chip obsolete (note: even before it's available!). (Hacking, of course, has been one of the main modes of subversion of informatic systems.) Predictably, court cases are pending, even though, as we've noted, the technology always manages to stay well ahead of any legal efforts to control it.[4]

Cyborg dreams

The same kinds of privacy issues arise with information generated by genetic coding technology. Do persons have a right to information about their virtual health status (or their children's), revealed by a comparison of their DNA against some universal genetic map? Which persons? Patients, doctors, insurers, men, women? Who regulates the reproductive process in cloning technologies? Who regulates their development, marketing, and distribution? Such questions can be read as symptoms of panic over the precipitous loss of agency that comes with the development of simulated forms of control. The recovery of agency, however, is kept open as long as it is conceived of as an exercise of power *over* these technologies. What does the clone dream of (to change only slightly the sense of the question in the title of Philip K. Dick's (1982) novel *Do Androids Dream of Electric Sheep?*)? It dreams of being an agent (again?), of being able to break the code, unplug the machine, literally, to break with what is dead in it. But this is the dream of something that is already a *hyper*agent (in *Blade Runner*, the film adapted from Dick's novel, the cyborg Roy kills his inventer/"father" when he learns he can't halt his programmed decommissioning – condemned to remain a simulacrum of agency, he finds out that only humans, not cyborgs, can control codes).[5] The contemporary panic over the reassertion of agency itself only reflects that agency is already far down the path of virtuality, like power and control (where everything partakes of the demand to be an agent, a subject, it is only because Agency itself, capital A, has disappeared). In one sense, we are all like Roy in this desire of hyperagents to return to being agents, human once again, and that plays itself out in a kind of frantic search for the keys to the secret code governing (one's own) death. For whatever reasons, we do not easily come to comprehend that that very search is too late. The dream of a possible return to human agency is deluded and only masks a final departure. The principles of resistance and subversion of such a system are no longer human, but always first cyborgian – "unplugging" the machine is a fantasy of crossing back over to a side (agency) we have already left behind. The main political question from the point of view of the hyperagent is: can one "unplug" from a space always already *inside* the system, assert a power *in and through* rather than over, utilizing the very elements of the system to push it past its limit?[6]

Instead, we see various parties, interest groups, etc., battling to secure their political control over codes, privacy and access to information. All this is certainly understandable. Much of what is at stake in the politics of agency has to do with the agent's claims to personal identity. New bio-surveillance technologies (like DNA screening) are, or will soon be, so definitive that they render all competing identity claims insignificant; at its imaginary limit – the clone – identity becomes entirely a function of the code. Unlike other forms of biosurveillance that test identity retroactively (blood tests, urine tests, fingerprinting, lie detection), genetic coding technology offers the fantastic possibility of *pre*-identification, i.e., identities assigned in advance, profiles that we have seen can be used to target bodies for all kinds of future interventions and diversions. (Do your genes indicate a disposition to alcoholism? No problem. We've got a program set up to treat predisposed alcoholics, i.e., your newly assigned identity.) And not only future problems, but past ones as well (cloning is always a matter of assigning a *past in advance* – the clone is the body that one *will have become*, i.e., a biological destiny). In the imaginary, sci-fi world of gene therapy, all normalcies, and by extension all pathologies, are virtual. Here, pathologies are not just problems in embryo, but *always already eliminated problems*. Normalization is not so much *effect-ed* as it is pre-operative. The imaginary ideal of genetic therapy is genet-ic *design*, the ultimate means of solving problems that never were problems, so that they *never will have become* problems (the impossible, Frankensteinian imaginary of eugenics, a pseudo-problematics of a genetic utopia – "imagine a perfect, beautiful body"). It's hardly surpris-ing that critics of genetic research have seen such work as the absolute erosion of privacy, if what is private is seen as equivalent to the body (*my* body), its workings, the pleasures and pains it experiences. What is pri-vate when the most intimate and revealing biological information is translatable according to the conventions of some universal code and available to all with access to that code?

In fact, by this time real privacy, the master signifier, like the real body, is already lost, and the apparent mechanisms to which it has been lost (surveillance apparatuses) are the very mechanisms that now gener-ate it as a hyperreality, launch it into orbit. In the politics of encryption, in the debate over genetic mapping and cloning, the distress over the dis-appearance of privacy is only the symptom of a general dynamic that now seeks in a positive way to simulate privacy, to make privacy (once again) absolute and inviolable. Paradoxically, it also seeks this for publicity, which has also disappeared. Behind the genetic debate about who controls sensitive bio-information is a process that in fact seeks not only perfect anonymity and closure, but perfect exposure and visibility. In a fully genetically mapped world, in an ideally genetically manufactured society, no one "stands out" from anyone else. At the same time, *everyone stands out* – no one is ugly, everyone is beautiful, no one is diseased or disfigured, no one requires "therapy," because all therapies are effected in advance, in utero, in vitro, ultimately, at the level of the code. Everyone is (can be) "different," in the same sense that fashion seduces us with the offer of difference (always the new, unique look!).[7] Genetic engineering is not just a harbinger of sameness (everything predictable, calculable, and therefore the loss of any meaning for the concept of privacy), but also an imaginary technology that promises everyone has the chance to be *singular*, unique (pick the sex, eye color, hair color, intelligence, aesthetic sense, whatever, of your baby, choose, so to speak, pick its *ancestry*, its past or line of descent, which doesn't necessarily have to be yours!). And it is this hallucination of absolute control over difference, absolute choice in matters of what and who gets reproduced, repeated – a hallucination generated, of course, by operations made possible by the "discovery" (read: positing) of a formal, universal code – that guarantees and in fact defines privacy and publicity in telematic societies. But despite the language of choice which infuses the frenzied drive to map the genome (or decode any body of information), neither privacy nor publicity here has anything to do with agency or human control, with a rational decision-maker who examines and selects from among the bio-info-options. Choice is strictly a function of the array of options within the already coded matrix, a function of the genetic, informatic simulacrum.

Leaving aside the question of publicity for now, all this signals not exactly the end of privacy, or that privacy disappears absolutely in some Orwellian sense (I shall return to this), but that paradoxically we are saturated with hyperprivacy. Privacy in telematic societies becomes one more reference in simulation, and to that extent something ironic. What's ironic about privacy today is that following its apparent "death" in surveillance societies it returns with a kind of vampiric and ghostly vengeance (the return of the repressed as simulation). If in the past, privacy could still be bought, could still enter into the system of exchange as a kind of property, in the postpanoptic age, privacy is *free*, offered as a gift that is (increasingly) impossible to refuse or return.[8] Telematic societies, in one sense, are where privacy for the first time becomes a *freely supplied necessity*. It's ironic (and necessary to protect yourself, that is, your data files) that encryption software is freely available *over the Net*, just as it will be ironic (and necessary) for everyone soon to have a genetically engineered body (free too, of course, in the sci-fi world we're talking about – the "gift" of being the clone of your choice!). These efforts, however, are always too late to redeem privacy, in its symbolic or enchanted sense (i.e., the unbetrayable secret life of one's thought, the secret experience of a singular body, both now defined as and absorbed in information). The enchanted, secret space of privacy no longer exists, if it ever did – the apparatuses of inspection whose formal operational principles were already articulated in the eighteenth and early nineteenth centuries have seen to that, substituting instead the disenchanted forms of secrecy characteristic of observation societies (the secret always defined as the unobservable, in terms of the *possibility* of its observation). In telematic societies this process is pushed to its imaginary limit. Secrecy is defined no longer in reference to what is potentially observable, but to what is virtually producible. Secrecy is a matter of the screen here, not the gaze, relative to information, i.e., the simulated gaze. If secrets exist on informated networks, it is only as informated secrets.

If secrecy (and by extension, privacy) can retain any of its sense in telematic societies, it would mean *to disappear within the matrix of information*, not just beneath the watchful eyes of the authorities, but from within the code itself (which encompasses the authorities themselves). To be unbetrayable and uncomprehendible in terms of information, to be uncoded, that would define the secret today, the subversion of the imaginary order of surveillance. That imaginary, we have seen, projects a passage from the order of the gaze to the order of the screen. Screens don't "watch" people or "invade" their privacy; increasingly, they *are* their privacy. The mildly pleasurable stupor induced by interacting with screens is the most pure form of privacy. "Watching" functions at a higher level here, as something designed into the circuitry, a pure functionality which defines the surveillance assemblage and its relations in its entirety. Privacy can only have parallel meanings here: not zones invisible to the gaze, but zones of scrambled or jammed information, or breaks in the flows of cybernetic control.

Most people today still speak as if privacy had to do with physical regions closed off to observation, invisible or otherwise inaccessible enclaves in space and time. In fact those enclaves, whether they know it or not, are in the process of being radically reconfigured in telematic societies. Home, work, the body, the spheres of sexuality and health – those regions and others have become far more penetrable, and the boundaries that once separated them less defined, as the mechanisms of observation and recording have become smaller, faster, and more sensitive. The new electronic and biosurveillance technologies available today easily overcome spatial and temporal barriers to inspection and control. They penetrate beneath surfaces, see in the dark, and transmit data at the speed of light. But these once enchanted enclaves are becoming increasingly irrelevant to means of hypercontrol employing virtual technologies. Oftentimes, to be effective, these technologies do not have to be intrusive at all (even though in many cases they justify or enable intrusion, and on a massive scale). Instead, they can simply be imposed on preexisting stores of data, utilizing various sampling and matching strategies to infer and deter potential lines of deviation.

Hyperprivacy, in the end, is about access to information, to those virtual zones that information creates and, in the strict sense, *is*. But even this formulation, we have seen, is inadequate. What is at stake in the privacy debate today – how is it threatened? how can it be protected? – is not who controls access to the data banks (against Lyotard's suggestion) (1979: 67). It is rather the informatization or telematization of access as such. To speak of access to digital information, especially as a mode of empowerment or resistance, is in one sense to engage in a kind of mystified thinking. Whoever or whatever "accesses" the data banks is already captured by the info-system and reproduces its operations from the very beginning. In hypersurveillance societies, the "accessor" is only another node in the Net, a cyborg. Today, any stakes concerning privacy must develop around not only its disappearance, but its reconstitution as a (technological) simulacrum, that is, as informatics and cybernetic systems. Today privacy, like control, is in the network; and the network is not precisely or exclusively a spatial or temporal phenomenon. In actuarial, diagnostic societies, the question of privacy is not about how to elude surveillance, i.e., how to elude exposure by creating secret enclaves in physical space or time. That question, again, comes too late. Rather, it is about how to elude simulation or otherwise to disappear in hyperspace (and hypertime), to subvert the process of being doubled or tracked not in the real world of access and control, but in the shadow realm of cyborg worlds.

The end of the observer?

If modern societies were ordered, in part, around a *myth* of privacy, telematic societies are ordered around a *delusion* about the end of privacy. The myth of privacy, which is still very much with us today, refers to the possibility of escape from observation, even if that means a retreat into the solitude of one's own thoughts. The delusion of the end of privacy is that one can never get away, that no secret, invisible spaces remain. The myth and the delusion are not opposite each other, but complementary. Both assume the possibility of privacy, that something that could be called a private space or time exists, is real but threatened. In fact, as I have suggested, privacy becomes more of an absolute with the advent of telematic societies, even as it appears at the same time that there is less and less of it to guard.

Consider two recent analyses of surveillance.

David Burnham (1983: 15, 120, 145ff.), in *The Rise of the Computer State*, writes that electronic surveillance "increases the influence of the major bureaucracies by giving these organizations a method by which they can anticipate probable future thoughts and activities." He notes that information is power, and that the "misuse of information" threatens American values of privacy, autonomy, choice, freedom, and checks and balances in government.

A recent report by the Office of Technology Assessment (1985b: iii) states: "Public policy on the use of information technology to electronically monitor individual movements, actions, and communications has been based on a careful balancing of civil liberty versus law enforcement or investigative interests ... New technologies – such as data transmission, electronic mail, cellular and cordless telephones, and miniature cameras – have outstripped the existing statutory framework for balancing these interests."

What these two analyses have in common with a host of others published on the topic of surveillance (or "intelligence-gathering") over the last thirty years is alarm over the rapid erosion of individual privacy in postindustrial societies and the inadequacy of current regulatory policies to protect it (at both the national and international levels). These are just some of the facts they cite: at work, computer-generated statistics form the basis of work evaluation for millions of office workers, and the trend is toward more computer-based monitoring. Women are disproportionately affected, since one in three women works in computerized service jobs – in wordprocessing, telemarketing, insurance claims, and reservations, or as bank tellers or telephone operators – which are routinely subjected to continuous performance checks. More workers are being watched on visual display terminals or having their phone conversations recorded. Electronic monitoring is only the tip of the iceberg. Other applications of surveillance technology in the workplace include polygraph testing, drug testing, genetic screening, and brain wave testing.

And this is only the workplace. We have already taken note how in the United States alone credit firms maintain millions of records containing individuals' names, addresses, phone numbers, spouses' names, place of work, salary, bankruptcies, lawsuits, purchases, etc. Government at all levels collects massive amounts of information on virtually everyone: taxpayers, drivers, entitlement recipients. Law enforcement authorities engage in both covert and overt intelligence-gathering using the latest electronic equipment. Polls track every current of opinion, every shift in preferences, every change in outlook. Since the early 1960s there have been calls to establish a centralized national database. By the late 1980s, however, personal computers and systems like the Internet had so expanded the potential for information sharing that a centralized data storage facility already seemed like an outmoded concept. In the 1990s, it looks like it's full speed ahead for the construction of "infobahns" that will link together homes, schools, businesses, government agencies, libraries, emergency response systems, whatever.

This is not simply an international or global system, but an *orbital and cellular* network linking the macro and micro levels of information-gathering, connected by satellites, microwave dishes, and miniaturized, personal communications devices. In this network, the distinction between observer and observed breaks down in the impersonal domination of the hypersurveillance assemblage. Observation becomes a general, diffuse condition, the precise locus of which cannot be discerned. Friedrich Dürrenmatt (1988) fictionalizes this condition in his book *The Assignment (Or, On the Observing of the Observer of the Observers)*, where a Möbius-spiraling configuration of information, images, screens, celebrities, cameras, and satellite spies overwhelms and surpasses the duality of visible and invisible worlds in a universal system of inspection.

The book begins with the investigation of a death. A famous filmmaker (F.) is summoned by the psychiatrist Otto von Lambert, to document and investigate the discovery of the body of his wife Tina near the site of some ruins in the Middle Eastern country of M. In Tina's journal, the last entry is, "I am being observed." This clue becomes the basis of a hypothesis. Maybe Tina fled to M. because she "dreamt of drawing upon herself the observing eyes of the world" and, "finding her disappearance remained unobserved, which is to say, ignored, may have felt impelled to seek out more and more audacious adventures, until, by her death, she achieved the desired end, her picture in all the papers and all the world observing her and giving her the recognition and meaning for which she had yearned." Tina, that is, desires her own simulation, her reproduction in the media as a celebrity, and achieves it precisely through her disappearance and death.

When F. arrives in M., she becomes caught in the middle of a struggle between the police chief and the head of M.'s secret service. Foreign journalists and photographers are everywhere. A prisoner, who as it turns out is also a journalist, is executed after having confessed to Tina's murder, but soon afterwards, F. sees newspaper photos showing Tina and her husband von Lambert reunited. F. investigates further and encounters a photographer named Polypheme filming a corpse in the countryside of M. Polypheme – the name of the Cyclops in Homer, a reference to the (blinded) gaze – leads her to an elaborate underground bunker. Polypheme tells F. the bunker was built to monitor the performance of electronic weapons. The western powers have been simulating a desert war in order to test their new equipment (Dürrenmatt published this book, prophetically, before the Persian Gulf War). Everything is now automated and under surveillance. The bunker is watched by satellite, which itself is watched by another satellite, and so on. Polypheme

himself was being observed as he observed, he knew the resolving power of satellite pictures, a god who was observed was no longer a god, God was not subject to observation, God's freedom consisted in being a concealed, hidden god, while man's bondage consisted in being observed, but what was even worse was the nature of those who observed and made a fool of him, namely a system of computers. (Dürrenmatt 1988: 109)

In *The Assignment*, surveillance slides imperceptibly but completely into its simulation. Tina's disappearance, the execution, the reunion in the media, the desert war, everything is staged to be observed. In the end the seer Himself is annihilated in universal observation, and what remains is a simulated God, a network of computers that is no longer invisible and indeed has no need to remain concealed. Is this the end of privacy and the beginning of a radical publicity (everybody witnessed and a witness), or rather a perverse and ironic privacy? Here everyone is famous but remains perfectly obscure. Who is F.? Where is M.? What territory is this drama played out on, what time does it take place? Is Tina dead, or alive, or even real (all we have are documents, photos)? Who (what) is Polypheme? Is there a war, or not? Everything is inconclusive in this novel, just as everything is paradoxically uncertain in a system of perfect surveillance (what does the gaze that sees all, including itself, see)? Just as everything is inconclusive in a system of (perfect) simulation – is this real? where is this place? When is this time? What,

precisely, *sees*? Or, maybe just the reverse, everything is perfectly con-
clusive – there is no more to see, everything is laid out, nothing is left to
the imagination, no secrets, nothing has to be known. In simulation, in
a hypersurveillant universe, knowledge disappears into information, each
bit of which is equivalent to any other, a cold, endless seriality.
Dürrenmatt in fact crafts his narrative as a long series of clauses separated by commas, an endless string of vignettes that blend seamlessly into
one another, spinning out in unanticipated trajectories, and that perfectly capture the rhizomatic, disenchanted, homogeneous realm of information and telematics.

Orwell in orbit

In Orwell's (1984) vision of the future, Big Brother watches you.[9] But in
a cyborg vision of the future, it's far more complex. There, you watch
Big Brother watching you watch Big Brother, in a continuous reversal or
oscillation of the poles of observation and power. And not only that. In
this oscillating space of watching and control, Big Brother definitively
disappears, and so do you, into the very technology and practice of
watching, which themselves dissolve into simulation. The cyborg model
goes Orwell one better. Big Brother doesn't just place you under surveillance anymore, but you become a fully integrated component of an
encompassing network of surveillance, both its target and its support. In
a cyborg world, *Big Brother is you and you are Big Brother*. This is true
to such a degree that it becomes generally useless to speak of a medium
of observation or, more generally, Big Brother at all.

In Baudrillard, the order of simulation is the sign of the end of the
media (he first presides over its last rites in his essay "Requiem for the
Media") (1981: 164–184). The mass media, he claims, are not mediatory
but actually anti-mediatory, in that they do not allow *response*, i.e., the
reciprocity of symbolic communication or exchange. Today we live not
in a media society but rather in an "ecstasy of communication" which
has nothing to do with the social, precisely because communication disappears in the implosion of the media in the masses (and vice versa). That
is, we transfer our waning capacity for sociality, for communication, to
the abstraction of an operation which specifies and governs the alignment
of biochemical and electromagnetic forces.[10] For Baudrillard (whose
views on these matters have changed somewhat over the years), the end
of the media is the point at which the obscenity of the media begins, its
viral incursion into all forms of communication, into the language and

practice of sexuality, politics, and the social, each of which is resurrected in an abstract and abstracting technology – and in an assemblage of power – that can only be called, from our perspective, cyborgian. Here there are no inputs or outputs, senders or receivers, no messages, but only pure cybernetic biofunctionality. No longer related externally to one another, bodies and screens, organisms and the apparatuses of recording and projection, form dense integrated living-circuits whose logic is simple, diffuse hypercontrol.

The cyborg model, as a frame for understanding the simulation of surveillance, is not so far-fetched and in fact is becoming more necessary every day. The interest in penal technologies that utilize integrated bio-surveillance – electronic leashes, body implants and sensors, chemical monitors – is rising. Foucault had already noted the tendency of practices of confinement to develop in directions in which physical restraint, enclosure, or isolation were no longer necessary.[11] To the modern electronic transduction equipment that allows confinement to transcend itself, we can add all the imaging, filing, sorting, and matching systems which analyze this information and circulate it over the Net. Electronic biopenality, that might be another name for cyborg control in the late twentieth century. And as Foucault knew very well, it is not just prisons that are meant here, but all contemporary institutions caught up in, reproduced by, and reproducing a cyborg order. We have seen that the contemporary discourse which has grown up around these practices and technologies is ergonomics. Here it is a question of how to match the machine to the body, to give it a perfect fit, to allow continuous monitoring and facilitate the conversion of bodies (their comportments, locations, metabolic functions, genetic instructions) to information and information back into bodies.

In *Nineteen Eighty-Four*, privacy is still a stake, a political and social value set against the intrusions of the observation-machine. The entire love affair between Julia and Winston, for instance, at least asserts this value against their forced betrayal of each other's secrets in the end. Already, however, it points to the paradoxes of the totalization of surveillance, where not even thought (especially thought!) escapes the machineries of inspection, confession, recording, and indoctrination. Orwell's work in effect concludes with the hypothesis that forms the premise of Dürrenmatt's work: the observer is observed, thus the end of the god of observation and the humiliation of human beings themselves reduced to false gods, i.e., to the very screens that envelop them.

All this, of course, is already present in Orwell. Goldstein, Big Brother, is a pure projection, a screen, not a watcher, but only the sign and the image of a watcher (guard, overseer, benevolent caretaker). Ideally, in this society, the apparatus of observation never has to touch the ground, never has to be real, since everyone is implicated in it in one way or another from the beginning. But for all that, *Nineteen Eighty-Four* appeals to a strong principle of reality, one linked to the domain of privacy. The enemy of Big Brother is the thought criminal, and in Orwell it is the free, private thought that is real. Winston suffers the purification rites of Room 101 to expose and correct his thinking. In the novel, Room 101 serves a double function. It names the physical space of a psychical cure, a site where the evil reality of private thought is exorcised. And it is the metaphor of a totalitarian society, an ideal space through which everyone passes (thought criminal or not). There, Room 101 is a simulacrum, a virtual reality. Here there is no thought crime (or perpetually undifferentiated thought crime, for there is no difference – everyone is equally innocent and guilty). Here there is no privacy (or perpetually undifferentiated privacy, a privacy so profound that at its highest point it is experienced as an absence). It is this tension, between the actuality and virtuality of privacy, the actuality and virtuality of free, criminal thought, that animates *Nineteen Eighty-Four*, and which has made it such a popular metaphor for surveillance in telematic society. Today, however, one is faced with a much more radical possibility. Not just the tension (or dialectic) between these poles but their compression and their collapse into one another. In hypersurveillance, simulation societies, there is no question of a return to some private realm (of thought, of space and time). Or rather, the return comes in the form of a hyperization. Today, the images of privacy, of private life, are endlessly replayed over the airwaves. Today, the first message coming from our screens is to get away, to be somewhere else, to elude the system, to escape the gaze and the routine it imposes – what else has advertising been telling us for years but that a private enchanted realm awaits us, and in fact is here, in our very homes, in our very bodies and brains. Privacy can indeed be found, and to the maximum possible degree, in the total immersion and cold solitude of video worlds, in watching our brains work on computer screens, in the lurking silence and terror of a defective gene, all techno-virtuo-hallucinogenic bridges to private (so totally private, so absolutely *remote*) realms.

Remoteness is the peculiar sensibility of telematic orders. Everything now is accessed remotely – the images on TV, society itself is on the Net – how long before the world is *only* accessible remotely? Remote doesn't simply mean distant here. It can mean, on the contrary, immediately present or available. The remote – most people own at least two or three

today – is an interface technology (in effect a translation device) for erasing the distinction between distant and close, present and absent, immediate and mediate, different and same. Remoteness, both in the
conventional sense and in the imaginary of virtual systems (which converge here), is a *problem for overcoming,* a problem which today is practically resolved (if never absolutely transcended) in the positing of a
general translatability of things into information, and information into
images, sounds, texts, etc.[12] The remote is a time/distance translator; it
literally "brings things (images of things) home," if we can still talk about
"home" – to our "node" would be better way of describing it (node only
indicates a point of diversion, a break point, through which a flow of
information passes, is decoded and observed).

Remote technology substitutes informated travel for physical travel,
the world on your screen at your fingertips. The whole idea of privacy
today is intimately related to the idea of immobility, of not having to
move, and thus remaining unseen. The military, we have seen, has long
recognized the strategic value of immobility as it relates to simulation
devices such as camouflage (the appearance of not moving, fading into
the background), but it has counterparts in other realms (see chapter 4
on military deception). Not moving is sometimes a tactic of animals, an
instinctual reaction to imminent danger, sometimes the last reaction possible. Is the freeze of a deer in a car's headlights something like the hypnotic "freeze" of people in front of their television sets or computer
screens? Transfixion as a passive mode of escape (like prisoners making
a break caught in a spotlight)? Are both efforts to disappear from sight,
from the light – or better, *into* the light, the only move left, a paradoxical invisibility? The deer's strategy can be fatal, of course, and so may be
our mode of disappearance, our immobility before the screen, before a
technology that connects us with everywhere and anytime and has no
intention of letting us escape (images of homage, prostration before the
screen, sacrifice, and the dream of non-detection).

What is unseen does not move, what is unseen is private, secret. And
in turn, what does not move, sees everything (from a strategic "point" in
front of the screen ... where "is" that point?). The whole imaginary of
virtual technology is one of not moving as a means of invisibility and
interiority, all the while exercising absolute power over images – in everyday terms, staying "home," "in one place," hooked up to the virtual
relays in your house (theater, mall, world, universe, "all places"), never
moving, but tuned in to the world (news, sports, life, love, emotion!), a
channeled world, relentlessly knocking on the back of your screen,
demanding that you turn on the power and let it enter. You don't move,

you "blend in," like a chameleon. You switch on the power, the images return. Are you *seen* by them? Does this remain a "private" experience, an experience of power, of controlling what is seen? Do you watch, or are you watched? You "welcome" the images into your "home" (or do they welcome you?). You make your home a world, without moving, by switching on the power. The world is here, now, present. It's like you're out there while staying in here, but there is here and here is there. Is this private? Even if the images are only the blind "eye" of the screen? Or is it the ultimate in publicity, everything here, now, at the touch of my remote? When you no longer move, you become the ideal target, always there, always available to the apparatus, always locatable, isolatable, online.

When the world becomes our screen (or our bodies become our codes), privacy and publicity dissolve into one another. The whole idea of exercising control over the distinction, the whole modern separation, of public and private spheres becomes paradoxical, implausible, finally impossible.[13] It is a curious sensation, being a "node," absolutely isolated (but absolutely connected), immobile (but moving anywhere instantly, remotely), alone (but everyone who's anyone is here, with me, onscreen!), absolutely connected (but home alone, unsupervised) – a feeling of being invaded by information and images at some level of what is supposed to remain a secret, unknown space (your house, your room, your sensorium, your brain, the chemistry of your microbes), but also a sense of complete security, absolute inviolability, because every transaction, every exchange, every movement, is accomplished without moving, within a perfect, enveloping interiority that cancels the gap between foreground and background. That is, we have seen, *from within and as* the cyborg apparatus. Privacy, we now realize, has nothing to do with escaping the gaze (I'll return to this below), but dissolving imperceptibly into the flow of information, into the cold gray "light" of televisuality. Likewise, the sensation of publicity is not produced by a gaze, which televisual technologies can only simulate, but by the mere fact of connection, and of the powerlessness to disconnect, the totalization of the simulated gaze.

Andy Warhol's old remark – in the future, everyone will be famous for fifteen minutes – still retains much of its paradoxical sense today, reflecting as it does the objective irony of the telematic situation. Fame only realizes itself absolutely in the absolute indifference of publicity and privacy. The old star system of American cinema was carefully constructed on the imaginary of that collapse between the private and the public (the meticulously organized but nonetheless notorious celebrity of the private lives of stars, their similarly notorious isolation and "singling out," the uniquely private and unapproachable character of their public lives, the loneliness and immobility, so to speak, of the spotlight). Today, that imaginary is rapidly becoming available to everyone in the general collapse of the real into its image, and the general diffusion of hyperreal, cyborg forms. Everyone gets to participate in the production and consumption of the simulacra of fame ("real" fame, just like "real" obscurity, having long ago disappeared). And anything, any trivial distinction, can be a ground for fame (the Guinness record syndrome). Fame, in the star system, was always a matter of according value to trivia, of making boring facts interesting differences. At least potentially, that path is now open to anyone – go online, create a whole new persona (as we'll see in the next chapter on sex), engineer your genes, create a unique child, a unique body, a slight difference to set you apart, get you noticed – and as that path opens to all, fame itself definitively vanishes as a mark of distinction.

We complain over and again how much surveillance erodes privacy in modern life, but how much of that is due to this more subterranean, more imaginary desire for fifteen minutes of fame? Even Warhol, though, had to assign that imaginary a real time, and so *misread* it. In the future history of telematics, fame, and anonymity, too, have no time – everyone is instantly famous, instantly forgotten, a node, a blip, a power surge, a crash. Fame is part of the menu (insert: distinction, awards, scandals ... delete: default identity, re-enter new identity ... paste: customized biography ... duplicate: informated persona ... send over network, undo text, etc.). What do simulated personae have to do with fame? They are already famous (on the air!), just like they are already unknown (today everyone's on the air, consigned to the oblivion of the media – all the "really" famous people are offline). This is a technology that pushes fame, *the very idea of fame*, and hence the very idea of anonymity, to its limit. In the imaginary of telematic systems, fame (notoriety, celebrity) becomes a fragile thing indeed, weightless and insubstantial. And this is true of one's isolation, too. Every moment is one of both potential exposure and absolute absorption. On the Net, in simulation, in virtual spacetime, everything and nothing is a secret, everything and nothing is seen. In systems where both celebrity and isolation are constructions of simulation, we really cross over to a new game.

The medical body and privacy

Where is the wisdom we have lost in knowledge? Where is the knowledge we have lost in information?

T. S. Eliot, *The Waste Land*

The profoundest secret is that which is enacted within the body.

Elias Canetti, *Crowds and Power*

The means of exposure (observation, examination) in telematic societies have really outdone themselves. Nowhere is this as true today as with regard to medicine, where simulated exposure is now a *prelude* to body probes. Here the body is *pre*tested before it's tested, its code is consulted before it is observed, and its code *guarantees* its observation, i.e., it insures that the body is something that *will have been observed* in a way that is translatable by and attributable to its code. The medical coding of the body in the modern age has gone from linguistic to informatic, and medical practice from diagnostics (reading signs from the body) to engineering, hyperdiagnostics, and virtualization (the body as an informational structure) – identifying and correcting coding errors at the microscopic chemical level, repairing defects in genetic structure, designing new structures and replicating them, etc. No more medical gaze, no more invasive probes, at least *not first* – the gaze, probing, all that comes *next* (although come it does, naturally and inevitably!). First, though, a consultation with an "expert" – the computerized clone or double, so to speak, of the medical practitioner him/herself, although one with a better memory. (The first and primary uses of so-called expert decision systems, or computer "consultants," were military, but medicine did not lag behind. Medicine has always found the technologies of war useful in the "battle" against disease, death, and the contaminated body.) First, *see* the model, then see the patient *in* the model. First, refer to the code (in telematic societies, all references are to and from codes); then make the body visible. First, prepare (stage, simulate) the conditions for medical surveillance. The genetic code is not just the ultimate, best diagnosis of the body (so this thinking goes) but the perfect *prescription for diagnoses*, the perfect training in diagnosis. As usual, we are referring to an imaginary (how difficult it is becoming to fix the sense of that concept!), a simulation model for medicine in which the body is already diagnosed and on the road to recovery well before the first appearance of any medical problem, i.e., before the development of a symptom, a sign. The code, properly constructed and set in operation, insures its possessor a *symptomless body*, a body without the *trace* of a problem. A weightless, insubstantial, virtual, but guaranteed, secure body, engineered to specs. A *eugenic* imaginary of the virtual body has existed from the beginning of modern medicine and throughout its development, an imagination, really, as much of the end of the medical gaze as it is of the intelligible body, the end of reading the signs of disease from the body, observing the functions and insides of bodies – to a *prestructuration of the signs of the body*, via genetic manipulation, always in the name and under the principle of life (genetic therapy/engineering are always framed by the authorities in terms of how they promote life). Genetic technology may be new, but its imaginary of the body, we have said, is still the pure, sterile, disease-free body, the body that presents no problems or even hints of problems, that is perfectly healthy, uniformly and predictably variable, according to instructions delivered by a code which surpasses it in all senses, and which because it's a secret, must be known, deciphered in full. We are today witnessing what happens when that imaginary begins to falter. The code, we know, can never be perfectly determined (knowledge of the genetic structure, like any physical system, is governed by the uncertainty principle). That doesn't, however, slow down the eugenic drive, which compensates for uncertainty with replicability (quality control), that responds to imperfection by contenting itself with simple repetition (perfect only means to be able to do it again, to clone it). So alongside research to map the code (the human genome project, surveillance), we get "practical" technologies of cloning, genetic therapy, and a whole new area of "free" choice opens up for us – for the first time, genetic "decisions." (What body would you like today? Choose your child, see what she'll look like in advance.) The look before the look. The simulation of surveillance.

The politics of the body in telematic orders is often articulated around the intersection of medical practice and the legal discourse of privacy. The debate on abortion, over biotruth technologies like drug testing and genetic screening, AIDS treatment – all from our point of view oriented around the problem of the disappearing body, of the body's simulation, and the simulation of its observation (we'll come back to these concerns in the final chapter). In places like the United States, these issues are immediately linked by various groups not to the relation of simulation and surveillance, but to "rights" of privacy, to concerns about access to and control of information about the body, and so forth. Undoubtedly, the experience of the body as something private is very old, rooted perhaps in the kinesthetic sense of the body as something singular, bounded, and continuous, something mine. But there was no conception, and no politics, of privacy in relation to the body until relatively recently in the history of the West. The private body as we know it – unseen, secret, interior, personal – was born simultaneously with the birth of modern disciplinary practices of examination that were themselves widely responsive to demographic and political changes sweeping European societies in the eighteenth century. The private body was both a counterweight to discipline and its alibi, a site of challenge and a locus of trouble for the authorities, but also discipline's necessary Other (read: necessary Evil), that unknown, secret outside that constitutes the possibility of authority and the Law, the "legitimate" exercise of power. It becomes the locus of a struggle, between forces that would conceal its operations and those that would expose them (not only medicine, but the biological and psychiatric-social sciences, the state actuarial machines, the military, the popular media, and so forth, all linked to a problematics of the visibility and intelligibility of the body). Tied early in the modern age, by Locke and others, to the discourse on property, privacy becomes the emblem of the body as a place of last refuge, as haven and escape, as *my* body, but also the last reminder of a vanishing body, intruded upon on all sides by the apparatuses of surveillance. Today, the private body is experienced as a place of perhaps irretrievable loss, disappearance, ruin, and sacrifice (complete loss of control to the surveillance apparatus, disappearance into information, sacrifice to the image, the perfect, beautiful, smooth-functioning body) (see Kroker and Kroker 1987). All these are indications that what is at stake in the present politics surrounding the privacy of the body is something beyond privacy altogether, and in fact is about the body's hyperreality, the indiscernibility and indetermination of the visible (actual) and virtual body. Here privacy means something else – an ironic privacy of the body, because the body is already precoded and overcoded, the absolute, inviolable privacy of the clone (the private hell of biotechnical repetition).

Medical science in conjunction with Capital's demand for fit, workable bodies (and the culture's demand for beautiful, desirable bodies) long ago assured that at least in matters of physical health and appearance, the body would have no special privileges in regard to privacy. The body as a concentrated repository of economic and cultural value was bound to be meticulously observed and its features categorized. Today, with the available battery of biological probes designed to gauge our immunities and plot our susceptibilities, to police our bodily fluids, and to regulate the flow of the body's "vital" information, with the craze in cosmetic surgery, with Wall Street investing in wetware and clone technology and ergonomicists dreaming of computer–brain–sex links, with the explosion of designer pharmaceuticals (e.g., Prozac – what information are you swallowing when you take this drug?), it is difficult for one to even imagine anymore a private, let alone a mysterious, secret body. Some see this as a new era of biomedical "normalization." But, again, what we are witnessing is not just normalization. It is cyborgization, not just body surveillance, but information–body integration (as Haraway notes, Foucault's examined body was only a "flaccid" precursor to the postmodern cyborg body) (Haraway 1985: 66). Cyborgs aren't "normalized." A norm requires a comparison, an inside and an outside, a difference; but the only difference between cyborgs can be an already programmed difference. The constitutive Other of medical authority we spoke of above, the private body, no longer exists, except as a reference in simulation (where it now "overexists" and simultaneously vanishes). I'll return to this. For now, I just reemphasize that this process is not just about privacy and its loss, but the orbitalization of privacy through the *erasure* of machinic–organic boundaries, and the forging of an indissoluble connection between simulation and surveillance technologies (cloning/eugenics alongside body probes). The cyborg and the clone as the paradoxical figures of the hyperization of privacy and its fantastic, absurd crash into nothing. The clone and the cyborg are the ultimate Others, inscrutable because they are perfectly known.

All this has tremendous implications for the constitution of postindustrial societies. Genetic research in the late twentieth century promises to change completely the relation of individuals to major social institutions, in fact to call this relation radically into question as more and more transactions go online. Information about susceptibility to inherited diseases, about lifestyles, physical and mental dispositions, etc., will be used to control the make-up of families (e.g., choosing the sex of children), to hire and fire workers (on their tolerance for hazardous work environments), to justify early intervention or therapy, to design educational or other disciplinary systems for specific target populations, to model ideal body images, to name just a few of the applications. Individuals no longer will "encounter" institutions, or feel dominated by them, but will rather be fitted, ergonomically, to their institutional circumstances and environments. We'll be matched to our families, our jobs, our preference structures (polls), our hospitals and schools before we can ask why, because our genes say it's so and it's right, and because our body probes confirm it. We'll be assigned a secure identity, a biomedical and biotechnical self constructed around our immunological profile – if we're lucky, we'll be immune to forces that interfere with work, immune to forces that interfere with sex, immune to forces that interfere with our programmed lifecourse. If we're not so lucky, if our biomedical index of future health (sanity, intelligence) does not coincide with the code, we will find ourselves out of work, out of school, out of pleasure, assigned to rehab or, in most cases, to the street.

All this has an actuarial history (see Eylenbosch and Noah 1988). Medical surveillance of populations really took off in the late seventeenth century, around the time when Leibniz suggested setting up the first Health Council to collect and analyze mortality statistics, even though the idea of observing, recording, and collecting facts about sickness and disease dates back to Hippocrates and before. In modern times, records of vital events had been preserved in many European towns from at least the sixteenth century on. The London Bills of Mortality, for instance, were enacted in 1532, although the information they generated was not used for scientific purposes until almost 100 years later, when Captain John Grant (1620–1674) published his *Natural and Political Observations*, the first serious attempt to estimate the population of London and count the number of persons that died of specific causes. Around the same time William Petty (1632–1687) published his *Political Arithmetik*, which among other things calculated numbers of physicians, medical students, and facilities needed to deal with the sick and dying in the city. In France during this same period Colbert introduced the practice of demographic statistics and Renaudot suggested setting up central offices to keep registers on health and disease.

These efforts developed in relation to prevailing political and economic philosophies of the time. The theory of mercantilism, for instance, provided an early justification for considering health care in terms of entire populations – the generation of an economic surplus depends on the state's means to guarantee a healthy, productive workforce. One of those means is formal record-keeping and analysis of demographic trends. In 1749, Achenwall (1719–1772) introduced the term "statistics" to replace the old "political arithmetic," and so-called "vital" statistics have been widely and routinely used since then and applied to increasingly diverse kinds of problems – rates of suicides, general mental health, lifestyles, medical topology, the relation of geography to pathology and public health policy.

Today, actuarial thinking supports medical surveillance in such diverse realms as prenatal care, birth defects, cancer research, general nutrition, immunization, occupational health, accidents at work and home, environmental hazards, mental illness, alcohol and drug abuse, poison control, and the list goes on. Information is collected, analyzed, matched, and profiled by national and world health organizations and centers for disease control. As with everything else, modern medical surveillance depends on high-speed computers, modeling and simulation technologies for everything from tracking AIDS in communities to monitoring region-al famines to supplying health data to insurers of workers in hazardous industries.

Insurance firms today are intensely interested, for rather obvious rea-sons, in genetic information. Armed with foreknowledge of clients' future health "histories" (and those of their children), they can choose to pro-vide or deny coverage as they wish. As usual, the current political debate centers around access to this kind of medical information, the privacy of records, procedures, and so forth, and not – or at least not so much – the technologies themselves. Inevitably, genetic and immunological tests are placed in the best light by those in the position to control and prof-it from them (their value as preventative, deterrent medicine; their poten-tial to keep insurance costs down by better identification of risks). But it is senseless to call genetic records "private" information. Any code that so positively individuates you and outlines your medical history in advance is no longer private, no matter who has "access" to it. (Do clones need "access" to their records? They *are* their record.) The battle for privacy of genetic records is only a symptom that those records have already been stolen, the code has already been pilfered and cracked (by the combined forces of three hundred years of medical surveillance). We have entered the age of simulated medical surveillance – the rewriting and replication of the biochemical program. Even if there continue to be bat-tles over the rights of individuals to their own genetic profiles, the genet-ic code itself, the model, can never be private in any political sense. When all the relevant decisions about how to live refer to that model – where and how to work, what to consume, what things to learn, when and whether to have children, how to arrange for one's death, etc. (all these things can be directly related to foreknowledge of future medical risks) – when this happens, privacy itself gets absorbed in simulation. Does a clone, to repeat the question in its most delusional form, have a "right to privacy," to the very information that has been used to create it?

The privacy/trust simulacrum

The conventional argument is that individuals in contemporary surveil-lance societies enjoy considerably less privacy than in times past. In a recent book, however, Steven Nock (1993) has argued for something quite different. He claims that the historical emancipation of young peo-ple from traditional family structures has in fact expanded the modern domain of privacy and produced in its wake a radical crisis of trust. Too much privacy, and no one knows anyone else intimately enough to inspire any confidence in social relations. In ways that recall Simmel's reflections on modernity and urban life, Nock identifies privacy with strangeness, and suggests that surveillance, by maintaining and verifying reputations (through credentialing, documentation, and intrusive "ordeals" like drug testing, polygraphs, and so forth), restores trust in social conditions of anonymity, i.e., in societies of strangers (Simmel 1950; Collins 1979). Surveillance, that is, literally fills the gap created by an explosion of privacy (fragmentation of families and the consequent isolation, estrangement, distance) in postindustrial societies, challenging the common belief that surveillance is the simple negation of privacy. Here, surveillance is a complex function that compensates for social isolation with a disenchanted, surrogate form of trust, viz., trust between documented, licensed, and screened individuals. I trust you and you trust me because our files (profiles, codes) say it's okay to trust one another; on the basis of the results of batteries of tests, through telematics and informatics, we redeem, as best we can, an eroded, disappearing sense of mutual confidence and reciprocity. Sensitive to the coming revolution in biotechnologies, Nock also notes how biochemical and genetic surveillance, unlike prior means of observation and control, project self-contained reputations (e.g., medical identities, health information) far into the future and allow "trust" to be established between individuals in risky relations without their ever needing to know one another intimately (or, as in the case of AIDS or other sexually transmitted diseases, as a prelude to a "disabused intimacy"). This loss of intimate knowledge or contact and its replacement by detailed information is, for Nock, the "cost" of increasing privacy in the late twentieth century.

But intimacy and privacy are not opposites in telematic societies. In fact, they are both *excessive* – everything is absolutely close-up and transparent and simultaneously absent and far away. Both closeness (as intimacy) and distance (as privacy, strangeness) are, like everything else, hyperized in simulation; no "real" gap separates them. For Simmel, the stranger is the one who is "both near and far," a double or marginal figure with feet in two worlds – prescient thoughts for someone writing decades before the explosion in virtual technologies. Today, strangeness is still one of the best terms to describe the experience of computer communication, virtual reality, genetic engineering, or just watching TV – one is near and far, or the scene is near and far, it matters little which we say because the self, the agent, the object, all dissolve in the general (imaginary) confusion of distances and times in these technologies. If Nock isn't wrong to say that information compensates us with a disenchanted form of trust in societies where privacy has become the predominant experience, he neglects to say that privacy – strangeness – itself comes in informated forms today. Information is not just the medium for another kind of sociality, the instant, abstract sociality and credential-ized, coded "trust" that exists among networked individuals. It is also not just the *absence* or loss of some form of natural intimacy. Information simulates the social *in its entirety*. Privacy still exists there, like trust, but in a coded, "clean," surrogate way (a construct, a designed and hyper-controlled experience). Likewise, intimacy is not lost, but purified and hyperized (in virtual space it is possible to be "closer than close," *more* than intimate, but still keep a safe "distance," just as it is to be "farther than far," but still retain an operational closeness). In our societies, the screen is what is close and far, intimate and distant, private and public. It is impossible to say whether there is more or less privacy in telematic orders, or more or less intimacy, because both refer only to their simu-lation model. Nock is right up to a point. In a realm where privacy cre-ates a crisis of trust, information networks substitute what "passes" for a society based on reciprocity, intimate knowledge, a digital simulacrum of the social order. But in doing so, it also constructs what "passes" for privacy in that order, that is, *informated privacy, a cold simulacrum of pri-vacy* – my password, my log-on, my genetic profile, all absolutely unique, but all absolutely standardized, referred to a precoded operationality. Nock is certainly right, there is more privacy today, but it is of a very different form than the privacy of the past. It is privacy as a virtual real-ity; not a world hidden from surveillance, but an already staged, pro-grammed isolation and strangeness. Simmel's impressionistic notion of strangeness is closer to this sense of privacy than Nock's, who begins from the fact of privacy rather than its facticity, i.e., the staging or per-formance of its scene in telematic orders. Simmel already sensed that pri-vacy in the modern age was not just compatible with continuous exposure, but that privacy, strangeness, had somehow already slipped into simulation, with its ecstatic dissolution of space and time. Near and far – today, that *can* mean *both* near and far, or *neither*; the question is undecidable and, yes, strange. Privacy in telematic societies is the experi-ence of the undecidability of distances and times. Strangeness is not just the isolation of the individual, but the ironic, perfect isolation of the cyborg, plugged in and alone at (in) the screen, intimate and fragment-ed, outside and in, perfectly known, perfectly indeterminate.

Not just private, but more private than private. The telematic imagi-nary is not just one of any escape, but *perfect* escape. Escape to your own private, exotic world ("personalized" vacations, outings, cruises, cars, etc.). Escape into work and into play. Flip the switch, escape into video, onto the Net (in the "privacy" of your home, in the privacy of your screen). Escape into escape. Escape, however – we all know this – is just a reality-delusion, and that is precisely its allure. You don't "really" escape into "vacations" (which more and more take on a hyperplanned character, managed leisure) or into video (video-games, computers, TV), but rather you *sacrifice* yourself, that is, give your complete attention, mind, soul, and body, to it, and it is the sacrificial element, the masochistic giving up one's attention for an exotic hyperisolation, that produces a kind of cold ecstasy, the kind we can read in the eyes of children in electronic arcades. But escape itself is fully simulated – you can't escape anything or anyone by playing Nintendo, by taking a planned vacation, or by cruising cyberspace. Escape here is always to another inside, or rather, from the interior to the interior; you never get outside the medium (which, of course, itself "disappears" under these conditions). This is especially true, even though at first it seems paradoxical, when you disconnect or unplug yourself from the system. The "outside," the "real" world beyond simulation can no longer link up to the idea of escape and instead becomes fixed to the idea of capture or confinement. The outside, in a word, is a prison, the sphere of unfreedom. Escape, privacy, "divine" isolation, today all this is on the Net. You too can get away (but who and where are "you"?).

It's not just that growing privacy produces (and explains) modern surveillance as a response to a growing crisis of trust, but that modern surveillance responds to the expansion of privacy by reproducing it on a higher level, giving us more privacy – perfect privacy – while simultaneously comforting us with the assurance that we are still – perfectly – connected (e.g., taking your cellular phone on a hike into the wilderness – you're never alone, *especially* when you're alone!). Here we return full circle to the collapse of private and public in information orders. We almost unthinkingly associate surveillance with publicity, and the totalization of surveillance with absolute publicity (exposure). But it is not only the signs and images of publicity (celebrity/notoriety/fame) that are everywhere today. It is just the same for privacy; its signs are everywhere – both effects of the surveillance-simulation assemblage. Privacy and publicity are no longer different here, no longer opposites; rather there is a subterranean complicity as both get taken up into simulation, a continuous transmutation and reversal of these poles. The image of the Private is exactly what is most Public today (in escapist ads, exposés of the lives of celebrities, in fashion, etc.), and what is most coldly fascinating and provocative (this reversal is the force behind pornography in all its forms). Reconstructed from vast swamps of information, the private world is precisely what is continuously on display today – staged privacy, programmed anonymity. It's nothing new to observe that telematic societies are voyeuristic societies, bound up in watching themselves watch themselves. What's new is that all this now reproduces itself on the level of simulation. When I observe the most intimate details of the Other onscreen, whether it is in the form of pornographic images or a genetic map (how similar today!), it is only the *mise en scène* of intimacy that I am given, a disenchanted, sterile (but not lost!) intimacy derived not so much from witnessing something hitherto unobserved or private as from plugging into a system where nothing is private and everything is, where the secret does not exist and everything is a secret at the same time – all this in the form of an ecstasy of orbitalization and dissolution, a mass mediated extravagance. Or again: a system where privacy slides over into its simulation through the very apparatus that compensates for its overproduction in modern society. The problem of too much privacy, and the crisis in trust which that excess produces, receives its answer today in a system that programs both privacy and trust as functions of its normal operation.

But one can also argue exactly the reverse (because the question is always undecidable): it is the Public that today is most Private. Information saturation always leaves one with the suspicion that nothing has been understood, that in fact the crucial information has been left out or excluded. This is precisely how tabloid news works and is the reason for its success. By raising the level of celebrity and notoriety to fantastic levels, the persons or events described recede and finally disappear. The very information that encloses and saturates them guarantees that they won't be known, that they will always remain obscure and mysterious. This in turn becomes the source of their notoriety, a *deep* (but delusionary) privacy that becomes all the deeper the more it is penetrated, until finally nothing is left but whatever gossip/rumor can be manufactured to fill the void. The "real" celebrity, the "real" public figure, is the one who has completely imploded into media, whose privacy is only a media affair, but who in every other sense, in the most profound sense, does not exist – an absolutely private nobody.

This is the privacy/trust simulacrum, and it produces the most exquisite paradoxes and ironies. The system allows for the perfect circulation of "personal" information among complete strangers, for a radical anonymity within the context of perfect, full disclosure. When everything that can be known about anyone is included in their electronic dossier and can be reduced to a simple 1:0, on:off logic, trust becomes a simple matter of having the right index (and so does privacy). Here we can imagine a society where everyone with a 1 is allowed a social identity (1 is a universal marker indicating freedom from disease, high intelligence, political conformism, whatever), everyone with a 0 is an outcast. But this absolute certainty would only be a superficial facade masking a more radical uncertainty. Trust, that is, rather than grounded in perfect information, instead takes the form of prophylaxis – sterility. I trust you (if you wear a condom, if you've had "the test"). I trust you (if you sign this document). I trust you in a world where absolutely nothing is certain and can be taken for granted anymore (the taken for granted world of the phenomenologist has disappeared). I know nothing about you, and to touch (see, hear, communicate with) you, I must have a medium that blocks our touch, yet allows it with as much realism as possible under the circumstances (a latex barrier against contamination, a screen, a filter, a surface of information, texts, documents, etc.). Everything is so uncertain today, nothing is known with assurance. Our batteries of tests prove nothing, and the more we use them the less confidence we can place in them. So we have a vicious spiral, madly constructing the media of examination, which only produce more uncertainty, greater isolation, intense erosion of the Social. All this is the very condition of possibility of our trust.

The full disclosure of the smallest details of individual lives on the Net becomes the basis of the perfect privacy and isolation of the Net itself, the perverse, collective privacy of a system spiraling in on and feeding on itself. Here the Net becomes the paradigm of isolation and anonymity in late twentieth-century society, literally a swamp of information in which, at the limit, one can discern no meaning. Here, we have moved from the strangeness of the individual, to the strangeness, and finally the unintelligibility, of the system, which is self-enclosed and does not connect to an outside. In a perverse way, modernity has succeeded in maintaining privacy against the operations of the surveillance machine by totalizing those very operations.

7

Sex in telematic societies

Cyborgs and the vanishing screen of sex

Telematic societies at the end of the twentieth century are distinguished by both an excess of sex – an expenditure of sexual energy beyond any conceivable utility – and the absolute disappearance of sex, its reduction to the zero degree. This isn't a contradiction. Rather, both are complementary effects of a general *obscenity* that characterizes the contemporary social order itself, an order where sex (and sexuality) is so thoroughly hyperreal and overcoded that it vanishes without a trace. The *ob*-scene, as Baudrillard calls it, is the contemporary scene of sex: an ultra-surveilled, virtual space where all the old gendered oppositions dissolve over the bionic horizon (Baudrillard 1990b: 50–70). Male: female, masculine:feminine, hetero:homo:transsexual, body:nature:culture:machine: if information and biotechnologies go the way of their imaginary, then we can say goodbye to these kinds of distinctions. Informated bodies – cyborgs – have no sex; or they have *any* sex.[1] In fact, we can say goodbye to the imaginary of sex itself, since in a radical and total state of exposure (everything observed, nothing hidden), sex no longer links up to *our* imagination, but only to the imagination we download onto virtual systems, onto *screens*. Here I mean screens of all sorts – prosthetic (sex surrogates), deterrent (sex security and sterilization measures), and proactive (sex diagnostics, replicant technologies) – not just the electronic variety. Sex "onscreen" is not simply porno, although that is one of its most ready images. Porno, the cliché goes, is only the tip of the iceberg, part of a more general implosion of sex into its media and the media into sex. Onscreen refers to the virtualization of sex across multiple functions, from risk assessment, to communications, to cloning (the ultimate screen of sex, since it eliminates the need for it). On one hand, virtual sex isn't sex at all, but on the other, it is *exactly* sex, in the

sense of being exactly what *stands in for* the scene of sex today. The "ob"
in obscene is a prefix for "in the way of," "in front of," like a screen. The
word, however, can be misleading. In telematic societies, the scene of sex
is nothing *other* than its screen. It *is* the screen. Not just the display, but
what displays.[2] Just examine the control functions of cyborg technology.
Scan, insert, close up, copy, reverse, slow-motion, freeze-frame. It is not
just the image, i.e., the *form of content* of the technology of display,[3] but
the technology, the medium, itself, the whole mediated environment or
envelope, that tends toward obscenity.

Penthouse magazine recently announced its entry in the new cyber
(read: cyborg) sex market – the first wave of interactive computer porno
("Porn, the Low-Slung Engine of Progress" 1994). What is the imaginary
of this technology? It is the same as other virtual systems: nothing less
than actualizing something impossible, viz., the real in hyperreality, a
perfectly convincing informated reality (i.e., not *merely* a representation).
The problematic around which pornographic perception is organized,
from the very beginning, is explicitness – the *display* is everything. It's in
that sense that Linda Williams (1989) is able to describe pornography as
a "frenzy" of the visible, a fantasy about viewing pleasure that transports
us to the "unseen world of the sexual other" (see also Brown 1981).
We've also seen that the visibility of the display technology itself interferes with explicitness, and that is why it develops according to a logic of
disappearance (a display has to hide its surface, be transparent, or undo
itself, to be a "really" convincing display, and there are many possible
solutions, some feasible, some fantastic, to this problem – miniaturization, non-reflective screens, high-density imaging, virtual headgear, even
direct brain wiring, the preferred methods of cyberpunk writers) (see
William Gibson's wet-wired "sim-stim" machines: 1988; 1986; 1984).
Cybersex is only porno with a refined means of display, a technical solution to the problem of sexual explicitness. In the imaginary (perfect)
development of cybersex technology, nothing in fact remains to get
explicit about; it's all there, the screen itself is perfectly transparent as
well as the user's connection to it. Nothing is left to the imagination –
the display itself becomes the imaginary and the user is "in" it, oblivious
to its artifice or illusion (or rather, to its absolute lack of artifice).[4] Who
needs "real" sex anymore (so this type of thinking goes)? Sex *is* the display, and like all virtual technologies, cybersex is about making the
(physical) display disappear, leaving just "sex itself," the "real thing,"
behind. Of course, sex "itself," "real" sex, is already long dead by this
time, a mere residue of its digitalized surrogate. Whether the virtual scene
of sex corresponds to or represents some real scene doesn't matter any

more. Nor, for that matter, is the issue any longer simply one of its visibility. Instead, that it *feels* real is the problem, and in fact the whole point, the essential fantasy, of this technology (the problem of making sex more visible pales in comparison to the problem of making its images convincingly tactile). Against Williams, who otherwise has much that's revealing in this context, this is not so much about a frenzy of visibility as a frenzy of *touch*. Williams brings a Foucauldian perspective to the description of porno as a complex, highly fictionalized, intersection of power, pleasure, and the visible (i.e., sexual surveillance). From our perspective, however, this fiction of sexual surveillance needs to be radicalized to account for new technologies of pornographic simulation like cybersex. With simulation, we pass from an imaginary of surveiling the sexual other and, as Williams says, attempting to "return with the story" (something never really possible) to an imaginary of *inhabiting* the space of the other – who is really no longer an "other" here but fully incorporated – the virtualization of sexual experience itself, not merely its relatively passive observation (Williams 1989: 279). We'll return to this at several different points in the text below. For now, it's enough to say that in the imaginary of cybersex, you go from the display of sex to sex *as* invisible display. Cybersex is about making a cyborg.

Nothing is apparently less sexual than a cyborg. At the same time, nothing exceeds its capacity to simulate sexuality. For the male:female double (for dualistic and categorical frames in general) cyborgs substitute a virtual universe of (hypergendered) connections. In this aspect, they perhaps contain certain emancipatory possibilities (as Haraway has suggested). But this interpretation is difficult to square with the fact that cyborgs are also the dissipation of sexual difference, reducing everything to abstract, internal relations of parts and wholes, to integrated bio-electronic monads. They are, in the imaginary line of their development, the ultimate cancellation of the "radical otherness" (Baudrillard 1993b: 113ff.) or strangeness that has always surrounded sexuality, substituting immediacy, hypercontact, and controlled uncertainty for the distance and pathos of sexual desire. If cyborgs break down sexual markers, it is difficult to think that they accomplish this in anything other than a thoroughly cold and disenchanted way.

In the 1960s, AT&T test-marketed the first TV phones. The technology didn't catch on then, because of cost and technical limitations, but in true postmodern form (recycling and repackaging the recent past), it has returned in the 1990s, and, given advances in channeling and display systems and possibilities for integrating different circuits of information – linking phone lines to data dumps like the Internet, for example – all this promises to send the porn business into orbit. If 1-900, dial-your-sexual-fantasy-for-a-fee numbers were the first wave in telephonic porn, it's not hard to see the possibilities of 1-900 pay-per-view telematic porn, connected to all the extravagant, dys-utopian possibilities of digital imaging: broadcasts limited only by available state-of-the-art resolution technologies; interactive systems that allow the user to control the time and space of simulated sexual encounters; or, down the road, fully programmed sim-sex (whatever turns you on), erotic video games, giant screen, wrap-around projection, electronic pleasure "environments," all approaching a level of production of hyperreal sex (read: super-cooled, clean, safe, improved) paralleled only by the sudden and catastrophic loss of real sexuality at the level of the human body.[5]

Here, the traditional voyeurism of pornographic perception (sexual surveillance) is elevated to the level of a vicarious experience – dive into the screen, exchange your body for a screen body (without being able to notice the difference). In the developmental logic of telematic systems, the idea of the body and of bodily contact loses its sense and coherence. The practical problem in the production of telematic porn is how the simulated body onscreen can become a surrogate for, and a prosthetic of, the real body, more attuned to the user's fantasies and pleasures. And also the reverse, how the "real body" of the observer can become more integrated into the apparatus of simulation. How can the cold interface between the observer and the mechanism be made sensual, i.e., re-sensualized? Again, this translates into a question not so much of vision, nor even exactly of the gaze (surveillance technology), but of *tactility* (McLuhan saw this in relation to television years ago). In virtual reality systems the current problem is not just the question of visual resolution and projection, but its ergonomic alignment to hand and body movements, its sensitivity to pressure and temperature, wetness and dryness. (Current solutions are still quite crude, to be sure, involving the use of treadmills, electronic gloves, etc. In science fiction, though, we can look forward to silicon implants, brain-jacks, midi-sex.) Interactive video in the mode of pornographic display only intensifies a problem that already existed at the origins of the technology, namely, the pleasure–power–knowledge relations of the interface, the conversion of the "feel" of the connection (keyboard, screen) into the feel, the warmth-coolness of bodies, the implosion of information into sex.[6]

Is this cyborg sex, or a sexualizing of cyborgs? An erotics of information, or a de-eroticization by information? Whatever the label, the traditional critique of pornography, as male exploitation and violence against women, doesn't go far enough here. In the "male" imaginary of cybersex, women are *already* eliminated; *in advance of everything*, they are reduced to codes, displays, options. Here, cybersex is not exploitation, but the purest form of male hysteria, a final, "clean" solution to the whole "problem" of female sexuality, i.e., that if it is uncontrollable, then it won't exist at all (Kroker and Kroker 1992). If cybersex is the intensification of a masculinist technology, then at its limit the screen alone is what remains of the "feminine," and as screen, under the absolute control of the (male) operator/observer. In fact, the screen becomes the projection of a phallocentric masculinity in crisis, the violence of its images the only compensation for a weak, parasitic power that has drained its host dry. Programmable techno-porn – what better strategy of male impotence against feminine power, against women?

This kind of critique starts to unravel, however, as soon as we consider the cyborg. In the cyborg, cybersex assemblage, there is no external relation between observer and observed. It is the dissolution of this relation, and between subject and object generally, that constitutes its operational principle. That means there is no external relation between masculine (observer) and feminine (screen), either, only an operational connection. We can think of cyborgs as either neuter (sexless, zero degree of sex) or hypersexed (hyperfemale:hypermale, informated female:male) – but they can't be identified as masculine or feminine, male or female. In this context, male and female are no longer located in anatomy. But we shall see that neither do they refer to culture (gender), or even strictly to "technology." The cyborg simply defies all these distinctions, associations, and categories, not by negating them, but fusing, shifting, mixing them together. It may say something about contemporary culture and sexual politics to talk about the information revolution in pornography, its exploitation of women, how men have devised this technology as a surrogate for female sexuality, which they can then control like any technology. But this ignores the subtlety of an operation which, in perfecting the connection between the body and the screen, vaporizes conventional sexual markers and substitutes for them a disenchanted *simulacrum of sameness and difference*. "Looking back at the year 2000," we can marvel at what electronic and biotechnology has done for sexual difference and sameness – canceled their relation to the symbolic and the heterogeneous, and reproduced them (ironically) in the homogeneous realm of information (Baudrillard 1987). Similarities, distinctions; whichever you choose matters little to the assemblage. This is a crisis not only of male sexuality, which may indeed still react today with violence and hysteria against everything feminine, a fantasy of extermination against all "other" sexuality in the name of its own sexual pleasure, but a crisis of sexuality itself, a violence against all pleasures, against all bodies, which everywhere are disappearing. Today sexuality, like everything else, filters through information, and the surface of contact between sexual bodies is an informated, electric surface.

So where is sex today? It is everywhere and nowhere, obscenely visible and invisible at the same time. Foucault once remarked that power isn't everything, it just seems to come from everything, every direction. It is the same for sex. In telematic societies, the screen of sex is like an environment, a climate. It is always *about*, and everything is *about* it. Cybersex is only one example of this general environment, although a particularly interesting one. Today, anything can be a screen of sex, a surface onto which sex is absorbed or projected; everything seems implicated in the problematics of its display (and further, its display's disappearance). Safe sex, risky sex, sex crime, cybersex. Sex as fashion, as art and politics, and religion. Sex as death (AIDS), as weapon (the phallus), sex as terror and predation (on the streets, at work, at home). A better question might be, where isn't sex today? Should we say that "real" sex is *gone* because the *spectacle* of sex is everywhere (Debord 1983)? This isn't adequate, because in telematic societies the spectacle *is* the reality and the truth of sex. In the imaginary of these societies, sex disappears, *but so too does its spectacle*, in the sense of a mere accumulation of images or signs, or a mere presence in the media. The postmodern spectacle of sex is not just a collection of sign-images, but a whole array of informated relations and virtual pleasures. It is about the *pleasure of screens*, and how to construct better, more interactive imagination machines and sensation-amplifying interfaces. And it is about the liquidity of sexual identity and desire over informatic networks. There, one's sex is completely and instantly reversible, in future (but already here!) electronic theaters of sex, complete with customized preferences (body types, bedroom scenarios), edit/format capability (the latest in software/wetware applications), file and hard copy capability.

Online networks now offer an array of log-on sex services, sex games, sex therapy, whatever you want. Again, what is the dream of these technologies? Nothing less than *realizing the dream of unlimited sex, sex without limits*. Or, put differently, nothing less than a permanent solution to the problem of sexual pleasure, viz., that sex is bound, ultimately, to death and power.[7] In virtual time-space, sex is freed once and for all from its Law. Nothing, no pleasure, is prohibited or too deadly, because all activity is mediated, and to that extent, there is nothing to transgress. That is the perverse, implosive allure of these systems. In virtual space-time, sex is like anything else, viz., anything goes. Anything, we have seen, object, event, experience, can be simulated (at least, according to the *rules* that constitute the operations of those systems). Simulation is an order of rules and games, not laws and their transgression. To violate a rule is not to transgress a limit. It is to leave the game (i.e., only to simulate transgression) (Baudrillard 1990d: 131ff.). Just as there is nothing really "explicit" about virtual sex, there is nothing "excessive" or transgressive about it, either; all the pleasures there are coded, cool, and supernormal pleasures, just as all the identities are fluid, all the dangers are controlled.

Take, for instance, the well-known story of Julie. Allucquère Roseanne Stone (1991: 82–84) recounts the story of a disabled woman who over the years became a trusted confidant and confessor to a number of women on a computer link-up.[8] Julie's accounts of how she dealt with her disability were so movingly rendered and passionate that a number of the participants began to reveal the most intimate sexual details of their own lives. Confidences were exchanged, advice was given, people were inspired, and lives transformed. Julie, as it turned out, was a male psychiatrist who logged on to the conference accidentally and found it too fascinating to log off. "I was stunned," he said. "I never knew that women talked among themselves that way." He concocted the neutralized sexual persona of Julie – vulnerable, victimized, confined to her small apartment – to learn more, and eventually became the center of conversation. The news that Julie was a man stunned many participants and prompted one woman to say she "felt raped." Others said they felt the sense of trust they had taken years to build had been violently shaken.

The point of Julie's story is not simply that people can *use* electronic networks in a deceitful way, but that in this medium all identities are virtual (this applies not only to one's sex, but to one's age, race, class, name, anything). In these types of encounters, the body is not a limiting case of identity. One is instead confronted with a cyberbody, an electronic, online identity. In Julie's case, which happened a number of years ago, when bulletin boards were just becoming common, this meant essentially a textual identity (Julie was only words on a screen). But in the imaginary of those who design cyberarchitectures, soon we will interact with virtual bodies, customize their appearance, even, if we look far enough ahead, feel them. It is the same for pleasure. Julie could as well have been a lover. Cybersex is only the next generation of simulated sexual encounters, one in fact that is already entering middle age. One must be careful not to couch all this too much in the language of deception, which still belongs to the order of law and transgression, or the false image (ideology). Julie, it is true, was "discovered." Her (his) ruse was exposed. But in virtual systems it is not about the reality to be discovered behind the surface (screen). It is about the reality *of* the surface/screen. Julie's discovery is less interesting than what the episode tells us about virtual sexuality. As Stone (1991: 84) notes, "ethics, trust, risk still continue [in these systems], but in different ways."[9] That is as "virtual ethics," etc. And as virtual sex, virtual identities, virtual pleasure. In the same way, there are only virtual dangers, banal dangers without real stakes. There are no "real" moral problems here; this is just the way these systems operate. Nor is this the "end" of transgression in the order of sex, only its apotheosis over digital nets. For "everything is transgressible," read "there is nothing left to transgress" (Kaite 1987).

Baudrillard (1993b: 51) writes that virtual reality devices, artificial intelligences, and so forth, are "celibate machines." They will never be able to experience pleasure. They are, alas, without feeling. The same is true for cybersex. It will never "really" be sex or pleasure. That "impossibility" doesn't, however, negate the intensity of our society's efforts in this direction, and in fact provokes those efforts. Today, perhaps, we increasingly assign the scene of sexuality and pleasure to these machines because secretly we sense the impending catastrophic ruination of our own sexuality, our own bodies, our own pleasures and pains, and we imagine that if we give these things over, i.e., if we *sacrifice* them now to the machine, we will be relieved of the great and monstrous burden they have become for us in the modern age (nothing is more worrisome today, more panicked and hysterical, than our relation to sex and pleasure).

What is sex today? It is everything and nothing or, alternately, it is a pure *residue*, the hyperreal projection of something dead, or left over from another time, that we can only recover in the dial-up, playback mode of postindustrial societies. Sex is a decoy, sex is a mock-up, a phantasm. It is dissolving into its screen, into information, its body is becoming a data phantom. As a function of bodies, sex is, or soon will be, history, that is, obsolete – too dangerous, too uncertain, too exhausting. Like everything else, soon your only "access" is a password. Sex is like history today, it just keeps being over.

The disaster of sex and the disappearance of the body

Postmodern sexuality is a sexuality in ruins. Of all the scenes we have sketched out so far – work, war, private life – no scene today is more catastrophic, more disastrous. Maurice Blanchot (1986: 1) writes that "the disaster ruins everything, all the while leaving everything intact ... We are on the edge of disaster without being able to situate it in the future; it is rather always already past." So it is with sex. Overexposed, overcoded, and hypercontrolled in telematic societies, sex today has the feel of irreparable damage.

The disaster of sex does not mean the end of sex, but rather its simulation. Nothing has changed, at least *apparently*. The disaster of sex is a virtual event, in simulated, not real, time. It is like Canetti's (1978: 69) imagination of the de-realization of history:

It is as if at a certain point, history was no longer real. Without noticing it all mankind suddenly left reality: everything happening since then was supposedly no longer true; but we supposedly didn't notice. Our task would be to find that point, and as long as we didn't have it, we would be forced to abide in our present destruction.

What does "finding" that point involve? Certainly not a rediscovery. Ironically, it involves the *renovation* of history, or more exactly, of time *before the disaster of history*, when history (once again!) is real and true. For posthistorical man, the "end of history" is an illusion, and in fact not even that. We "supposedly didn't notice" it, Canetti says. As it turns out, we were too busy deterring the disaster of history. The deep meaning of Canetti's idea turns on the impossibility – and the perversity – of this task. History is already in ruins; it is not possible to deter the disaster. Simulating history, however, provides the illusion of deterrence, of the mastery of real history. History can be real and true again as a reference in simulation. Posthistorical mankind maybe doesn't recognize the difference. But "our present destruction" is not just some void at the end of history; positively, it is renovation within the ruination of history (a good formula for postmodernity).[10]

Like the disaster of history, the disaster of sex in telematic societies is a crisis of its truth and its reality, and not its end. Nothing, Baudrillard writes, is more uncertain today than sex. The symbolism, seduction, and otherness of sexuality – those elements that grounded the play between the illusion and the reality of it – all these are gone. At the same time, we are plugged into a mediascape saturated with the signs and images of sex, a field that is now our return for two centuries of interminable analysis and surveillance of sex. If sex lies in ruins at the end of the twentieth century, it is because it is now in everything, more real than ever, captured and recorded by a vast array of info- and biotechnologies. Via informatic and telematic networks, sex, like history, is miraculously and ecstatically restored to the real and the true; the disaster (the past) of sex is returned to the future, for the present; and sex itself, the "real thing," is granted an (imaginary) reprieve to exist in a twilight zone of disenchanted forms, haunting its own ruins.

Like the Bomb, "real" sex appears today as an "impossible," if not exactly "unthinkable," event (Herman Kahn [1984] years ago described global nuclear war the latter way and even linked it to sex by calling it "wargasm"). Because it's too dangerous, too hooked up with death, because it threatens to destroy everything, we must deter it, which means relegate it to an imaginary field. This means more than just keeping it under close surveillance. It means, in one sense, just the opposite, viz., designing it so that its observation is unnecessary. Like total war as a concept in computer programming, sex is not so much a matter of seeing as of programming. It has to play itself out in virtual, i.e., less lethal, ways (this despite the fact that virtual systems can end up having more lethal consequences than the systems they replace) (see Bogard 1994). In postdisciplinary societies, this amounts to the endless *preparation* for sex (planning for it, scripting it, training persons for sexual encounters that they can never have, like the soldiers who train for doomsday in concrete missile silos, or like elementary school children instructed about the dangers of "unprotected" sex). But if total war and sex are equally impossible today, they are both references in simulation. Maybe we should even start to think about this state of affairs in terms of the *hyper*deterrence of sex, equivalent to the hyperization of deterrence as a military-political strategy: from organized displays of weaponry to organized arrays of electronic data. Sex then parallels war in moving from behind its screen (its deterrent forces) to *on*screen. Onscreen, sex, like war, is *more than* deterred, even *over*deterred. When we simulate the nuclear holocaust, a monstrous burden is lifted from our shoulders – responsibility not only for the reality, but the imagination, of the event and, ultimately, responsibility for its deterrence; leave it to the machine. The same is true when we sacrifice sex to simulation (our accountability for the disaster, our imagination of it, is downloaded to the system). In war simulations, deterrence itself is deterred – we can annihilate the world as many times and in as many ways as we can imagine. The same could be said today for sex. In the imaginary of simulation, we can abandon our desires to its lethality however and whenever we want.

So the end of sex is just the beginning of sex as simulacrum, the regime, we might say, of the telematic trans-sexual, an electronic rhizomatics of sex, sex fully de-realized and dematerialized/hyperrealized on the Net. The scenario is both provocative and chilling. Here, in the future-past of postindustrial societies, the scene of sex is channeled directly to the human cranium; just jack in to a theater of pleasures – someone else's, anyone else's, as your own – the ultimate vicarious experience (second only to the vicarious experience of death).[11] Sex today just keeps disappearing, despite (and because of) all our immense, panicked efforts to keep it in view, under the gaze, out in the open. But the more we see, the less there is to see; i.e., the less seeing counts for anything and the virtual experience matters most. We are passing from an age where sexuality is fixed and disciplined by a gaze to one which de-realizes sex and then orbitalizes it. The virtual sensorium of sex – safe, programmed, interactive.

What happens to sex happens to the body in general in telematic orders (Ostrander 1987; Baudrillard 1989; Baudrillard 1990b; Stelarc 1983). These are orders obsessed with observing the body, body parts, and the insides of bodies, but they are also dream cultures of the body – the perfect body, the beautiful body, bodies that are young, beautiful, healthy, and complete; but also the nightmare of the body as decay, disease, the body in pain (see Scarry 1985). Our obsession with the body is driven, in part, by age-old fears of death and disfigurement; surveillance as control here, as we have seen, takes the diagrammatic forms of the medical examination and the autopsy (Foucault 1975). The corruptible, contaminated body, as a medical-moral object, is at the core of what both fascinates and terrorizes contemporary societies, which expend massive resources on problems of prophylaxis and immunity. Once at the arbitrary mercy of sovereign power that exercised an absolute right to its death, today the contaminated body is the object of ceaseless efforts to manage, develop, and enhance its life, to reconstruct it and prolong it and assign it its proper place in the order of things (in the order of production and consumption, the order of signs and images, the order of health and disease, and so forth). Foucault, we have said, calls this bio-power, bluntly, the power over life, and we can easily understand how sex, linked as it is with issues of reproduction and health, with fantasies of politics, education, and fashion, becomes a kind of hinge through which this modern form of power can function. Already in the eighteenth and nineteenth centuries, he writes, sex was

at the pivot of the two axes along which developed the entire political economy of life. On the one hand, it was tied to the disciplines of the body: the harnessing, intensification, and distribution of forces, the adjustment and economy of energies. On the other hand, it was applied to the regulation of populations, through all the far-reaching effects of its activity. It fitted in both categories at once, giving rise to infinitesimal surveillances, permanent controls, extremely meticulous orderings of space, indeterminate medical or psychological examinations, to an entire micro-power concerned with the body. But it gave rise as well to comprehensive measures, statistical assessments, and interventions aimed at the entire social body. (Foucault 1980: 267)

Today, we could describe this as a kind of ultra-functionality, an obscene promiscuity of sex that has nothing to do any longer with its morality, but with the ceaseless recording and analysis of its operations. From genome research to education and health to the porno business, sex has little to do with prohibition and everything to do with breaking and creating flows, with *translation* – translation into formulae, onto film and video and disk, onto the airwaves, into popular codes of all sorts; sex is converted into *liquid*, it flows into and fills up every space and time today. Foucault (1980: 17ff.) associates this with the general provocation and incitement of sexuality into discourse in the modern period. Today we could just as well speak about informating sex, literally an *information ocean* of sex. However we wish to describe it, the effect of all this has been a dispersion of sexual information and images beyond anything remotely informative or imaginative, in any case, an end, at the close of the twentieth century, to what we could once call the mystery and seduction of sex (it's hard to imagine just how much more boring sex can get today). The modern surveillance assemblage has managed to produce a thoroughly disenchanted, neutralized sexuality and a thoroughly disciplined body.

At the same time, it's not only surveiling and disciplining sex that constitutes relations of power in telematic societies. Today, power hinges on the *disembodiment* of sexuality and the *desexualization* of the body, i.e., a double movement that drags both sex and the body into simulation, constructing both as virtual realities, not just surveilled objects (i.e., real representable objects). Because it no longer inhabits the real, sex is rendered sterile and absolutely risk free, the body is fully screened, sealed in a perfectly transparent medium – a cyberbody, or a body encased in a protective shell (like the bubble-boy we spoke of earlier who was born without an immune system) (Baudrillard 1985). In the future, we could say crudely, sex will happen either through information, pills, or plastic, whatever "surface" works best for protection (and whatever surface is most transparent, least disruptive). Safe, clean, secure, immune sex translates into simulated sex between simulated bodies – that is, if you want to *live*, to avoid *exposure* (here, not in the sense of surveillance but of viral contamination, as with AIDS, STDs). Sex in telematic societies is about immobilizing and sterilizing the environment of real bodies in order to make possible cybersex with cyberbodies, all under the sign – or rather, the hyperization – of deterrence. The (simulated) deterrence of sex, of the disease, decay, and death that come with it, in the bio-informational sense, is about decoding life itself, laying its foundation in information, the better to disinfect it in advance, before it becomes too much of a risk or burden to itself. This obviously entails an impossibility – no less than the elimination of sexuality and the body. That nonetheless is the imaginary solution offered by simulation technology – the quick(est) fix for contaminated sex and bodies. With these safely out of the way, virtual sex and bodies can have free rein, pleasure can be linked, again, with all the signs of excess (and all the "reality" of excess if the simulation is a perfect one) at the same moment that everything is sterilized. Excess no longer requires elimination; it can be made safe! Clean excess, no-risk pleasure (like non-alcoholic beer, no-tar cigarettes – drink and smoke as much as you like!). All this, of course, is not unrelated to the surveillance of sex and bodies in modern societies. Far from it, as we shall see below. Telematic societies are still bio-power societies, still oriented, as Foucault says, to the surveillance and control over life. Only now the game, as we've said so often, is one of hypersurveillance. Here sexuality is *over*exposed – this time in both the viral and the graphic, observational sense. So filtered of possible contaminants, it leaves itself open to the most random, unpredictable attacks (like the bubble-boy, one dies of a completely opportunistic bacterium or virus of the kind that can only arise in a rigorously sterilized environment) (Baudrillard 1993b: 66ff.). So at the focus of an immense information-gathering assemblage that never rests, it disappears in the white image produced by a shutter that never closes. So it goes in the imaginary of these societies, and this is how a surfeit of sex can be no sex at all.

Today the overexposed body is the body that is transparent, a surface *seen through*, but also the body *as* (disappearing) surface/screen. In a state of general obscenity, the flesh – subject to decay and obsolescence – vanishes beneath the apparatus that watches it, only to be resurrected as simulacrum. It's a blind spot, but not in the sense of a quality of the apparatus, but rather of the object, i.e., the body, itself. This is the virtual body, the completely personalized, personalizable body. Whatever you want to be, however you want to appear. Turn on the screen, and there it is, here *you* are. Here, in simulation, the body can find both its highest and lowest forms – a perfect, immaculately conceived body (any body can be simulated, why not have the best?), and no body at all (a pure sign-image, a data construct, a cold screen). And this is precisely what happens to sex and sexuality, too. Lost in the consuming brilliance of a gaze that continues to test, record, and replay its smallest movements in every conceivable way, it simply and finally supernovas. It moves into a virtual timespace, a kind of evasion by the object of the surveillance assemblage that has evolved and clustered around it in the modern age – in medicine, in psychoanalysis, in the biological sciences, in police functions, in law, in pornography. A sexuality about which there is nothing more to see or do (it's all there, in simulation; that means, it's everywhere, in excess).

Virtual touch and sterilization

The terror of AIDS is only one illustration of how sexuality gets pushed into simulation today, by an abreaction to sexual contamination (and death) that increasingly hypernormalizes and sterilizes all expressions of sexuality. With the advent of AIDS, the condom becomes a new master signifier of deadly sex in the same movement that the display of sex explodes in the culture. You can see sex everywhere – it's difficult, in fact, *not* to see it everywhere – but you can't get too close or touch it without protection of some kind. In the most graphic sense of postmodern sexuality, AIDS means: look, but don't touch; if you touch, you're dead. Or rather: if you touch, put a screen, a surface, between you and whatever you touch, something without any holes. *Renew the capacity to touch by breaking a flow*: it's a simple question of immunity, a problem of maintaining a sterile environment. Today, of course, that can take any number of forms, not just the condom, which is only one icon among many marking the general putrefaction and hysterical disempowerment of the postmodern phallus (another is the clone, to which we'll return one last time below). Whatever it is, the means of immunity has to be, in every sense, a screen, a surface across which the game of sexual contact can play itself out in absolute security, but without too much concomitant loss of realism (ideally, without any!). In telematic societies, the problem is recovering the reality of touch, to redeem the experience of sexual *contact* with none of the risk – the sterile touch, to be sure, but one that, given the technology, retains all its pleasures, and cancels all its "dangers." The perfect condom, in this perverse logic, is the indiscernible condom, in other words, the shrink-wrapped, hyperreal phallus itself. The condom as superconductor, bridging a gap in feeling, a distance that for reasons of death and danger can no longer be traversed by bodies.

The revolution in information and virtual technologies, we have said, has never been exclusively about vision and observational control at all, but about feeling and tactility. Baudrillard (1993b: 55) has noted that,

Reading a screenful of information is quite a different thing from looking. It is a digital form of exploration in which the eye moves along an endless broken line. The relationship to the interlocutor in communication, like the relationship to knowledge in data-handling, is similar: tactile and exploratory. A computer-generated voice, even a voice of the telephone, is a tactile voice, neutral and functional. It is no longer in fact exactly a voice, any more than looking at a screen is exactly looking. The whole paradigm of the sensory has changed. The tactility here is not the organic sense of touch: it implies merely an epidermal contiguity of eye and image, the collapse of aesthetic distance involved in looking.

But in another sense, screens are precisely to be understood in relation to organic touch, specifically, about the imaginary of reproducing it perfectly in simulation. More than ever, sex today is about controlled proximities and prophylaxis. Sexual technologies are oriented to security, comfort, and closeness, to the whole problem of the impossibility of tactile pleasure across (or better, *with/wearing*) an informated medium. Simulated pleasure is all we can afford today, all other varieties being lethal. This is the case not only with sex, but with almost anything having to do with the body. Our society's panic-obsession with health and aging, diet, exercise, beauty; our fascination with prosthetics, implants, cosmetic surgery, cloning; all these reflect, to a greater or lesser degree, the collapse of the poles of pleasure and death in telematic orders, where the least indulgence becomes fatal, where purging follows every gratification (societies are anorexic, not just individuals). Sex is death – an ancient connection, to be sure, but one whose tension is particularly acute in postmodern societies. Today, the technics of simulation develops as an imaginary solution to that tension, a solution that would virtualize, and thus break, that connection. The new bio-informatics of sex (from cloning technology to cybersex to disease prevention) is organized around resolving the contradiction between safe (sterile) sex and tactile (unsterile, unsafe) pleasure, and at its core is an imaginary ergonomics of screens. The perfect screen for sex is not just about the tactility of the image. It is the ideal deterrent – unseen, unfelt, a non-medium producing the sensation of real, natural contact, but absolutely impenetrable. This is what the simulation of sex is all about, real, tactile sex (once again!) beyond sex linked with disease, mortality, damage, immune deficiency. Basic innovations in simulation have to do with the surface of the screen, to make it more transparent to touch, to allow touch (or any contact that would otherwise contaminate), paradoxically, to pass through to the other side of a surface *without a hole*. The ultimate protection would be a technology that perfected the simulation of touch – of contact – and that thus reconnected sexuality with sensuality. The "new paradigm of tactility" (electric touch) in effect is just the old paradigm (organic touch) in an indiscernibly different form. At least, that's the ideal.

For a long time, sexuality has been subject to the admonition "look, but don't touch" (an *admonition*, i.e., a prohibition *plus* an incitement, a warning to pay close attention). The surveillance apparatus resolves this problem with reality checks. (HIV-positive? Don't touch.) The simulation apparatus, on the other hand, resolves it with hyperreality, designing an order where sex can be seen and touched without limit (no HIV in hyperspace or clone-world; touch all you want, so this thinking goes). In the imaginary that drives these mythic tasks of engineering an absolutely safe form of sex, an absolutely sterile body, touch only gets more real (better than real). We move away from – or rather, link in complex ways – solutions based on isolating deviant cases, keeping them under close scrutiny, confined and quarantined, to solutions that dream of the perfect simulation of touch. The simulation of touch is another impossible, of course, but as we have seen, simulation always aims for the impossible, a technological miracle. The miracle is what is impossible, but there it is! That, in theory, is what simulation is about, and sex in simulation is like miracle sex, safe sex, impossible sex, but above all, *real* sex (read: hyperreal, more satisfying than the real thing). The surveillance apparatus, of course, aims for an impossible, too – the absolute visibility of sex and the absolute knowledge of its dangers. In the future development of this apparatus, perhaps, everyone's risk factors will be a matter of automatic record – updated HIV status, chromosomal damage report, sexual behavior history, etc. But that approaches the radical kind of front-end control characteristic of simulation. The difference is that where surveillance technology exposes reality to control dangers, simulation technology, in theory, creates a dangerless reality ex nihilo. Where the former identifies and measures the risks, the other eliminates them (radically, entirely). And so telematic orders at the end of the century fuse together two impossible technologies of sex, each, in its own fashion, aiming at the reality of sex, in both competing and complementary ways – one through recording and one through programming, both wired together, a sexual reality–safety assemblage. If telematic societies are about the disappearance of sex, they are always simultaneously a (re)capture and a (re)configuration of sex into a higher form. The dominant technologies of sexual control, like those we discussed for work, are analogous to two methods of preserving a threatened species, either by confining surviving members to zoos (surveillance) or, when that fails, by taxidermy and dioramic presentation (simulation). These are two sides of the same coin, however, two means of resurrecting a dead (or almost dead) object, two ways of killing it just the same.

In the imaginary of these societies, sexual surveillance and sexual simulation are inextricably connected. The more sexuality is monitored and recorded, the more its reality and its vitality dissolve. The less real sexuality becomes, the more its observation (and its experience in general) is virtualized. Simulation technology is not only a solution to the dangers of sex, but to the basic problem of its surveillance, viz., that sex, ultimately, is uncontrollable, undisciplined. For the surveillance machine, sexuality is always an Other, i.e., something to regulate or assimilate, an Object to transform into a Subject (or vice versa). Surveillance, like any technology, is only perfect in the imaginary. No matter how radical and comprehensive the gaze, sexuality always escapes this machinery, eludes capture (observation, recording, analysis), and reasserts itself as something excessive. In that sense, pornography has nothing at all to do with sexuality, which always, in a basic sense, remains at a distance, inscrutable. Pornography rather is about the mastery of this distance or gap, whatever lies on the other side. "Mind the gap."[12] It is this unbridgeable distance that the surveillance-porno machine attempts to close by increasing its power of observation, and which the simulation-porno machine proposes to ignore altogether by converting its object to information. Simulation hyperizes the control of sexuality by *refusing to pay attention to distance*,[13] to the external relation between (or the duality of) the object and its means of manipulation, between sex (and the body) and machine/observer. Cybersex, to return to this example, has nothing really to do with older forms of surveillance or discipline – which require a human multiplicity to act on, bodies and objects to watch and relations to regulate – but rather with writing better programs, devising better interfaces and imaging technologies. What is being manipulated are not bodies, not even images or data, exactly. Rather, in cybersex, one enters a control envelope that has no real boundaries (in the same way that my visual field has no edges). Cybersex is sexuality as a closed circuit, forever circling in on itself. There is no room for control in that kind of environment because, as I've argued in previous chapters, the whole environment is control, i.e., sexual hypercontrol. Here simulation opposes and overcomes the limits of the surveillance machine. The latter is in fact no longer necessary, since its aim has been achieved by other means; it, along with its object (sex, the body), gets incorporated into the assemblage for projecting image-signs. Sex no longer has to be observed, because the observation of sex has already been coded (further observation is only a matter of refining the code, building better hardware and wetware). Here, in the imaginary of the perfect simulation of sex, the surveillance of sex, the discipline of the body, is perfectly passé.

Sex and the genome

Biogenetic research and diagnostics, and the vast information network that supports both, also feed the contemporary hyperization of sexuality and reflect, in the effort to control risk and limit liability, the dominant moods of sexual panic and uncertainty that characterize postindustrial societies. In their various functions – disease screening and prediction, sex typing and selection, genetic engineering – biological testing and the new genetics are radical intensifications of bio-power technologies, at the center of the effort to medicalize sex in populations at the level of the basic chemistry of the cell. The assumptions of nineteenth-century eugenics, the whole imaginary of biological determinism and organic/racial/sexual purity, haunt these new technologies, with their potentials for selective breeding, absolute identification, biocredentialing, cloning, functional adaptation and qualification, and exclusion (matching, for example, the biologically or medically "fit" to certain forms of work, denying the "unfit" insurance coverage, health care, education, reproductive choice, etc.) (Duster 1989; Nelkin and Tancredi 1989).[14] The aim of these technologies is proactive – to prevent risks from becoming actualities (disasters!), plotting information on individuals against risk profiles and targeting for elimination, treatment, or confinement those that do not fall within normal or acceptable ranges. This is nothing new, and follows various threads of ideas of selective breeding that have been around since ancient times. The current wave of genome research and mapping simply carries this tendency to its logical conclusion. In this dream of absolute control, a genetic screen exists for whatever disposition, unfortunate or otherwise, you can imagine (disease, crime, intelligence, sexual orientation) and a means of its *disposal*. The *disposal of dispositions* – in the widest sense of that concept, that is what genetic mapping is all about, viz., the adjustment, ordering, furnishing, marshaling, or discarding of possibilities in advance, before they have the chance to develop into problems (whether medical, educational, juridical, psychological, sexual, or social) – this is the whole focus, the whole imaginary, of biogenetic technology (see Nolan and Swenson 1988; Kevles 1985; Latour 1986; Rothman 1986). Expressed positively, it is to identify and isolate "normal possibilities" and actualize them in normal bodies, normal populations, normal cells. It's not just "possibilities" (possible bodies, cells, populations) the new bio-engineers are interested in, however, but virtualities – the design and fabrication of bodies, cells, and populations *in advance of life itself*. Not just converting possibilities (i.e., dispositions/chances) into realities, not just normalization, but transforming imaginaries (of absolutely perfect bodies, etc.) into hyperreal objects (codes, chains of genetic information). Contemporary bio-engineering imagines nothing less than the *perfection of the norm, of possibility itself, and that means the absolute cancellation of both norms and possibilities.*

Cloning is the most extreme case. Even in its technical infancy, its imaginary of perfect bodies projected from an end (engineered outcome) given in advance is absolutely clear. Here, there is only one norm, i.e., the genetic code itself. A norm, however, requires some kind of comparison. In this imaginary there is none – it makes no sense to say one clone is closer to the norm than another. A clone is a clone is a clone. There is, in fact, *only* the Norm here (with a capital N), and all clones *are it.* The "dream" of cloning is really to be done with the work of normalizing once and for all (in a perfect clone-world, who needs anything normalized?). In that world, moreover, clones are not "possible bodies," defined in terms of what "real" bodies lack – the right sequences, markers, etc. – but designer bodies that lack nothing. Genetic engineers in the everyday, workaday world might genuinely want to make "real" bodies better, to compensate and correct for all their deficiencies, but the imaginary figure of the clone that drives their efforts is itself never deficient. It signals, at the highest stage of its development, the end of the body's "possibilities." That doesn't mean all clones have to be the same. Differences can also be cloned, and whatever differences you like (blue eyes, green hair, detached earlobes, dominant moods, whatever – a "diverse" population can also be a cloned population). But this fact doesn't change anything fundamental. Difference amounts to little when it is programmed difference (just as sameness is meaningless when reduced to programmed sameness).

Cloning follows a simple rule (in the dream/nightmare logic of its development): isolate a function (genetic sequence) and *reproduce* it, or disallow its reproduction. Genetic engineers dream of customized (beautiful) bodies equipped with all the latest immunities, programmed to live long (immortal?) lives with no surprises (like inheriting some bad DNA and dying). A clone in the pure sense, however, is not a reproduction at all, but a simulation. Like all (ideal) simulations, it is always already reproduced. DNA is the purest example of reality – meaning *life* – in advance. Life in advance of life, a future in a past and a past in a future. And that is why cloning is the ultimate sim-sex technology – it is an effort to transcend the problem of reproduction entirely, i.e., all the uncertainty, chance, risk, failure, i.e., *all the sex*, associated with it. If there is a paradigm of "the hyperization of sex," it is the clone. Clones, like

cyborgs, don't have parents (or siblings or families) – they are programmed parts of an assemblage. Here, sex as reproduction doesn't matter or, at best, it amounts to gene-splicing and implantation. Cloning is
not just mass production technology, an assembly line for bodies, which
would still be to view it in terms of an industrial metaphor. It is virtual
technology, and thus depends on the support of an information-gathering, storage, and retrieval network (mapping the genome requires huge
amounts of information and would be impossible without modern computers).[15] Cloning is the simulation of production, because nothing in a
world of clones is really (re)produced (or pro-duced, in the sense of creating something *new*). Clones, like cyborgs and everything else we have
mentioned so far, are closed circuits. In the imaginary of these systems,
nothing enters, nothing exits, everything is a modulation. They are not
the end of sex (not simply that, at least), only the breaking of its connection to reproduction. They are, again, a pataphysical solution to sex
(the final solution, its last decoding).

Biogenetic technologies are good examples of how surveillance and
simulation technologies follow each other in telematic societies. The biosurveillance machine ("body probes," medical tests, and screens of all
sorts) and the simulation machine (genetic mapping, profiling, cloning)
work together to initiate and perpetuate divisions in populations along
dominant gender (and racial and class) lines. Prenatal testing, for example, is one area that not only explicitly targets women's bodies as objects
of observation and control but, in some cultures, planning the "perfect
child" can intensify the tendency to abort female (over male) fetuses (see
Rothman 1986). In the workplace, some companies – predominantly
firms manufacturing chemical products or handling hazardous wastes –
have developed "fetal protection policies" that have attempted to bar
women from occupations that could harm their unborn children (these
companies see mothers as liabilities, as insurance risks, or as potential lit-
igants). In the same way, AIDS testing is not only a screen for the disease, but a political/panic vehicle for the militant reassertion of
heterosexual values. Biosurveillance and simulation technologies can create sexual underclasses, ghettoizing everyone who fails the screen (Nelkin
and Tancredi 1989). Members of that class are disadvantaged and dis-
qualified not only on the basis of their anatomy – i.e., penises or vaginas
– but on a whole range of behavioral predispositions that in one form or
another can be related to sex.

Simulation and biosurveillance are risk technologies, i.e., they attempt
to deter the disaster of sex by a kind of panic reaction that focuses all its
energy into preparing for the disaster. In fact, they don't deter the disas-

ter of sex at all, but instead create its very conditions, in the same way that medicine, as a system of technology for the creation of sterile environments, creates the conditions most favorable for opportunistic, catastrophic infections and diseases,[16] in the same way that military hyperplanning and the continuous scripting of war scenarios creates the conditions most favorable for insuring the inevitability of future wars.

The paradox of surveillance and simulation technologies is that if together they reinforce sexual divisions in society, they also, as we have suggested, erode sexual difference (on which such divisions rest); they reduce sex to a neutral, neuter space, a dead zone, where everything is equivalent to everything else. While prenatal testing supports sex control, it also has nothing to do with sex. Male or female, it is ultimately a matter of indifference to the technology. The details of sexual bodies are only that to these technologies – details.[17] It is the form, not the content, of sex that matters. Sex, gender, penises, and vaginas, whatever, all become the equivalent of other body parts or characteristics on the menu of choices: hair and eye color, skin color, weight, resistance to various diseases, intelligence, artistic sensibility – the list, at least in the fantasy of genetic engineers, is endless. It is as if in focusing so relentlessly on sexuality, biogenetic research, unaware of what it was accomplishing, made it disappear, and the more it attempts to bring it into focus, the more sexuality eludes capture.

Time, space, hypergender

This connection of bodies to nets of information, of organisms to cybernetic systems, as Haraway clearly saw, destabilizes conventional gender meanings and dualisms, the political effects of which, according to her, can be either confining or subversive, depending not just on how information is used and by whom, but on the openness and freedom of connections themselves. Foucault, likewise, focuses on the multiplicity of gendered connections, if not as cyborg relations, then as effects of more inclusive relations of power, knowledge, and pleasure. Together, Foucault's and Haraway's ideas on the intersections of sexuality and control – on gender reversal and dissolution, on the discipline and spectacle of sex pushed to their limit – are far more intriguing than a view like Berger's, which takes up the themes of power, imagination, and sex, but assumes the old dualisms even while critiquing them:

A woman must continually watch herself. She is almost continually accompanied by her own image of herself . . . [and] comes to consider herself the surveyor and the surveyed within her as the two constituent yet always distinct elements of her identity as a woman. She has to survey everything she is and everything she does because how she appears to others, and ultimately how she appears to men, is of crucial importance for what is normally thought of as the success of her life. Her own sense of being in herself is supplanted by a sense of being appreciated as herself by another. One might simplify this by saying: men act; women appear. Men look at women. Women watch themselves being looked at. This determines not only most relations between men and women but also the relation of women to themselves. The surveyor of woman in herself is male; the surveyed, female. Thus she turns herself into an object – and most particularly an object of vision; a sight.   (Berger 1972: 46–47)[18]

In this passage, Berger places under the male sign what in Foucault's work is a far more comprehensive connection between discipline, hierarchical observation, and self-examination, between visibility, the incitement to discourse, and the experience of pleasure. In Foucault's writings, the gaze is not essentially male or even phallic. If it serves to reproduce patriarchal systems – and there is no doubt about this – it also reinforces heterosexual over homo- or transsexual practices, the administration and control of children's sexuality, the "proper" comportment and display of the body, the policing of sexual health matters and the varieties of sexual excitement and satisfaction, and so forth. All these, while never severing the close link between maleness, objectifying forms of perception and the historical subjugation of women, implicate the gaze in a far wider, more diverse network of power–pleasure–knowledge relations, one in which the hierarchical relations between men and women, or the masculine and feminine, are *immanent effects* of a broader anatomo- and regulatory politics of sexuality. That is, those relations reproduce themselves within a diagrammatic machinery of power relations (disciplinary, panoptic, virtual) that both passes through them and makes them operate in predictable ways. The gaze (panoptic discipline) is not gender- or sex-specific, but orders the multiplicity of human sexualities into discrete, functional relations across a multiplicity of social fields (e.g., the gendered division of labor, the gendered political sphere, the gendered domestic sphere, gendered economy, etc.). It is not a categorical form of dominance, but a complex web of provocations, dividing practices, and detailed manipulations that come to have a general application in telematic orders.

Foucault (1979: 195ff.), we have seen, shows us how architecture can embody relations of power and how relations of power themselves constitute an architecture. Gender relations, like all power relations, are organized in time and space. The architectural arrangements of homes, workplaces, schools, and other institutional settings, as well as geographical ordering in the broader sense, are simultaneously gendered spaces (Spain 1993). This is certainly an old story. Practices of gender exclusion (confinement, segregation) by physical means have a long history. Almost all societies devise men's and women's "places" and control them by partitioning space, into zones of access and visibility, open territories, secret spaces, etc. "A man's home is his castle" is a ridiculous maxim, but it also reflects the historical and material ordering of households into strategic places under women's maintenance but men's control. Already in the fifteenth century, the architect Leon Battista Alberti was describing the home as masculine territory, a space for enhancing masculine status and power. This pattern is reproduced in countless ways in building design and construction, both public and private, in the modern age (Spain 1993: 137; Wigley 1992).

The same is true of time. Gender/power relations are structured and reinforced by clocks, calendars, a whole meticulous ordering of sequences, repetitions, postponements, anticipations, and so on. At some of its most basic levels, gender politics plays itself out in struggles to control the temporality of speech – silences, interruptions, timing of premises and conclusions – in phenomena like waiting, planning, and so forth (who can speak and when, who must delay or postpone acting). It is reflected in how time is valued (in labor time, free time, useful versus wasted time): historically, women's time counts for less than men's, a fact that is reproduced not just in structures of economic inequality but in the myriad of details of everyday life, the thousands of disciplinary tactics and devices that regulate gender interaction as a daily routine.

In the modern period, the technologies of discipline still orient themselves to a problematics of the real. Spatial and temporal orderings are in the service of revealing, stripping away appearances, penetrating surfaces – a political technology of control over real spaces and times. As we have seen many times in the course of this book, however, it is precisely the order of real space and time that virtual, hypersurveillant systems call into question. This is the whole of their imaginary, to suspend the "rules" of time, to enable its reversal, the modulation of its tempo and rhythm, to repeat it (at will, endlessly). Virtual time is not linear, real time. In virtual time, events in the future are always already in the past, in the sense in which their code precedes them; they unfold according to a logic of repetition in advance (Bogard 1994). Every video game, every simulation, is over before it begins, no matter how complex or how large the number of variations it can accommodate; in these games, when you gaze into the screen, you are staring into an imaginary scene that is the simulation of your own gaze (your gaze before it happens!). Playing these games is like having someone else's eyes, someone else's experience, *but they're your own*; you're somewhere else but here, too. To break down the limits of space and time, to travel anywhere, instantaneously, or even better, *to arrive before you leave*, that's the logic of a virtual machine. In virtual space, there are no "destinations," no "origins." There are no "visibilities," no loci of control (control is diffuse across the connections). Virtual reality is not an architecture, but a cyberarchitecture. Virtual time is not clock time – computers don't connect people in "real time," but in simulated time (see Benedikt 1992: 1–27). "Where" and "when" are categories of simulation – homes, schools, workplaces, all these "real" places with their "real" rhythms, dissolve in a digital field without edges, or rather, they are reincarnated as hyperreal sites within that field. Finally, in virtual time and space, gender loses its sense as an aspect of "real" culture (in the same way sex is radically dissociated from the real body). Virtual "cultures" (such as those we hear about developing on electronic networks) are not cultures at all, not in any conventional sense at least. They have, as Baudrillard's work continually reminds us, nothing to do with symbolic systems, with meaning, or even with communication, but only the simulation of these things, a simulation that strives to replicate or counterfeit culture, but in the last analysis is always the zero degree of culture.

How do we analyze this state of affairs? In thinking about the effects of modern information and biotechnologies, it would be absurd to doubt that they reproduce, in one form or another, dominant gender (and also class and racial) hierarchies. In chapter 5 we saw how many of the least valued, most stressed out, stupor-inducing jobs in the cyborg workforce – electronic filing and retrieval, order recording, and other clerical computer work, sales, reservations, etc. – are done by women, or, more accurately, information systems *served* by women. In the same way, women will fall in disproportionate numbers into the new biological/sexual "underclass," because of their historically marked position in reproductive politics and morality. Dominant gender interests continue to fuel the massive expansion of actuarial information in postmodern societies, exacerbating the ghettoization of women by virtue of defining them against normative and normalizing criteria that are overwhelmingly masculinist (security, protection, insurability, etc.). Finally, the development of virtual reality and compu-televisual systems promises not only to hyperize the domestic sphere, canceling the boundaries between home and work, but, as we have seen, to informate and amplify the presentation and circulation of pornographic images. Both, certainly, will operate to the social, economic, and political detriment of women as well as other marginalized groups in society. Making home like work and work like home doesn't eliminate gender relations of domination and subordination, it just decodes and *standardizes* them. And cybersex isn't just software to realize male fantasies of rape, but marks a more fundamental identification of the feminine and technology in general, as a screen for the compensation of masculine impotence and the projection of male hysteria – the machine and the female, in this imaginary order, share the same characteristics: they are slaves, passive, receptive, on call. It is not difficult to show how much of the technology developed in the modern age perpetuates the myth, the delusion, and the hallucination of male power. Cybersex is only the latest and most extreme example.

If all this is true (factual), it is also a completely inadequate way of conceptualizing things from the point of view of their imaginary. Virtual systems hyperize gender/power relations, the same way they do for sex. The conventional language of differences in power, knowledge, or pleasure doesn't account at all for the simulation of these differences. If cyborg technology is a degendering (as well as a desexualization) of social relations, it is also a *re*gendering (and resexualization) of *informated* relations (assuming one is still allowed to speak of "relations" in cyborg logic). The problem is how to describe this concretely while avoiding the very dualist framework of feminine/masculine that bio-informatic technology shatters. Gender/sexuality, we have said before, matters nothing to this technology except as material for restoration and renovation. The cyborg *is* the simulated gender relation, just as more generally it *is* the simulated social relation in postmodern societies. It is the screen of contemporary gender relations, the surface where gender implodes in the media. Just like the case of Julie, what matters is not simply the construction of gender in the medium – how a man could appear to be a woman, or a woman a man, or a woman as a man as a woman – but the *hypergendered medium itself*, how screen becomes (indifferently) masculine and feminine, simulates a context, virtualizes a world. It is less helpful to think of men and women "using" or "communicating over" or "being exploited by" these systems than as virtual nodes or switches in cyberspace and cybertime, whose gender is more intimately related to the logic and design of the technology than to any "real" social context of the operator. The "social," if there still is one here, is on the Net. Certainly, one group (gender, class, race) may be more oppressed by these technologies than another. But the far greater danger of these systems lies in their radical implosion of distance, bodies, the disenchantment of time itself, in their relentless translation into codes, keys, and screens.

In many ways, gender has always been a matter of simulation, if by simulation we mean artifice, illusion, and seduction. The spectacle of gender has always been linked to inhabiting secret spaces, the control of illusions of time and timelessness, to the symbolic order. The new technologies, however, disenchant all this. Virtual imaging, computers and communications, biomodeling are entirely without artifice and symbolic content. In the end, they are not imaginaries at all, but rather completely lacking imagination, just like they are without feeling, flat and passionless. The new technologies do not seduce, they are only coldly fascinating. There, gender relations have no risks, no dangers, and no stakes either. Everything converts into a game. When I log onto the Net, when a person in an electronic sweatshop in Malaysia processes corporate sales information, when an AIDS death figures as a blip in a vast medico-statistical apparatus for tracking disease in the population, gender – its seductions, its stakes, its politics – disappears and begins to haunt its own ruins.

Maybe this is just demonizing the technology and there is a positive side to all this. Choosing the lesser of two evils, Haraway (1985) writes that she would "rather be a cyborg than a goddess," meaning, I suppose, that it's better to be a human-machine, with all its dirty, messy contingencies, than something timeless and pure. But isn't the cyborg, in its imaginary form, just another absolute, god-like power (dissolving boundaries, simulating time and space, replicating bodies)? Haraway's "blasphemous faith," with which she begins her cyborg manifesto, is in the multiplicity of connections, even if that means sacrificing standpoint, ignoring the gap between organism and machine, living and dead forms, or departing from what she takes to be certain essentialist orthodoxies within feminist discourse. Her challenge is to stake out a positive space for new (feminist) praxis within the cyborg assemblage itself.[19] The question, though, is what, if any, kind of politics can survive in such a radically decentered and homogeneous field, where experience, identity, and sociality assume entirely hyperreal forms.

Epilogue

"Hugh"

I am reminded of an episode of *Star Trek: The Next Generation* where the captain of the ship, Picard, is captured and turned into a cyborg. The "Borg," as they are called, are not so much enemies of humankind as simply following their programmed instructions to assimilate humans to their own form of existence, where each unit is just a miniature expression of the collective. Borg are fond of reminding the humans they encounter that "resistance is futile," that "all who resist will be assimilated" or, barring that, annihilated. Of course, in *Star Trek: The Next Generation*, resistance is never futile. The captain was rescued, and the Borg, when the series ended last year, were being threatened by a "virus" placed in their midst, a captured Borg, one of their own, who has become self-conscious and taken a name – "Hugh" – and who will now return, reprogrammed and enlightened, to spread to the whole of the Borg the fatal "diseases" of identity, uniqueness, and humanity.

There are two morals to this story. One is that "normal" kinds of resistance to a cyborgian system don't work – the resister just gets incorporated. Unplugging doesn't help here; the system actively searches you out. In telematic societies, the fact that someone is unplugged is a matter for surveillance, all the forms of insistence and pressure that one get online, connected. On another level, however, the system is totally indifferent to resistance. It expands and transforms itself by its own logic and life unplugged just gets increasingly more difficult, inconvenient, finally impossible (telematics, like all interconnected technological systems, are just webs of formal necessities). The Borg's imperative to assimilate humans whenever they resist is only the outward expression of a more radical indifference to human life in general. Humans, for them, are a lower form of existence – their resistance really doesn't matter, or at most it is an irritant, a minor delay. Time is on the side of the cyborg – it has all the time in the world. Setbacks may affect the parts, but not the whole. Eventually, there will be no more "delays."

The second moral, however, is just the opposite. It is that such a system itself is not resistant to the right kind of attack. The right kind of attack, in this story, is one where the system's defenses are penetrated by one of its own kind – they fail to scan it, it doesn't register on their equipment. Hugh is a copy of all Borg, different in only one detail, a small one, in fact *the least one*, from the point of view of the collective – Hugh has become human. An indiscernible if nonetheless ominous distinction – a "gap" that fails to register (at least until Hugh rather stupidly attempts more conventional forms of resistance, like blasting his way to the Borg command center). Cloned societies like the Borg, it turns out, are very fragile. Despite a formidably hard outward appearance, they are deceptively delicate; any tiny connection which fails might transmit that failure to the entire system. A cyborgian system, it seems, is vulnerable to chance infections, minor unseen anomalies, mutating cells, that end up crashing its code (its "immune system"), allowing the disease to spread to the entire body – a kind of cyborg cancer. In this, it is like all simulated systems, so disconnected from reality, so self-referential and informated, that the slightest internal change occurring at the right moment can bring it down. The process is gradual, unnoticeable, but once initiated, irreversible. This moral, unlike the first, gives us a happy ending. When we last see "Hugh," he is still fighting a "human" war against his fellow Borg (laser guns, guerrilla tactics, infiltration, surveillance). He is infinitely outnumbered, but that doesn't matter. We are left with the certainty that daily more and more Borg are becoming infected with a sense of individuality, with "selves," freedom of choice and the Federation (read: the American) way. We sense that in the end, the cyborg "virus" with the indiscernible human difference will win out and force won't be necessary. A non-violent, stealthy victory. The Borg will become more like real "people," and less like Borg. Though they will always be human machines, now it will be the machine that doesn't matter (which now will become the least difference, definitively transcended).

We won't speculate any further on the morality of all this – either the happy humanist morality of *Star Trek: The Next Generation* or how our own experiment in becoming cyborgs will end. Cyborg logic doesn't operate by any moral imperative; as we've said, it just operates. No forces of good versus forces of evil here, no global threat followed by a happy ending: the end of the cyborg is a moral illusion, one that, if we want, we can watch on TV anytime (or act out on any video game – in the popular game "Terminator 2," anyone who plays can be like Hugh, a good

Borg out to kill a bad Borg). The issue here is not the morality or even the power of resistance, but its simulation. As a form of power, resistance to cyborg logic works only when the gap between the machine and the human remains intact. That gap is what's at stake – literally, politically, pragmatically – in the effort to relocate real people and real things within a technoculture that insists on de-realizing them and promoting its own hyperversion of reality. When that gap disappears, though, so do the stakes. Power thinks it can contain simulation, but it is simulation that in fact absorbs power. Against what we could call the objective fantasy of simulation, against the totalization of simulated forms, resistance is indeed quite futile. Or more accurately, once the circuit between the actual and the virtual closes, it also closes between actual and virtual forms of resistance. Power isn't negated or subdued by simulation; it becomes hyperreal, perhaps even deadlier than before.

Hugh can't recall a time when he was ever human, because he never was. Maybe he could be programmed with human memories, but how would that make a difference? Even with his new name and sense of self, in one way Hugh will always be a Borg, a clone. What does "becoming human," then, signal for Hugh? Perhaps not at all what we might hope it signals for us, viz., victory and a happy ending. If Hugh "infects" the Borg, will it make the machine die? Maybe instead it just *makes the machine Hugh* (exactly replicating the process that Hugh himself underwent). This is precisely the alternative (also fictional, to be sure) which the "humanist" moral of Hugh's story misses. What it doesn't consider is the possibility that the final encounter with the Borg will not be with a bunch of individual Hughs, but with Hugh himself, the collective, the Borg *as* individual. The return of Hugh, all right, but what a Hugh! Here's the other ending – not that the virus doesn't work, but that it works flawlessly in a way completely unintended. We thought the Borg were bad enough. Now we've got a real problem (especially if the "collective" Hugh now wants to "individualize" us, bring us the joys of freedom and absolute subjectivity – you too can be like Hugh, and will be). The return of the virus, only now a supervirus, and no longer unquestionably friendly.

Today, the gap separating the imaginary and the real is narrowing, but we shouldn't simply conclude from this that telematic systems aim to close it for good. More accurately, they aim to absorb it in simulation, to simulate the difference. The more resistance to closure, the more the system itself resists closure, but in a higher register. The system, it turns out, doesn't cancel out resistance at all. Quite the contrary. It feeds on it in order to reproduce it; reproducing resistance – reproducing power – is what it's all about, to repeat the gap continuously, only this time at the level of the virtual. The Borg as resister par excellence, the Borg as Hugh, and Hugh as real, an individual, but someone who stands apart from the crowd and knows where he's going – just a regular cyberguy. In the ultimate ploy, the system counters resistance not with any moral imperative or forceful repression but with the pleasure of resistance itself – to limits, finalities, boundaries. No pain, no suffering, just a delusion of mastery over everything final, the hypnotic, integrated satisfactions of the screen and the code. No limits, no worries. Rather, be the limit, be the end. No waiting, but a frenzy of simulated (instantaneous, undelayed, "real") contact. No need to go to the extremes when you can start from the extreme – control by the end.[1] In exchange for this delusionary power over limits, the system only "demands" your complete individuality, your total humanity, your absolute uniqueness.[2] This is nothing new. It is precisely what the modern apparatuses of surveillance have been demanding for two hundred years. Is individuality possible in a system of total surveillance? Just ask Hugh (the big Hugh). Now (soon) we can all be watchers. Better, we can design, watch, and record our own dreams, and wire them to the dreams of others. Where surveillance cannot capture an event, its simulation can, and offer this (delusion of) power to anyone (just call it up onscreen); where surveillance cannot make a body conform, the code can, and make it fun (a completely editable body, just choose from the list of options). In exchange for the trouble of exposure – the fact that many will resist it, that it takes time and effort – the system compensates with an ecstasy of exposure, the cancellation of time, the reprogramming of resistance. And where exposure is impossible, virtual images also make it unnecessary – everything fantasizable now seeable, touchable, without having to "see or touch" it at all. Just jack in to your dreams. The system, in effect, offers human beings the unlimited pleasure of their own superfluousness. It dreams for them. Who needs to see, touch, think, who needs to dream what can be simulated? The screen is our eyes and skin, the code our brain and dream-work. Who needs *to be* anything different, when everything different is instantly *be-able*? It's fine to resist this system because, to the system, resistance is what makes it go. If you want to resist being simulated, simulation can arrange that for you. Picture living in a time or place without information systems, without the frenzied pace and all the pressures of electronic, biotelematic civilization. Now picture being transported there by virtual reality. If this is science fiction – and certainly it is – it's only to illustrate that being a Borg has its pleasures, and that those pleasures don't exclude resistance to the imperatives of the system. The system seduces with the image of what resistance *can be* – that's its whole message, that you're in charge, that you program the limits and the gap, a simulated agent at the controls in a simulated world.

We must break off the text here with this barely discernible clue. Resistance to biotelematic systems cannot be anti-technological, at least from the point of view of their imaginary. Luddism is not an option here. Biotelematic systems are themselves profoundly "anti-technological" – they begin from the premise of their own end, their own disappearance. Unlike the Borg in *Star Trek: The Next Generation*, they have no problem with becoming human, becoming Hugh. All the better, if that's what it takes. Maybe we can learn something from the Borg here – not to resist becoming Hugh. At least we can still gamble on the ultimate fragility of the system. That fragility, for all we know, is an effect of boredom. Being connected, we dimly sense, is not what it's hyped up to be, not even close. Once everyone is Hugh, what's the difference? You can turn on the power, but nothing's on, there's nothing to watch (the familiar lament of the TV addict). Oversimulated systems are always prone to sudden reality-crashes, and perhaps today that means they simply become transparent and uninteresting. The Internet is exciting for a while, but the novelty quickly wears off – it's all the same. CDs sound great until the day you close your eyes and suddenly all they sound like is a CD and you'd rather hear the orchestra (or even the record!). Even the best virtual images eventually get tedious, their "fidelity" starts to wear thin – even photographs start to look better, more real. The high-tech gloss of electronics, the screen, the rush of hypercontrol, the fascination with decoding: the time is coming, perhaps sooner than we think, when all this will be excruciatingly boring, the endlessly dull fantasy, the simulated pleasures, of virtual systems. Only then, perhaps, will the cyborg run out of time.

Notes

1 A social science fiction

1 For a similar approach, although one that produces a quite different style of text, see Pfohl (1992). Donna Haraway also discusses the deep similarities between scientific (factual) and fictional discourses in western culture in *Primate Visions* (1989: 3ff.).

2 "The entire universe of objects that can be known scientifically must be formulated as problems in communications engineering (for the managers) or theories of the text (for those who would resist)" (Haraway 1985: 81). In focusing on an informatics of domination, like Haraway, I certainly don't wish to argue that all uses of informatic technology are oppressive. The systems that I describe in this book enter into complex relations of power and elusion whose consequences at best are never entirely foreseeable, and which constitute solutions to problems – of politics, economy, desire, and pleasure – that, depending on other conditions, could be either coercive or liberating. No one would deny that information technology has opened up a number of possibilities for political resistance and creative expression in the late twentieth century. Still, as this book hopes to make clear, the cost of such "freedoms" has been very high, in terms of the intensification of worktime, the loss of privacy and magnification of social isolation, the virtualization of pleasures, and the global militarization of social relations.

In the same way, it could also be argued that many contemporary uses of simulation technology have enhanced our ability to save lives or reduce risks. Earthquake simulations, for example, have been used to promote stronger building codes along fault lines. Vulcanists have developed models of possible rates and directions of lava flows, allowing for higher levels of preparedness and the design of safe evacuation routes in the event of an eruption. There are many such potential benefits of simulation modeling that could be cited. It is worth remembering, however, as I have argued in another book (1989), that such technical "mitigation" efforts themselves can often carry hidden costs, or produce unintended, and perhaps devastating, consequences. If, for instance, more people move into areas whose hazards have been simulated in an effort to control dangerous outcomes, results may be more, not less, deadly. A dam whose simulation had indicated the ability to withstand a 500-year flood may induce migration into and development of a flood-plain that, if and when such a disaster does occur, might produce even heavier damage and loss of life.

3 Hyperrealism, then, is simply realism pushed to its limit, i.e., the real as anticipated and generated in advance by its code, to the point where both the real and its reproduction "fall out" of consideration and the code itself becomes the "encapsulated" form of reality. Virtual reality machines, along with a host of other modern reproduction technologies that we will discuss – audio CDs, tele-presencing, video games, flight simulators – aim for precisely this kind of effect, viz., a kind of fantastic or excessive realism, imaginary scenes "so real" that it becomes increasingly difficult, finally impossible, to distinguish them from "the real thing" – the real and its reproduction both become functions of ever more sophisticated sets of instructions (programs, codes, models) that precede them in time – control, we could say, not toward an end, but *from* an end. We'll return to this point later in the text.

4 Even if technically, from the point of view of the programmer, it was always clear.

5 The term is Shoshana Zuboff's, from *In the Age of the Smart Machine* (1988).

6 The distinction between social and system integration is Jürgen Habermas's, from *The Theory of Communicative Action, Vol. 2* (1987), who uses it, much like Weber, to describe the increasingly instrumental-rational character of social relations in the modern age.

7 Almost to the point of already being boring in popular culture. In the cartoon "Life in Hell," Matt Groening lists "virtual" as one of the main words he wishes would disappear in 1994.

8 Virtual light is the cold steel-gray light of the computer or television screen. *Virtual Light* is also the title of one of William Gibson's recent cyberpunk novels (1993).

9 Elias Canetti's work on power is very significant here, tracing these functions back to elemental processes of seizing and incorporating, making flee and immobilizing. See *Crowds and Power* (1960: 203ff.).

10 "[P]ataphysics is the science of imaginary solutions, which symbolically attributes the properties of objects, described in their virtuality, to their lineaments" (Jarry 1960: 131). From our point of view, pataphysics is the description of a technology in the mode of its future past (the technology as hyperreal). See Bogard 1994.

2 Surveillance, its simulation, and hypercontrol in virtual systems

1 The principles that war (military power) is based on deception and demands foreknowledge of the enemy for its successful conduct are, of course, Sun Tzu's, and date back to the Warring States period in China in the fifth century BC. See *The Art of War* (1963: 66). Virilio discusses the "observation-machine" as a logistics of perception linked to deception in *War and Cinema* (1989). Chapter 4 will explore these themes in greater depth.

2 Literally, you don't *matter*, you're not even real, or more exactly, "less real" than the profile. For an interesting and provocative discussion of how cultural and historical productions create "bodies that matter" versus bodies that are assigned to the margins of indifference, see Judith Butler, *Bodies That Matter* (1993).

3 On deterrence as dominant strategy of postindustrial, telematic culture, see also Baudrillard, *Simulations* (1983b: 59–60), and "The Beaubourg Effect: Implosion and Deterrence" (1982).

4 In *Discipline and Punish*, Foucault shows how panoptic surveillance is designed to foster self-control (1979: 201ff.). Mark Poster also emphasizes the self-participatory and self-regulatory nature of contemporary informational systems of control in *The Mode of Information: Poststructuralism and Social Context* (1990).

5 On how informated control systems produce "mobile" or floating subjects, see Scott Lash and John Urry, *Economies of Signs and Space* (1994). We shall return to this idea many times. Chapter 6, on privacy, notes one of the fundamental ironies of virtual systems – that in being able to "travel" anywhere onscreen (e.g., channel cruising), the subject who views the screen remains fixed and immobile in front of it, collapsing the dialectic of mobility and immobility. The collapse of the poles of mobility and immobility, Subject and Object, human and machine, observer and observed, is a general theme in much of the postmodern literature on technology and control. Again, one of the main theorists here is Baudrillard, especially his book *Fatal Strategies* (1990b). See also the collection of articles in Michael Benedikt (ed.), *Cyberspace* (1992). For a critique of Baudrillard's position on this subject, see Douglas Kellner, *Jean Baudrillard: From Marxism to Postmodernism and Beyond* (1989): 154–167.

6 Foucault's discussion of the gaze in *The Birth of the Clinic* is still the best, especially chapters 7–9 (1975: 107–173).

7 For a discussion of some of the paradoxes of experience in virtual systems, see Allucquère Roseanne Stone, "Virtual Systems" (1992).

8 In Baudrillard, "crystalline perception" (simulation and virtuality as pure event and Object) has a high price, however, precisely because it absorbs the Subject – absolutely, finally – in the field of projection: the triumph of the Object. See *The Revenge of the Crystal* (1990c).

9 See chapter 6 on the implosion of privacy and secrecy in hypersurveillance societies.

10 On the distinction between an organization and an order, see the account of Gilles Deleuze's work in Michael Hardt, *Gilles Deleuze: An Apprenticeship in Philosophy* (1992).

11 "It is no longer a matter of bringing death into play in the field of sovereignty, but of distributing the living in the domain of value and utility. Such a power has to qualify, measure, appraise, and hierarchize, rather than display itself in its murderous splendour; it does not have to draw the line that separates the enemies of the sovereign from his obedient subjects; it effects

distributions around the norm" (Foucault 1980: 144).

12 For Canetti (1960), survival is perhaps the key measure of power, and the survivor is the one who stands over (surveys) the crowd of dead bodies. The experience of being left alive while seeing that everyone else has died is, Canetti says, the moment and the "passion" of power. For us, however, the survivor is still a figure of an order of surveillance, still playing off the distinction between the living and the dead. In an order of simulation, the "survivor is a cyborg" (living or dead?), and its "power" is virtual, its passions informated.

13 In fact, this is already being done. New CD technology being tested today aims to reproduce the entire range of the listening experience, including random noises. Some manufacturers are even experimenting with making CDs sound more like records, which some listeners claim have a warmer, if "noisier," sound. The difference, and the paradox of all this, I suppose, is that CD noise is somehow cleaner, better reproduced, than record noise.

14 I return to the bubble-boy and related issues in the chapter on sexuality in telematic societies.

15 Deleuze and Guatarri's discussions of machinic-desiring assemblages are also scattered throughout their *A Thousand Plateaus* (1987), especially the chapter on nomadology and the war-machine.

16 In *Anti-Oedipus* (1977), Deleuze and Guattari refer to three syntheses of machinic production: (1) the production of production (connective synthesis of partial objects and flows in desiring production), (2) the production of recording (disjunctive synthesis, or selection, which in this book refers to the surveillance machine – recording is selective, it breaks into a flow and creates segments), and (3) the production of consumption, what I shall refer to as simulation, and which Deleuze and Guattari place in the context of a discussion of the "celibate machine" and the experience of pleasure. Baudrillard, we shall see, also discusses simulation technology in terms of celibate machines (video games are a good example) – they produce pleasure but cannot experience it.

17 On the imaginary and its role in the generation of social structures, see also Cornelius Castoriadis, *The Imaginary Institution of Society* (1987).

18 On "the impossible" and the miraculous, see George Bataille, *The Accursed Share, Vol. 2* (1991: 206ff.).

19 A recent *New York Times* article documents the emerging battle over the government's right to enforce PC manufacturers to incorporate certain encryption technology in their machines. As more "personal" information is converted to home electronic files, these struggles will only become more intense in the future. We shall discuss this further in chapter 6. See "Cyberspace under Lock and Key" (1994).

20 When the tennis star Andre Agassi announces in a popular television commercial that "image is everything," we can be sure that the "image" is dead (i.e., virtualized onscreen).

21 Baudrillard, in a piece on the Gulf War a few years ago (1991), provocatively claimed that it never happened. That doesn't mean no one was killed. Hardly. It means, for Baudrillard, that the Gulf War, like all wars today, had no beginning and no end. War, i.e., in telematic societies, is a continuous *preparation for war* (training, simulation of combat, the militarization of industry and social relations generally). The lethality of war, if anything, is intensified even as the bounded time of war collapses in its absorption by informated systems. We'll return to these themes in chapter 5.

22 See chapter 6 on the simulacrum of privacy.

3 Social control for the 1990s

1 David Lyon notes some of the conceptual problems of the concept of "new surveillance," in *The Electronic Eye: The Rise of Surveillance Society* (1994: 53ff.).

2 See Lyon (1994) on "seeing as knowledge" in surveillance societies: 205ff. There is a real sense, however, in which these systems do not even produce (store, file, transmit) knowledge. Information systems are not exactly systems of knowledge, and a good case could be made that knowledge, as a difficult, complex process of trial and error, learning, practice, etc., is precisely what is sacrificed in a telematic order. Turn on the TV, flick on the computer, and sit back. Who needs to "know" anything?

3 Much of the following information was distilled from a series of publications by the Office of Technology Assessment on the effects of new surveillance technologies. See OTA, *Federal Government Information Technology: Electronic Record Systems and Individual Privacy* (1986); OTA, *The Electronic Supervisor: New Technology, New Tensions* (1987); OTA, *Federal Government Information Technology: Electronic Surveillance and Civil Liberties* (1985b). See also Kenneth Laudon, *Dossier Society: Value Choices in the Design of National Information Systems* (1986).

4 See also Paul Virilio, "Negative Horizons" (1987). Virilio traces the "end of relief" to the problem of speed – at absolute speed (what Virilio calls the "light of speed"), all depth, all distance collapses. The experience of absolute speed is virtual – movement anywhere, anytime, instantaneously. We shall return to Virilio's ideas throughout this book.

5 Poster, we have already noted, develops this idea in a discussion of Foucault and the relation of the latter's theory to the development of modern electronic databases. I would prefer the more descriptive term "virtual panopticon."

6 Gary Marx (1986), for example, has noted from the beginning how new surveillance technologies have transcended distance, time, and darkness, how they have become dispersed and decentralized, and foster self-policing. But, like Cohen, Giddens, Dandeker, and many others, he sees these developments only as a historical evolution of surveillance technologies and strategies, not as having anything essential to do with simulation.

4   Sensors, jammers, and the military simulacrum

1   Friedrich Dürrenmatt, *The Assignment (Or, On the Observing of the Observer of the Observers)* (1988). We'll return to a more extended discussion of Dürrenmatt's interesting work and its relation to military forms of simulation and observation in chapter 6 on privacy.

2   The new generation of military surveillance apparatuses are not exactly "optical" or "panoptic," but rather "panspectral," searching bands of information rather than lighting spaces as means of decrypting encoded messages (see de Landa 1991: 205).

3   The publicly televised debate preceding the United States's entry into the Gulf War was routinely framed by the administration in terms of how it would be totally unlike Vietnam, that it would be efficient, clean, quick, that it wouldn't involve the extensive and drawn-out deployment of ground forces, etc. It is interesting to note how that rationale has increasingly played out in the current US policy to get involved only in future, post-Cold War, conflicts that it is sure it can win easily, and that present relatively few moral or public relations problems (presumably as a result of conducting extensive simulations of them) – Panama, Somalia, and Haiti versus Bosnia and Chechnya, for example.

5   Simulation, surveillance, and cyborg work

1   See also Foucault's remarks on the relation between Capital and bio-power technologies in *History of Sexuality, Vol. 1* (1980: 141ff.): "bio-power was without question an indispensable element in the development of capitalism; the latter would not have been possible without the controlled insertion of bodies into the machinery of production and the adjustment of the phenomena of population to economic processes ... But ... it also needed the growth of both these factors, their reinforcement as well as their availability and docility; it had to have methods of power capable of optimizing forces, aptitudes, and life in general without at the same time making them more difficult to govern." The growth of bio-power technologies and their support of Capital, in short, was grounded upon the development and continuous refinement of the disciplines.

2   The computer, like writing, signals the advent of a new medium, not just a new tool. It took some time to realize that the computer had far greater capabilities than simply doing computations or manipulating texts. It has, in that sense, no general use, and produces no general use-values. Information is less the computer's "product" than its "element" or environment, the virtual world in which it "operates" rather than "produces."

3   Marx, *Wage-Labour and Capital/Value, Price and Profit* (1933: 19). See also Marx, *The Economic and Philosophic Manuscripts of 1844* (1964: 110): "The [alienated] worker therefore only feels himself outside his work, and in his work feels outside himself. He is at home when he is not working, and when

he is working he is not at home." With cyborg work, however, this external-ity of home and work is definitively solved (e.g., home computers linked to the Net), and certainly not in the way Marx would have intended.

4 See also Ruth Schwartz Cowan, *More Work for Mother: The Ironies of Household Technology from the Open Hearth to the Microwave* (1983), who argues that domestic appliances have increased the intensity and duration of household labor. Also Harry Braverman, *Labor and Monopoly Capital: The Degradation of Work in the Twentieth Century* (1975).

5 See Baudrillard's remarks on radical otherness in *The Transparency of Evil: Essays on Extreme Phenomena* (1993b: 146–155).

6 It is interesting to note the parallels between de Certeau and Marx here, par-ticularly the connection between temporal strategies and an idea of authen-tic labor (production for one's own, rather than another's, use). This also points to a limit of de Certeau's critique of Capital. It is not that time is on the side of Labor and Space on the side of Capital, but that both employ the simulation of time and space in reciprocal efforts to subvert one another.

7 For an extended discussion of lost dimensions in relation to an art of disap-pearance, see Paul Virilio, *Lost Dimension* (1991); and also Baudrillard's dis-cussion of the lost dimension in regard to *trompe l'oeil* in *Seduction* (1990d: 60–66).

8 See Office of Technology Assessment (OTA) reports from mid-1980s: *The Electronic Supervisor: New Technology, New Tensions* (1987); *The Automation of America's Offices* (1985a). See also R. Howard, *Brave New Workplace* (1985).

9 Telephone operators are perhaps the most blatant example today of workers caught up in the cyborg apparatus of hypersurveillance, their conversations randomly monitored, the record of their performance (time and length of ser-vice, efficiency, courtesy) continuously displayed to their supervisors (who are themselves routinely monitored!), and so on. And, of course, we should not neglect how the consumer also enters into this web of recording and simula-tion.

10 See Deleuze and Guatarri's remarks on the "production of recording" (the "disjunctive synthesis of recording") in *Anti-Oedipus* (1977: 75ff.). Informated work can be this ... or this ... or this ... or anything. Whatever process can be informated (i.e., anything at all), can also be work.

11 Deleuze's notion of a "static ontological genesis" in relation to sense and nonsense can be applied to the operation of virtual reality technology, which from a field of static impermeability and impassability generates a moving, dynamic world of infinite connections. See his *Logic of Sense* (1990), espe-cially 109ff.

6   Privacy and hyperprivacy

1 Westin 1967: 39: "[The right to privacy] is the claim of individuals, groups, or institutions to determine for themselves when, how and to what extent information about them is to be communicated to others." When the Privacy Act of 1974 was debated in the early 1970s, government recordkeeping systems were still made up of paper documents. Access to those documents was largely a matter of having the appropriate credentials. With the advent of computers, increasingly privacy concerns also became a matter of knowledge of their electronic encryption methods (alphanumeric, alphabetic, and various types of chronological systems).

2 The exemplary figure of the "private" person in the information age is the one confined to his virtual space capsule, whose only contact with the "outside world" is a screen.

3 This is the age, Baudrillard claims, of virtual system *crashes*, orders of relations that collapse because they are overcoded and oversimulated – crash markets (computer stocks), crash immune systems (AIDS), crash sexuality, crash art. All virtual phenomena, when their means of verisimilitude (staging) are exposed, immediately lose their sense of reality and concreteness (holographic images, for example, can seem very real until we place our hand "in" them and are able to touch nothing but the flat surface from which they are projected). Also see J. G. Ballard's *Crash* (1985), one of the sources of Baudrillard's reflections on these themes.

4 The Office of Technology Assessment (1986) estimates that current privacy legislation is approximately two generations behind new digital technologies. At a more general level, we could say that simulation, with its capacity to erase boundaries and free fixed forms, is always the *undoing* of power. See Baudrillard, *Seduction* (1990d: 45ff.).

5 See Giuliana Bruno, "Ramble City: Postmodernism and *Blade Runner*" (1987). The only sense in which cyborgs are subjects is in their *subjection* to codes.

6 This is the "political" question today, if we can still speak in these terms, not whether the system can be transcended or made to function according to the demands of a particular political agenda (Left–Right–Center). As a dialectical process, politics, like everything else in this imaginary, gets swallowed up in simulation. It is one thing to change the politics governing the uses of modern telematic technologies, quite another to change the dream that fashions those uses in the first place.

7 On the structural interplay of difference and sameness in fashion, see Roland Barthes, *The Fashion System* (1983).

8 On gift exchange and the power of the gift that cannot be returned, see Marcel Mauss's discussion of the potlatch ritual in *The Gift: Forms and Functions of Exchange in Archaic Societies* (1967). In the potlatch, the one who has the most power (prestige) is the one able to give up the most personal possessions, i.e., make the greatest sacrifice. The gift that can't be

returned creates the most sublime form of dependence and submission in the other.

9 Orwell looms as a major figure behind most contemporary discussions of surveillance. For a welcome exception to this trend, see David Lyon, *The Electronic Eye* (1994). Lyon argues persuasively that postmodern "surveillance societies" are as much oriented around the issues of consumerism and pleasure as they are control, and that the appropriate fictional analog for these societies is to be found in Huxley's *Brave New World*, where information technology can be likened to the stupor-inducing "Soma," not in *Nineteen Eighty-Four*. See my remarks in the next chapter on the perverse "pleasures" of cybersex.

10 Along with everything else we sacrifice to simulation technology – knowledge, intelligence, desire, imagination, understanding, meaning – everything, that is, in the Subject.

11 See Gilles Deleuze's remarks in *Foucault* (1988: 42). See also my remarks in chapter 3 on Stanley Cohen's work on the diffusion of social control.

12 Just like magic, translatability into information is always a second-best, merely "adequate" solution to the problem of remoteness. The ideal solution, of course, and one which constitutes the imaginary of informatization, is instantaneous time travel, i.e., the absolute overcoming of distance defined in terms of time.

13 See the interesting collection of articles on this issue in Michael Sorkin (ed.), *Variations on a Theme Park: The New American City and the End of Public Space* (1992).

7 Sex in telematic societies

1 See Haraway 1985: 67. Haraway writes that the cyborg "is a creature in a postgender world. It has no truck with bisexuality, pre-oedipal symbiosis, unalienated labor, or other seductions to organic wholeness through a final appropriation of all the powers of the parts into a higher unity." I would argue, though, that it has "truck" with all these things, only at the level of the hyperreal. Not "postgender," or postsexuality, but hypersex, ultra-gender. Part of the problem with Haraway's otherwise tremendously insightful analysis of cyborg technologies is that on occasion she still contrasts them in a dualistic way to earlier modes of domination (representation versus simulation, organicism versus biotic component, sex versus genetic engineering, mind versus artificial intelligence, etc.) (ibid: 80). This kind of analysis sits uneasily with her clear recognition in other places that cyborgs are *multiplicities* (although within the "higher unity" of the code, the program, etc.). Simulation, we have argued, does not so much replace representation with a "new form," as absorbs it into an order where it can be anything – representation still subsists, but only within the frame of simulated references; sex

still exists, but within the general context of the multiplicity of forms of simulated sexuality, etc.

2 Berkeley Kaite discusses the sexualization of recording and display media in "The Fetish in Sex, Lies, and Videotape: Whither the Phallus?" (1992).

3 See Gilles Deleuze's comments on a form of content versus an "environmental" form (1988: 31ff.). This parallels Marshall McLuhan's (1964) distinction between the form and the content of a medium (the latter is also a medium).

4 Virtual systems, we have said, aim at nothing less than total mastery of the real, i.e., the complete absence of illusion, the secret, and the "scene." See Baudrillard, *Fatal Strategies* (1990b: 50) and Baudrillard, *L'Illusion du fin* (1994).

5 See Baudrillard on the ecstasy (simulation) of sex as a form of "disembodied lewdness" (1990b: 53).

6 See Foucault's discussion of the arrangement of letters on the typewriter keyboard as a network of relations of power actualized as a tactile interface between keys and fingers in *The Archaeology of Knowledge* (1972: 86). Also in Deleuze (1988: 2).

7 Undoubtedly from the beginning this is a masculine dream that works to the advantage of masculine interests. But it is still a dream that ultimately signals the limits of sex, gender, and power, and in this sense, the limits of "the masculine," too (as a fixed, universal signifier or "master narrative").

8 Even the name "Julie" may be wrong here. The original story appears in Lindsy Van Gelder, "The Strange Case of the Electronic Lover" (1985). In that article, it was "Joan."

9 See also Judith Perrolle, "Conversations and Trust in Computer Interfaces" (1991).

10 It is Baudrillard's formula in *Cool Memories* (1990a: 171).

11 See Larry Niven's sci-fi work, "Death by Ecstasy" (1976), where jacking in can be so pleasurable that people will do it until it kills them (like the old addiction experiments with rats and cocaine – just press the button).

12 Frontispiece of Baudrillard's *Xerox to Infinity* (1988b).

13 And to time, for that matter, since it aims to control how sexuality unfolds as event and process.

14 Nelkin and Tancredi cite a chilling quote from Bentley Glass, past president of the American Association for the Advancement of Science: "the use of the new technology [will] assure the quality of all new babies ... No parent will have the right to burden society with a malformed or mentally incompetent child" (1989: 12).

15 That is, cloning depends on a surveillance apparatus that one day it hopes to transcend. Once the genetic map is complete, so this reasoning goes, all that remains to be done is application, the design of better bodies.

16 See Ivan Illich, *Medical Nemesis: An Expropriation of Health* (1976); Baudrillard makes the same point about AIDS, not a disease of sexuality per se, but an effect of medicalization itself (1993b: 66).

17 In *Discipline and Punish* (1979), Foucault emphasizes the disciplinary assemblage's attention to and control of details. For the simulation machine, though, details are, to put it bluntly, no problem.

18 See Also E. Ann Kaplan, who argues along similar lines in a psychoanalytic interpretation of cinematic representation in "Is the Gaze Male?" (1983).

19 Susan Bordo (1990) criticizes "postmodernist" ideas like Haraway's for valorizing an impossible "view from everywhere" to challenge the neutral, objective (male) "view from nowhere" that has dominated western thinking for centuries. But Bordo herself doesn't see that both perspectives are compatible with the imaginary of simulation technology (virtual reality is precisely the view from both nowhere and everywhere, simultaneously!). What is needed is a language that escapes such spatial (and temporal) dualisms. While falling into some of her own dualisms (see footnote 1), Haraway still signals a way out, one that may or may not be effective, but that at least reintroduces some political and gender stakes into a thoroughly disenchanted game.

Epilogue

1 An ironic reformulation of Baudrillard's critical remark, "Better to die from going to extremes than starting from the extremities" (1993b: 1).

2 All the joys of "possessed individuality." See Arthur Kroker, *The Possessed Individual* (1992), who makes precisely this point about the kind of "freedom" virtual systems offer us.

References

Althusser, Louis. 1971. *Lenin and Philosophy and Other Essays*. London: Monthly Review Press.

Athanasiou, Tom. 1989. "Artificial Intelligence, Wishful Thinking, and War." In *Cyborg Worlds*, Les Levidow and Kevin Robins (eds.), 113–134. London: Free Association Books.

Attewell, Paul. 1987. "Big Brother and the Sweatshop: Computer Surveillance in the Automated Office." *Sociological Theory* 5 (1): 87–100.

Ballard, J. G. 1985. *Crash*. London: Faber.

Barthes, Roland. 1983. *The Fashion System*. New York: Hill and Wang.

Bataille, George. 1991. *The Accursed Share, Vols. 2 and 3*. New York: Zone Books.

Baudrillard, Jean. 1994. *L'Illusion de la fin, ou la grève des événements*. Paris: Galilée.

1993a. *Symbolic Exchange and Death*. London: Sage.

1993b. *The Transparency of Evil: Essays on Extreme Phenomena*. New York: Verso.

1991. "La Guerre du Golfe n'a pas eu lieu." *Libération*. March 29.

1990a. *Cool Memories*. New York: Verso.

1990b. *Fatal Strategies*. New York: Semiotext(e).

1990c. *The Revenge of the Crystal*. London: Pluto Press.

1990d. *Seduction*. New York: St. Martin's Press.

1989. "The Anorexic Ruins." In *Looking Back at the End of the World*, Dieter Kamper and Christoph Wulf (eds.), 29–45. New York: Semiotext(e).

1988a. *Selected Writings*. Mark Poster (ed.). Stanford, CA: Stanford University Press.

1988b. *Xerox to Infinity*. London: Touchepas.

1987. "The Year 2000 Has Already Happened." In *Body Invaders*, Kroker and Kroker (eds.), 35–44.

1986. "Clone Boy." *Z/G* 11: 12–13.

1985. "The Child in the Bubble." *Impulse* 11 (4): 13.

1983a. *In the Shadow of the Silent Majorities or . . . The End of the Social.* New York: Semiotext(e).

1983b. *Simulations.* New York: Semiotext(e).

1983c. "What Are You Doing After the Orgy?" *Artforum* (October): 42–46.

1982. "The Beaubourg Effect: Implosion and Deterrence." *October* 20 (Spring): 3–13.

1981. *For a Critique of the Political Economy of the Sign.* Trans. by Charles Levin. St. Louis: Telos Press.

Baudrillard, Jean and Sylvere Lotringer. 1987. *Forget Foucault and Forget Baudrillard.* New York: Semiotext(e).

Benedikt, Michael (ed.). 1992. *Cyberspace.* Cambridge, MA: MIT Press.

Beniger, James. 1986. *The Control Revolution: Technological and Economic Origins of the Information Society.* Cambridge, MA: Harvard University Press.

Benjamin, Walter. 1969. "The Work of Art in the Age of Mechanical Reproduction." In *Illuminations*, Hannah Arendt (ed.), 217–251. New York: Schocken Books.

Berger, John. 1972. *Ways of Seeing.* Harmondsworth: Penguin.

Bergson, Henri. 1991. *Matter and Memory.* New York: Zone Books.

Bergstrom, Janet. 1986. "Androids and Androgyny." *Camera Obscura* 15: 37–64.

Black, Bob. 1987. "The Abolition of Work." In *Semiotext(e) USA*, 15–26. New York: Semiotext(e).

Blanchot, Maurice. 1986. *The Writing of the Disaster.* Trans. by Ann Smock. Lincoln: University of Nebraska Press.

Bogard, William. 1994. "Baudrillard, Time, and the End." In *Baudrillard: A Critical Reader*, Douglas Kellner (ed.), 313–333. Oxford: Blackwell.

1991. "Discipline and Deterrence: Rethinking Foucault on the Question of Power in Contemporary Societies." *Social Science Journal* 28 (3): 325–346.

1990. "Closing Down the Social: Baudrillard's Challenge to Contemporary Sociology." *Sociological Theory* 8 (1): 1–16.

1989. *The Bhopal Tragedy: Language, Logic, and Politics in the Production of a Hazard.* Boulder, CO: Westview Press.

Bordo, Susan. 1990. "Feminism, Postmodernism, and Gender Scepticism." In *Feminism/Postmodernism*, Linda J. Nicholson (ed.), 133–156. New York: Routledge.

Braverman, Harry. 1975. *Labor and Monopoly Capital: The Degradation of Work in the Twentieth Century.* New York: Monthly Press.

Brown, Beverly. 1981. "A Feminist Interest in Pornography – Some Modest Proposals." *m/f* 5/6: 5–18.

Brown, Geoffrey. 1990. *The Information Game: Ethical Issues in a Microchip World.* London: Humanities Press.

Bruno, Giuliana. 1987. "Ramble City: Postmodernism and *Blade Runner*." *October* 41 (Summer): 61–74.

Burnham, David. 1983. *The Rise of the Computer State.* New York: Vintage.

Butler, Judith. 1993. *Bodies That Matter*. New York: Routledge.

Canetti, Elias. 1978. *The Human Province*. Trans. by Joachim Neugroschel. New York: Seabury.

1960. *Crowds and Power*. New York: Farrar, Strauss, and Giroux.

Castoriadis, Cornelius. 1987. *The Imaginary Institution of Society*. Cambridge, MA: MIT Press.

Cohen, Stanley. 1985. *Visions of Social Control: Crime, Punishment, and Classification*. Cambridge, UK: Polity Press.

1979. "The Punitive City: Notes on the Dispersal of Social Control." *Contemporary Crises* 3: 339–363.

Collins, Randal. 1979. *The Credential Society: An Historical Sociology of Education and Stratification*. New York: Academic Press.

Cowan, Ruth Schwartz. 1983. *More Work for Mother: The Ironies of Household Technology from the Open Hearth to the Microwave*. New York: Basic Books.

"Cyberspace under Lock and Key." 1994. *New York Times*. February 13: E3.

Dandeker, Christopher. 1990. *Surveillance, Power, and Modernity: Bureaucracy and Discipline from 1700 to the Present Day*. New York: St. Martin's Press.

De Certeau, Michel. 1986. *Heterologies: Discourse on the Other*. Minneapolis: University of Minnesota Press.

1984. *The Practice of Everyday Life*. Berkeley: University of California Press.

De Landa, Eduard. 1991. *War in the Age of Intelligent Machines*. New York: Zone Books.

Debord, Guy. 1983. *Society of the Spectacle*. Detroit: Black and Red.

Deleuze, Gilles. 1990. *The Logic of Sense*. New York: Columbia University Press.

1989. *Cinema 2: The Time Image*. Minneapolis: University of Minnesota Press.

1988. *Foucault*. Minneapolis: University of Minnesota Press.

Deleuze, Gilles and Felix Guatarri. 1987. *A Thousand Plateaus*. Minneapolis: University of Minnesota Press.

1977. *Anti-Oedipus: Capitalism and Schizophrenia*. New York: Viking.

Der Derian, James. 1990. "The (S)pace of International Relations: Simulation, Surveillance, and Speed." *International Studies Quarterly* 34: 295–310.

Dick, Philip K. 1982. *Blade Runner (Do Androids Dream of Electric Sheep?)*. New York: Ballantine Books.

Dürrenmatt, Friedrich. 1988. *The Assignment (Or, On the Observing of the Observer of the Observers)*. New York: Random House.

Duster, Troy. 1989. *Back Door to Eugenics*. New York: Routledge.

Dvornik, Francis. 1974. *Origins of Intelligence Services: The Ancient Near East, Persia, Greece, Rome, Byzantium, the Arab Muslim Empires, the Mongol Empire, China, Muscovy*. New Brunswick, NJ: Rutgers University Press.

Edwards, Jeff and Neal Mayer. 1990. "Low Altitude, High Speed Flight, and the Politics of Simulation." *National Defense* 74 (March): 34–38.

Eylenbosch, W. J. and N. D. Noah (eds.). 1988. *Surveillance in Health and Disease*. Oxford: Oxford University Press.

Foucault, Michel. 1991. *Remarks on Marx.* New York: Semiotext(e).

1988. "The Prose of Actaeon." In *The Baphomet*, Pierre Klossowski, xxvii–xxxviii. Hygiene, CO: Eriadnos Press.

1982. "The Subject and Power." In *Michel Foucault: Beyond Structuralism and Hermeneutics*, Hubert Dreyfus and Paul Rabinow (eds.), 208–226. Chicago: University of Chicago Press.

1980. *The History of Sexuality, Vol. 1.* New York: Vintage.

1979. *Discipline and Punish: The Birth of the Prison.* New York: Vintage.

1975. *The Birth of the Clinic: An Archaeology of Medical Perception.* New York: Vintage.

1972. *The Archaeology of Knowledge.* New York: Harper and Row.

Garson, Barbara. 1988. *The Electronic Sweatshop.* New York: Penguin.

George, Alexander L. and Richard Smoke. 1974. *Deterrence in American Foreign Policy: Theory and Practice.* New York: Columbia University Press.

Gibson, William. 1993. *Virtual Light.* New York: Bantam Books.

1988. *Mona Lisa Overdrive.* New York: Bantam Books.

1986. *Count Zero.* New York: Ace Books.

1984. *Neuromancer.* New York: Ace Books.

Giddens, Anthony. 1990. *The Consequences of Modernity.* Stanford, CA: Stanford University Press.

1987. *Social Theory and Modern Sociology.* Stanford, CA: Stanford University Press.

1984. *The Constitution of Society.* Berkeley: University of California Press.

Godfrey, David and Douglas Parkhill. 1979. *Gutenberg Two.* Toronto: Porcépic.

Gray, Chris Hables. 1989. "The Cyborg Soldier: The US Military and the Post-Modern Warrior." In *Cyborg Worlds: The Military Information Society*, Les Levidow and Kevin Robins (eds.), 43–71. London: Free Association Books.

Habermas, Jürgen. 1987. *The Theory of Communicative Action, Vol. 2: Lifeworld and System: A Critique of Functionalist Reason.* Boston: Beacon Press.

Hagedoorn, John, Paul Kalff, and Jaap Korpel. 1988. *Technological Development as an Evolutionary Process: A Study in the Interaction of Information, Process, and Control Technologies.* Amsterdam: Elsevier.

Haraway, Donna. 1989. *Primate Visions.* New York: Routledge.

1985. "A Manifesto for Cyborgs: Science, Technology, and Socialist-Feminism in the 1980s." *Socialist Review* 15 (2): 65–108.

Hardt, Michael. 1992. *Gilles Deleuze: An Apprenticeship in Philosophy.* Minneapolis: University of Minnesota Press.

Heidegger, Martin. 1977. *The Question Concerning Technology and Other Essays.* New York: Harper Torchbooks.

Howard, R. 1985. *Brave New Workplace.* New York: Viking.

Illich, Ivan. 1976. *Medical Nemesis: An Expropriation of Health.* New York: Pantheon Books.

Jarry, Alfred. 1960. "What is Pataphysics." *Evergreen* 4 (13), May–June: 131–132.

Kahn, Herman. 1984. *Thinking about the Unthinkable in the 1980s*. New York: Simon and Schuster.

Kaite, Berkeley. 1992. "The Fetish in Sex, Lies, and Videotape: Whither the Phallus?" In *The Hysterical Male*, Kroker and Kroker (eds.), 171–186.

1987. "The Pornographic Body Double: Transgression is the Law." In *Body Invaders*, Kroker and Kroker (eds.), 150–168.

Kaplan, E. Ann. 1983. "Is the Gaze Male?" In *Powers of Desire: The Politics of Sexuality*, Ann Snitow et al. (eds.), 309–327. New York: Monthly Review Press.

Kellner, Douglas. 1992. *The Persian Gulf TV War*. Boulder, CO: Westview Press.

1989. *Jean Baudrillard: From Marxism to Postmodernism and Beyond*. Stanford, CA: Stanford University Press.

Kevles, Daniel. 1985. *In the Name of Eugenics*. New York: Knopf.

Kroker, Arthur. 1992. *The Possessed Individual: Technology and the French Postmodern*. New York: St. Martin's Press.

Kroker, Arthur and Marilouise Kroker (eds.). 1992. *The Hysterical Male: New Feminist Theory*. Montreal: New World Perspectives.

1987. *Body Invaders: Panic Sex in America*. Montreal: New World Perspectives.

Lacan, Jacques. 1981. *The Four Fundamental Concepts of Psychoanalysis*. New York: Norton.

Lash, Scott and John Urry. 1994. *Economies of Signs and Space*. Thousand Oaks, CA: Sage Publications.

Latour, Bruno. 1986. *Science in Action*. Cambridge, MA: Harvard University Press.

Laudon, Kenneth. 1986. *Dossier Society: Value Choices in the Design of National Information Systems*. New York: Columbia University Press.

LeFebvre, Henri. 1991. *The Critique of Everyday Life*. New York: Verso.

Lehner, Paul E. 1989. *Artificial Intelligence and National Defense: Opportunity and Challenge*. Blue Ridge Summit, PA: TAB Books.

Lyon, David. 1994. *The Electronic Eye: The Rise of Surveillance Society*. Minneapolis: University of Minnesota Press.

Lyotard, Jean François. 1979. *The Postmodern Condition*. Minneapolis: University of Minnesota Press.

Marx, Gary. 1995. "The Engineering of Social Control: The Search for the Silver Bullet." In *Crime and Inequality*, J. Hagan and Ruth D. Peterson (eds.), 225–246. Stanford: Stanford University Press.

1990. "The Case of the Omniscient Organization." *Harvard Business Review* (March–April): 4–12.

1988. *Undercover: Police Surveillance in America*. Berkeley: University of California Press.

1986. "I'll Be Watching You: Reflections on the New Surveillance." *Dissent* 22: 26–34.

Marx, Karl. 1973. *Grundrisse: Foundations of the Critique of Political Economy*.

Trans. by Martin Nicolaus. New York: Random House.

1964. *The Economic and Philosophic Manuscripts of 1844.* New York: International Publishers.

1933. *Wage-Labour and Capital/Value, Price and Profit.* New York: International Publishers.

Mauss, Marcel. 1967. *The Gift: Forms and Functions of Exchange in Archaic Societies.* New York: Norton.

McLuhan, Marshall. 1964. *Understanding Media: The Extensions of Man.* New York: McGraw-Hill.

Munro, Neil. 1991. *The Quick and the Dead: Electronic Combat and Modern Warfare.* New York: St. Martin's Press.

Negri, Antonio. 1991. *Marx Beyond Marx.* New York: Autonomedia.

Nelkin, Dorothy and Laurence Tancredi. 1989. *Dangerous Diagnostics: The Social Power of Biological Information.* New York: Basic Books.

Niven, Larry. 1976. "Death by Ecstasy." In *The Long Arm of Gil Hamilton*, 1–65. New York: Ballantine.

Noble, Douglas D. 1989. "Mental Materiel: The Militarization of Learning and Intelligence in US Education." In *Cyborg Worlds: The Military Information Society*, Les Levidow and Kevin Robins (eds.), 13–41. London: Free Association Books.

Nock, Steven. 1993. *The Costs of Privacy: Surveillance and Reputation in America.* New York: A. De Gruyter.

Nolan, Kathleen and Sara Swenson. 1988. "New Tools, New Dilemmas: Genetic Frontiers." *Hastings Center Report* 18: 40–46.

Office of Technology Assessment. 1987. *The Electronic Supervisor: New Technology, New Tensions.* Washington, DC: GPO.

1986. *Federal Government Information Technology: Electronic Record Systems and Individual Privacy.* OTA-CIT-296. Washington, DC: GPO.

1985a. *The Automation of America's Offices.* Washington, DC: GPO.

1985b. *Federal Government Information Technology: Electronic Surveillance and Civil Liberties.* Washington, DC: GPO.

Olalquiaga, Celeste. 1992. *Megalopolis: Contemporary Cultural Studies.* Minneapolis: University of Minnesota Press.

Orwell, George. 1984. *Nineteen Eighty-Four.* San Diego: Harcourt Brace Jovanovich.

Ostrander, Greg. 1987. "Foucault's Disappearing Body." In *Body Invaders*, Kroker and Kroker (eds.), 169–182.

Perrolle, Judith. 1991. "Conversations and Trust in Computer Interfaces." In *Computerization and Controversy: Value Conflicts and Social Choices*, Charles Dunlop and Rob Kling (eds.), 350–363. New York: Academic Press.

Pfohl, Stephen. 1992. *Death at the Parasite Cafe: Social Science (Fictions) and the Postmodern.* New York: St. Martin's Press.

"Porn, the Low-Slung Engine of Progress." 1994. *New York Times.* January 9: B1.

Poster, Mark. 1990. *The Mode of Information: Poststructuralism and Social Context*. Chicago: University of Chicago Press.

Rothman, Barbara Katz. 1986. *The Tentative Pregnancy*. New York: Viking.

Rule, James. 1973. *Private Lives, Public Surveillance*. London: Allen-Lane.

Scarry, Elaine. 1985. *The Body in Pain: The Making and Unmaking of the World*. New York: Oxford University Press.

Schor, Juliet. 1991. *The Overworked American: The Unexpected Decline of Leisure*. New York: Basic Books.

Schwab, Gabriele. 1987. "Cyborgs: Postmodern Phantasms of Body and Mind." *Discourse* 9: 64–84.

Shelley, Mary. [1818] 1992. *Frankenstein*. Boston: St. Martin's Press.

Shorris, Earl. 1985. "Reflections on Power: A Dissenting View." *Harper's* (July): 51–54.

Simmel, Georg. 1950. "The Stranger." In *The Sociology of Georg Simmel*, Kurt Wolff (ed.), 402–408. New York: Free Press.

Sloterdyck, Peter. 1987. *The Critique of Cynical Reason*. Minneapolis: University of Minnesota Press.

Solzhenitsyn, Alexander. 1968. *Cancer Ward*. New York: Dial Press.

Sorkin, Michael (ed.). 1992. *Variations on a Theme Park: The New American City and the End of Public Space*. New York: Hill and Wang.

Spain, Daphne. 1993. "Gendered Spaces and Women's Status." *Sociological Theory* 11 (2): 137–151.

Stelarc. 1983. "The Body Obsolete." Interview by Paul McCarthy. *High Performance* 6 (4): 14–19.

Stone, Allucquère Roseanne. 1992. "Virtual Systems." In *Incorporations*, Jonathan Crary and Sanford Kwinter (eds.), 609–621. New York: Zone Books.

1991. "Will the Real Body Please Stand Up?: Boundary Stories About Virtual Cultures." In *Cyberspace*, Michael Benedikt (ed.), 82–118. Cambridge, MA: MIT Press.

Taylor, Frederick W. 1984. "Scientific Management." In *Critical Studies in Organization and Bureaucracy*, Frank Fischer and Carmen Siriani (eds.), 68–78. Philadelphia: Temple University Press.

Turkle, Sherry. 1984. *The Second Self: Computers and the Human Spirit*. New York: Simon and Schuster.

Tzu, Sun. 1963. *The Art of War*. Oxford: Oxford University Press.

Van Gelder, Lindsy. 1985. "The Strange Case of the Electronic Lover." *Ms. Magazine* (October): 94ff.

Virilio, Paul. 1991. *Lost Dimension*. New York: Semiotext(e).

1989. *War and Cinema: The Logistics of Perception*. London and New York: Verso.

1987. "Negative Horizons." In *Semiotext(e) USA*, 163–180. New York: Semiotext(e).

1986. *Speed and Politics*. New York: Semiotext(e).

1983. *Pure War*. New York: Semiotext(e).

1980. *Esthetique de la disparition*. Paris: Balland.

Weber, Max. 1958. "Bureaucracy" and "Science as a Vocation." In *From Max Weber*, H. H. Gerth and C. Wright Mills (eds.), 129–156, 196–244. New York: Oxford University Press.

Westin, Alan. 1967. *Privacy and Freedom*. New York: Atheneum.

Wiener, Norbert. 1948. *Cybernetics: Or Control and Communication in the Animal and the Machine*. Cambridge, MA: MIT Press.

Wigley, Mark. 1992. "Untitled: The Housing of Gender." In *Sexuality and Space*, Beatrice Colomina (ed.), 289–327. New York: Princeton Architectural Press.

Williams, Linda. 1989. *Hard Core: Power, Pleasure, and the Frenzy of the Visible*. Berkeley: University of California Press.

Wingerson, L. 1990. *Mapping Our Genes: The Genome Project and the Future of Medicine*. New York: Dutton.

Yurick, Sol. 1985. *Behold Metatron, the Recording Angel*. New York: Semiotext(e).

Zuboff, Shoshana. 1988. *In the Age of the Smart Machine*. New York: Basic Books.

Index

actual image
  passing present and 14–15
actuarials 146
AIDS 42, 143, 147, 148, 164, 166, 172
Alberti, Leon Battista 175
Althusser, Louis 47
artificial intelligence 85
assemblages 8, 42–43
  biomachinic 30
AT&T 155
Attewell, Paul 99

Babbage, Charles 2
battlefield management systems 85
Baudrillard, Jean 5, 10–13, 41–42, 46,
  70–74, 108–109, 126, 136, 153, 155,
  160–161, 166–167, 188n21, 191n3
  see also hyperreality; obscenity;
  simulacra, orders of; social, the
Beniger, James 1
Benjamin, Walter 33
Bentham, Jeremy 18
Berger, John 173–174
Big Brother 136–138
biological determinism 170
biological underclass 176
bio-power 39, 165, 170, 189n1
  sexuality and 163
  see also Foucault, Michel
biosurveillance 41, 172
  genetics and 40
Blanchot, Maurice 160
body, the 105
  as corruptible 163
  as disappearing screen 165
  as information 63
  desexualization of 164
  disappearance of 62
  disciplines of 39, 163
  medical coding of 142
  panic over 63–64
  privacy and 143–144

simulation of 42
surveillance of 39, 61
without symptoms 142–143
boredom
  resistance and 182–183
Borg, the 179–182
breaks and flows 42–43, 46, 164, 166
  surveillance as 43–44
Bryson, Lyman 84
bubble-boy, the 41–42, 165
bureaucracy 1, 12–13, 17–18, 28, 67
  secrecy and 38–39
Burnham, David 2, 133

Canetti, Elias 161, 185n9, 187n12
capital
  and labor 101–105
  as consumption of living labor 102
  as death machine 102–103
  crises of 116
  simulation of 109
Clipper chip 127–128
cloning 41, 143, 147, 153, 171, 193n15
  perfect bodies and 171–172
  sex and 171–172
codes 20, 30, 55, 71–72, 125
  genetic 142–143
Cohen, Stanley 67–69
computer state 2, 133
computer sweatshops 99
computerization 2, 32–33, 189n2
condoms 166
control 1, 28
  architectures of 19
  cybernetic 8
  deterrence and 32–33
  dialectic of 17, 76, 101
  disappearance of 122
  ecstasy of 34
  fiction of 19
  hypercontrol 4, 9
  imaginary of 4–5, 34